JUAN CARLOS OF SPAIN

Also by Charles Powell

EL PILOTO DEL CAMBIO

Juan Carlos of Spain

Self-Made Monarch

Charles Powell
Research Fellow
St Antony's College, Oxford

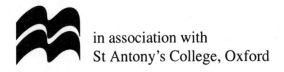

in association with
St Antony's College, Oxford

First published in Great Britain 1996 by
MACMILLAN PRESS LTD
Houndmills, Basingstoke, Hampshire RG21 6XS
and London
Companies and representatives
throughout the world

This book is published in the *St Antony's Series*
General editor: Alex Pravda

A catalogue record for this book is available
from the British Library.

ISBN 0-333-54726-8 hardcover
ISBN 0-333-64929-X paperback

First published in the United States of America 1996 by
ST. MARTIN'S PRESS, INC.,
Scholarly and Reference Division,
175 Fifth Avenue,
New York, N.Y. 10010

ISBN 0-312-12752-9

Library of Congress Cataloging-in-Publication Data
Powell, Charles T.
Juan Carlos of Spain : self-made monarch / Charles Powell.
p.   cm. — (St Antony's series)
Includes bibliographical references (p.   ) and index.
ISBN 0-312-12752-9 (cloth)
1. Juan Carlos I, King of Spain, 1938-   . 2. Spain—Politics and
government—1939-1975. 3. Spain—Politics and government—1975-
4. Monarchy—Spain—History—20th century. 5. Spain—Kings and
rulers—Biography. I. Title.
DP272.4.J8P69   1996
946.083'092—dc20
[B]   95-15318
                                                                CIP

10   9   8   7   6   5   4   3   2   1
05   04   03   02   01   00   99   98   97   96

Printed and bound in Great Britain by
Antony Rowe Ltd, Chippenham, Wiltshire

For my **mother** and **father**

Contents

Foreword

Although King Juan Carlos I is one of Europe's most well-known and respected heads of state, to date very little has been written about him outside Spain. The immediate aim of this book is therefore to satisfy the curiosity of English-language readers who may wish to learn more about this remarkable figure. More specifically, this political biography of Juan Carlos aims to provide a cogent interpretation of his career, and in particular of his decisive contribution to the transition to democracy in Spain. Although some of this ground was covered in an earlier publication of mine, *El piloto del cambio* (Barcelona, 1991), it is in many ways a new book.

Reigning monarchs are not often described as 'self-made', but in many ways Juan Carlos may be said to fit this description. Born into a royal family which had recently been forced into exile, the son of a pretender whose chances of ascending the throne were slim, much of his early life was marked by an overwhelming sense of uncertainty. On settling in Spain he soon found himself competing with others, including his own father, for the post of successor to General Franco, until his nomination in 1969 eventually paved the way for his proclamation as king of Spain in 1975.

Juan Carlos may be said to have ruled under two very different monarchies: the authoritarian monarchy inherited from Franco and the parliamentary monarchy embodied in the democratic constitution of 1978. This book argues that Juan Carlos's determination to redefine his constitutional role, in turn motivated by both a highly-developed instinct for self-preservation and a deep sense of justice, greatly facilitated the ensuing transition to democracy. What is perhaps most remarkable about the king's pivotal role in this process – which largely explains its very nature and ultimate success – is that due to the absence of suitable precedents, he was constantly forced to break new ground. Indeed his role in aborting the attempted military coup of 23 February 1981 was merely the most extreme example of this.

In more recent years Juan Carlos has continued to prove innovative, defining his own role as king of a fully consolidated parliamentary monarchy. Here again, the absence of well established models may have proved a blessing in disguise; indeed by shaping the institution in his own image, Juan Carlos appears to have secured its survival, something very few Spaniards had dared take for granted in 1975.

CHARLES POWELL

Acknowledgements

I would like to take this opportunity to thank all those who have contributed, directly or indirectly, to make this book possible. I am particularly grateful to the Warden, Fellows and staff of St Antony's College, Oxford, for their continued friendship and support over the years. Raymond Carr, who supervised my D. Phil. thesis on the transition to democracy, has remained a major source of inspiration and entertainment. In Spain, my friends and colleagues at the Instituto Universitario Ortega y Gasset have helped me more than they can imagine. My work was also greatly facilitated by Bela Ortiz de Solórzano, of *El País*, and Elisa de Santos Canalejo, of the Spanish Foreign Ministry Archive, who battles on against all odds. Luis de Avendaño often came to the rescue with his word-processing skills, as did Carolina Labarta and Julio Crespo when it came to checking references at the PRO. Nicholas Neill-Fraser, whose knowledge of European royal families never ceases to amaze me, was also extremely helpful. Finally, I would like to thank my parents, who put up with me in Madrid while I was finishing the book, and of course Sylvia, who endured my absence with characteristic stoicism and good humour.

FAMILY TREE OF THE SPANISH ROYAL FAMILY

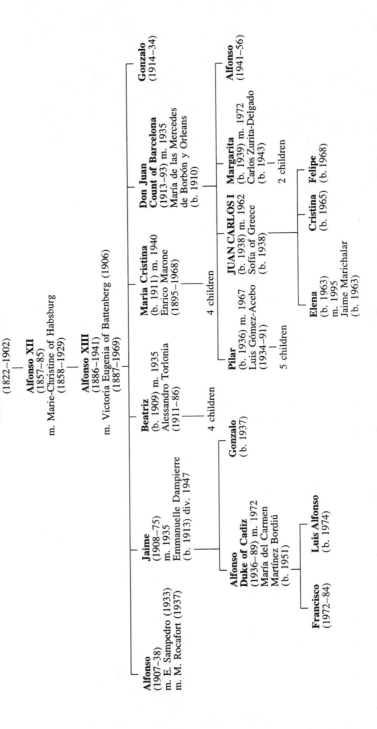

1 Years of Exile and Uncertainty

The birth of the future king at Rome's Anglo-American hospital on 5 January 1938 went virtually unnoticed in Spain, coinciding as it did with the battle of Teruel, one of the cruellest in the civil war. The child was the third born to Don Juan de Borbón and Doña María de las Mercedes de Borbón Orleans, who had married in the Italian capital in 1935 and settled there two years later, after being forced to leave Cannes by the French Popular Front government. Cardinal Pacelli, the future Pope Pius XII, christened the boy on 26 January with the names Juan, after his father, Alfonso, in honour of his paternal grandfather, King Alfonso XIII, and Carlos, after his godfather, the Infante Carlos de Borbón-Dos Sicilias. As a child, his family and friends invariably referred to him as Juan or Juanito, and it was not until he became a public figure several decades later that he came to be known as Juan Carlos.[1]

The child's father, Don Juan, was the third son of King Alfonso XIII, who had chosen to leave the country with his family in April 1931, following the victory of socialist and republican candidates in Spain's larger cities in the nation's first democratic local elections. On coming to the throne in 1902, Alfonso XIII had inherited the political system of the Restoration, established in 1876 under his father, Alfonso XII, which proved incapable of accommodating newly emerging sectors of Spanish society, represented by republicans, socialists and the peripheral nationalists of Catalonia and the Basque country. Largely in response to growing hostility to the monarchy, and with the king's full acquiescence, in 1923 General Miguel Primo de Rivera carried out a bloodless coup, which inaugurated a seven-year dictatorship. By failing to uphold the 1876 Constitution, Alfonso XIII effectively guaranteed that his reign would not long out-live the dictatorship. Primo de Rivera's dismissal in early 1930 thus led to a political crisis that was only solved with the proclamation of the Second Republic in April 1931.

Following the collapse of the monarchy, the Spanish royal family went into exile in France and later Italy. Alfonso XIII's eldest son, Don Alfonso, was afflicted with haemophilia, a disease he had inherited from his mother, the British princess Victoria Eugenia, a favourite granddaughter of Queen Victoria, who had become queen of Spain on marrying Alfonso XIII in 1906. Although the disease had been diagnosed as early as 1910, the king

1

had been reluctant to remove him from the line of succession, possibly because his second son, Don Jaime, had had his hearing seriously impaired after an unsuccessful ear operation carried out in 1912, when he was four years of age.[2]

Ironically it was not until after he had lost the throne that the king – who had refused to abdicate on his departure – finally clarified the succession issue. In 1933 Don Alfonso requested his father's permission to marry a young Cuban whom he had met while undergoing treatment in hospital. The king acceded to his request on the condition that he formally surrender his rights to the throne first, which he did on 11 June 1933.[3] Alfonso XIII subsequently called a meeting of prominent monarchists, who persuaded Don Jaime to follow his brother's example. Don Jaime, who was single at the time, surrendered his claim to the throne on his own behalf and that of his future heirs, a decision that was to prove highly controversial in years to come.[4] In the wake of these events, Alfonso XIII telegraphed his third son, Don Juan, who was in the Indian Ocean serving with the British Navy, to inform him that he was the new heir to the throne. Don Juan was greatly enjoying life on board HMS *Enterprise* and did not reply for over a week. As he was to confess many years later, the prospect of becoming heir to a throne that had been toppled with such ease only two years earlier, in a country where the restoration of the monarchy seemed extremely unlikely, filled him with apprehension. After several months of naval duty, however, Don Juan returned to his father's side.[5]

From their Roman exile the king and his heir – who soon had to leave the Royal Navy in order to retain his Spanish nationality – actively encouraged every conspiracy aimed at overthrowing the Second Republic. Given that the more authoritarian sectors of the monarchist opposition were also the most active, Alfonso XIII found himself under growing pressure to disown his liberal past. At one point he even sought an understanding with the ultraconservative Carlists, who had waged three civil wars in the nineteenth century against successive Bourbon monarchs, amongst them his own father, Alfonso XII, but was prevented from doing so by his more liberal supporters.[6]

By the mid-1930s many of those who wished to overthrow the Republic and set up an authoritarian system of government in its place no longer regarded the former constitutional monarch as a suitable figurehead, and began to look to his son for leadership. In October 1935 a contingent of monarchist leaders took advantage of their presence in Rome during Don Juan's wedding to encourage Alfonso XIII to consider abdicating in his son's favour, a possibility he refused to contemplate. By this stage the king had effectively been abandoned by his wife, Victoria Eugenia, who refused to attend the wedding, providing conservative monarchists with fresh ammunition.[7]

Both the king and his heir actively supported the military rising of 18 July 1936 against the Republican government, which was to trigger a bloody three-year civil war. On 31 July, the day after the birth of his first child, Pilar, Don Juan crossed the French border in the company of a group of conservative monarchists with the intention of joining the insurgents, but was turned back by one of the chief protagonists of the uprising, General Emilio Mola, who may have feared a hostile reaction from his Carlist troops. Undeterred, in December he wrote to General Francisco Franco, who had recently been appointed head of the Nationalist state, requesting permission to join the battlecruiser *Baleares*, which would later be sunk with great loss of life. In a characteristically skilful letter, Franco politely turned down his offer on the grounds that Don Juan's life was too precious to the nation to be put at risk in this manner, given the importance of the role he might be called upon to perform one day. In mid-1937 Franco justified his decision further with the argument that 'if one day a king returns to rule over the state, he will have to come as a peace-maker and should not to be found amongst the victors'. Ironically this was precisely the role Juan Carlos was to perform some forty years later, though hardly at Franco's bidding.[8]

Though enthusiastically supported by monarchists of all varieties, the uprising of 18 July 1936 was not specifically monarchist in character. Most insurgents revolted in the name of 'God and Spain', whilst some military units rose to the cry of 'Long live the Republic!' When the insurgents restored the red and yellow flag and the royal anthem introduced by the Bourbons in the eighteenth century, which had been banned by the Republic, they did so not out of loyalty to the monarchy as an institution, but because they regarded them as Spain's traditional national symbols. Initially, the only objective unanimously shared by the Nationalists was the overthrow of the Republic; given the disparate nature of their coalition, its leaders wisely refrained from committing themselves to potentially controversial political options.[9]

Most of those who favoured the restoration of the monarchy greeted General Franco's appointment in September 1936 as Caudillo of the Nationalist state with satisfaction. Franco had been Alfonso XIII's gentleman-in-waiting, and the king had honoured the young general by agreeing to be his *padrino* (best man) at his wedding. Following the conquest of Málaga by the Nationalists in November 1936, Alfonso XIII sent Franco a telegram openly identifying with his cause. In July 1937, however, the general clarified that a restored monarchy would have to be very different to that which had existed until 1931; indeed 'different in its content and, though it may grieve many, even in the person who incarnates it'.[10]

In late 1937 Alfonso XIII wrote to Franco expressing concern at his apparent lack of interest in restoring the monarchy. The latter replied somewhat brusquely, blaming him for Spain's decline, which he attributed to his earlier association with liberalism. In view of this Franco advised him to invest in the education of his son, Don Juan. Ironically, before long the general would be writing very similar letters to Don Juan, in connection with his son Juan Carlos. In spite of this treatment Alfonso XIII continued to congratulate the Caudillo on his military achievements, as did his son. In December 1938 Franco revoked the Republican edict that had condemned the king for his role in the Primo de Rivera dictatorship, as a result of which he had been officially deprived of Spanish citizenship and stripped of all his property.

Throughout the war Franco had personally informed the king after each major victory, but he failed to do so after the conquest of Madrid in March 1939. Alfonso XIII rightly saw this as evidence of his unwillingness to restore the monarchy, but nevertheless wrote to him placing himself at his orders, while at the same time suggesting that he be rewarded with Spain's highest military distinction, the *Laureada de San Fernando*. Later that year, however, Franco publicly stated that he had no intention of following in the footsteps of Primo de Rivera, who had been unceremoniously dropped by Alfonso XIII in 1930 when the dictatorship came under attack from all sides.

Franco was initially uncertain as to the type of regime that should replace the defeated Republic, but was careful not to rule out a possible restoration of the monarchy. Like him, however, by 1939 many monarchists had come to regard Alfonso XIII as a liability, due to both his incompatibility with the Carlists, who had made a significant military contribution to Franco's victory, and to his former association with a system of government that had been repudiated by the Nationalist camp.[11] Aware of this mounting opposition, and partly in the hope that he would be allowed to return to Spain, Alfonso XIII finally agreed to abdicate in favour of his twenty-seven-year-old son, Don Juan, on 15 January 1941, but died in Rome only weeks later. Thereafter, Don Juan's more enthusiastic followers came to know him as Juan III, though he was generally referred to as the Count of Barcelona, one of the King of Spain's traditional titles. It was thus that Juan Carlos became heir to the Spanish throne shortly after his third birthday.[12]

The young boy's future was largely to be determined by his father's relations with Franco. As we have seen, these were extremely cordial up until Alfonso XIII's death in 1941. In September that year Franco wrote to him acknowledging him as the legitimate pretender to the throne, and looking forward to the *instauración* (establishment) – as opposed to *restauración* (restoration) – of the monarchy, a distinction he was to observe henceforth. In his reply Don Juan proposed the creation of a regency, which would gradually pave the way for the monarchy. This suggestion was indeed taken up by Franco in 1947, by which time it had become a ruse to postpone the restoration indefinitely.[13]

Juan Carlos spent the first four and a half years of his life with his parents in a modest flat in the Roman residential suburb of Parioli. With Italy's entry into the second world war, however, his grandmother Victoria Eugenia, whom the authorities still regarded as a British princess, became *persona non grata* in Rome, in view of which she moved to neutral Switzerland. In 1942 Don Juan and his family followed her to Lausanne, where she was to live for the rest of her life. A year later Don Juan entrusted the child's education to Eugenio Vegas Latapié, a prominent ultra-conservative intellectual who had been chased out of Spain by Franco for conspiring against the regime. Vegas was hardly the obvious choice as a young boy's tutor, but the Count of Barcelona needed someone who could ensure that his son would speak Spanish fluently. When he was old enough, the child also began to attend classes at the Rolle school in Lausanne.

In the wake of his father's abdication and death, Don Juan gradually realised that Franco had no intention of restoring the monarchy in the near future. At first he hoped to achieve this restoration with the support of many of those who had fought with Franco in the civil war, in other words, the more conservative sectors of Spanish society, including the armed forces. Forced to choose between Don Juan and Franco, however, the vast majority opted for the latter. It was only then that Don Juan began to appeal to the general's opponents both at home and abroad.

In keeping with his efforts to favour the Axis powers without unduly antagonising the Allies, Franco initially sought to enlist Don Juan's support for his own cause. In May 1942 he urged him to identify himself publicly with the new single party, *FET y de las JONS*, in return for which he would be offered the throne of a 'totalitarian' monarchy, comparable, in his view, to that of the Catholic monarchs in the late fifteenth century. Several months later the dictator's undersecretary for the presidency, Luis Carrero Blanco, a naval officer who was to become his most influential adviser, produced a report in which he observed that, given Franco's refusal to proclaim himself king, Don Juan was the only serious candidate to the throne.[14]

By this stage, however, the Count of Barcelona had come to believe that once the Axis powers were defeated, the Allies would invade Spain and remove Franco from power on account of his former association with their enemies. His aim was therefore to present the monarchy to the Allies as the only viable alternative to the establishment of another Republican government, which would sooner or later lead to a second civil war. In carrying out this strategy he was enthusiasitically assisted by Pedro Sainz Rodríguez, Franco's first minister of education, who had fled Spain in 1942 to avoid being sent into exile by the regime for conspiring to restore the monarchy.

The timing of Don Juan's decision to distance himself publicly from Franco was thus largely determined by the Allied landings in North Africa in November 1942. In an interview with the *Journal de Genéve* that month, Don Juan presented the monarchy as the ideal instrument for a national reconciliation, and clearly stated his hope of occupying the throne soon, while admitting that the future government of Spain 'depended on the will of the Spanish people'. In March 1943 the count finally replied to Franco's earlier letter, refusing to associate himself with any single ideology and warning him that his 'provisional regime' was exposing Spain to grave risks, in view of which he should move quickly towards restoring the monarchy. In his reply, Franco admitted that he still considered him his potential successor, but only if he endorsed the *Movimiento* beforehand.[15]

Allied military success in Europe encouraged Don Juan's supporters to become ever-more explicit in their opposition to Franco. In June 1943, 27 *procuradores* of the newly created Cortes (parliament) petitioned him to complete the 'definition and ordering of the fundamental institutions of the state' by restoring the monarchy, thereby safeguarding Spain's neutrality and integrity. Three months later, eight of the Army's twelve lieutenant-generals requested his resignation, a challenge Franco successfully outmanouevred. Finally, in March 1944 a large group of influential university professors signed a manifesto in support of monarchism, resulting in four of them being exiled to remote provinces.

The Allied landings in Sicily and the subsequent fall of Mussolini encouraged Don Juan to present Franco with an ultimatum in August 1943, on the grounds that only the immediate restoration of the monarchy could save Spain from external reprisals and guarantee his personal safety. Years later the Count of Barcelona would privately admit that Franco had never forgiven him for this telegram, even though his reply had indicated that he did not wish to break with him altogether.[16]

Later that year Franco intercepted a letter from Don Juan to his supporters indicating that he was considering breaking off relations with the regime for good. In view of this, on 6 January 1944 he wrote the count a letter reiterating his own position, and denying that he was a usurper. In his reply Don Juan, confident in the belief that he enjoyed the full support of the Allies, insisted that 'it is necessary to offer Spaniards something which is neither Your Excellency's totalitarianism nor a return to a democratic republic'. As he later explained in an interview with the Argentine daily *La Prensa*, Don Juan's own alternative was a British-style monarchy capable of achieving a lasting national reconciliation.[17]

Don Juan's ultimatum, written at a time when many anticipated an imminent Allied invasion of Spain, created a poor impression in conservative circles, for it was felt that it was unpatriotic of him to seek to exploit Franco's external difficulties in this manner. The count apologised to Franco in February 1944, but the dictator did not accept his excuses and openly accused him of opportunism. Franco could afford to respond in this manner because by that stage it was becoming increasingly clear that the Allies were having second thoughts about invading Spain.

In an attempt to clinch Allied support for his claim to the throne, in March 1945 Don Juan issued his so-called Lausanne Manifesto. In it the count presented himself and the monarchy he wished to embody as the only viable alternative both to Franco's totalitarian regime, which he judged incompatible with an Allied victory in Europe, and a republic destined to fall under communist control. Amongst the future monarchy's priorities listed by Don Juan were 'the immediate approval, by popular vote, of a political constitution; recognition of all the rights inherent in the human personality, guaranteeing the corresponding political liberties; establishment of a legislative assembly elected by the nation; recognition of regional diversity; a broad political amnesty; a more equitable distribution of wealth and the elimination of unjust social distinctions . . .' In the wake of this manifesto Don Juan ordered all monarchists who had been collaborating with the Franco regime to resign their posts, an order that went largely unheeded.[18]

The Lausanne Manifesto was to have a decisive impact on Juan Carlos's future. It was in its wake that Carrero Blanco submitted a report to Franco in which he observed that 'it is necessary to start thinking about preparing the young prince [who is only six or seven years old] to be king'. As this could only be done with his father's consent, Carrero advised Franco not to react too violently against the manifesto. Instead Franco and his alter ego set out to win Don Juan for their cause once again, and even offered him the possibility of establishing himself officially in Madrid, at the state's expense. This decision was probably also motivated by the need to prove to the Western democracies that the regime was still compatible with a future monarchy, an option they undoubtedly preferred to that of a republic.[19]

Much to Franco's chagrin, however, Don Juan refused to occupy his gilded cage, and issued an even more belligerent statement to the *Gazette de Lausanne* in December 1945, in which he advocated the establishment of a parliamentary monarchy such as the British. Anxious not to lose him altogether, Franco agreed to allow Don Juan and his family to leave Switzerland for Portugal, in theory so as to facilitate a long-overdue interview with him. The Caudillo would soon regret his decision, as Don Juan's arrival in Portugal was greeted with the publication of a document signed by over four hundred members of the Spanish financial, military and academic élite pledging their support to his cause.

One of the pretender's major difficulties during this period was that, in his determination to win the support of all monarchists, regardless of their ideological preferences, he was forced to make contradictory, even incompatible promises. The ambiguity of Don Juan's position is best illustrated by the *Bases de Estoril* of February 1946, drawn up on his behalf by José María Gil Robles, the leader of the major Catholic party during the Republic, with a view to establishing a programme acceptable to the Carlists. The *Bases* had little in common with the Lausanne Manifesto, and were clearly inspired by the ideals of Catholic corporatism. What was more, the *Bases* failed to win him the unanimous support of the Carlists, whilst greatly antagonising both liberal monarchists and their potential anti-Francoist allies. Ironically, many of the ideas contained in this document were later taken up by Franco when he introduced his own pseudo-constitution, the Organic Law of the State, some twenty years later.

Determined not to go down in history as another Primo de Rivera, Franco was anxious to consolidate his regime by giving it a firmer institutional base. Given his own Catholic, conservative mentality, the only source of political legitimacy available to him was the monarchy, which he invariably associated with Spain's supposedly glorious imperial past. It was this that led him to promulgate the Law of Succession in March 1947, according to which 'Spain, as a political unit, is a Catholic, social and representative state which, in accordance with its traditions, proclaims itself to be a kingdom'. Franco thereby created a monarchy without a king, of which he would be regent in perpetuity. The law effectively established an elective monarchy, and gave him total control over the appointment of his successor, who could be either a king or a regent. Rubber-stamped by the Cortes in June, a month later the law was overwhelmingly endorsed in a referendum, which effectively became a plebiscite on Franco's continuity as head of state.[20]

Carrero Blanco had been sent to Estoril on 31 March to inform Don Juan of these developments, but 'forgot' to mention that the text of the law would be made public that same evening by Franco.[21] Outraged by the latter's behaviour and the content of the law, on 7 April 1947 Don Juan issued his famous Estoril Manifesto, in which he took a strong stand on the principle of hereditary succession. The Count of Barcelona declared that Franco's so-called monarchy would lack both dynastic and democratic legitimacy, and accused the Caudillo of seeking to perpetuate his personal dictatorship indefinitely. Several days later the *Observer* published an interview with Don Juan in which he openly advocated a democratic monarchy, promising the legalisation of parties and unions banned by Franco, such as the Socialist PSOE and the anarcho-syndicalist CNT. Additionally he envisaged a degree of decentralisation, religious freedom and a partial amnesty. Years later Franco would tell his private secretary that it was this interview that finally convinced him of the need to begin to prepare Juan Carlos as his successor. By way of reply the dictator modified the terms of the law, enabling him to elevate to the throne any candidate 'of royal lineage', regardless of his place in the line of succession.

Don Juan's increasingly difficult relations with Franco determined that Juan Carlos should remain at Lausanne when his parents moved to Portugal. In January 1946 he duly became a boarder at Ville Saint-Jean, a school run by the Marian Fathers at Fribourg and attended mainly by French children. The boy, who felt that his parents had abandoned him in the company of complete strangers, was extremely unhappy at first, but his misery was partly alleviated by the proximity of his doting grandmother, who saw him every weekend. Juan Carlos did not speak Spanish fluently at this stage, and Victoria Eugenia (or 'Gangan', as her grand-children called her), who had suffered considerably in Spain on account of her English accent, was so anxious to ensure that her grandson was spared her embarrassment that she spent many an hour giving him phonetic exercises to improve his pronunciation. Juan Carlos's teachers at Ville Saint-Jean remember him as a child of normal intelligence and exceptional physical stature and beauty, who badly needed disciplining after spending too much time in the company of indulgent nannies.[22]

The political climate in Spain was such that the prince's tutors were instructed to destroy any edible presents he might receive from well-wishers lest they be poisoned. Don Juan became increasingly uneasy at having left Juan Carlos behind in Switzerland, and in early 1947 he was finally allowed to rejoin his parents in Estoril. The prince was accompanied by Vegas, to whom he had become genuinely attached, in spite of the latter's intransigence. After attending a lecture of his on the ultra-conservative nineteenth-century political thinker Donoso Cortés, a liberal Catalan priest jokingly warned Don Juan that with such a tutor his son might turn out to be a new Philip II, a remark that Vegas took as a compliment.[23]

According to one of his early biographers, it was in January 1947, shortly after his first communion, that Juan Carlos was first given a detailed account of the Spanish Civil War by a friend of his father. After listening attentively, the child, who had just celebrated his ninth birthday, asked Don Juan: 'And why does Franco, who was so good during the war, treat us so badly now?'[24]

Unhappy with the ad hoc arrangements he had been forced to make for Juan Carlos's schooling in Portugal, in late 1947 Don Juan decided that he should return to Fribourg under the supervision of Vegas. The latter had been responsible for the release of the count's statement to the *Observer*, which was increasingly seen as a tactical error, and was anxious to withdraw from political activity altogether. Years later Juan Carlos would recall that it was his tutor's belief that 'the heir to the dynasty should be brought up without any concessions to the weaknesses which seem normal to ordinary people', and therefore 'educated me to realise that I was someone apart, with far more responsibilities and duties than other people'.[25]

The Law of Succession of 1947 put paid to Don Juan's hopes of ascending the throne against Franco's will and convinced him of the need to reach an agreement with the dictator. At the instigation of the Francoist monarchist Julio Danvila, the two men finally met on 25 August 1948 aboard the general's pleasure boat, the *Azor*, off the coast of San Sebastián in northern Spain. Gil Robles and Vegas, who had been largely responsible for Don Juan's strategy since 1942, were not informed of the meeting, which coincided with a fresh round of talks between monarchists and exiled socialists in southern France. As was to be expected, news of the interview largely stymied recent efforts to win the support of the moderate left for Don Juan's cause.[26]

It was in the course of this three-hour meeting that Franco and Don Juan decided Juan Carlos's immediate future. From the outset the Caudillo refused to discuss the restoration of the monarchy, but showed great interest in Juan Carlos completing his education in Spain, a goal shared by Don Juan. The latter nevertheless objected that it was impossible to send his son to a country where it was considered a crime to shout 'Viva el Rey!', and where monarchists were constantly harassed by the authorities. Franco assured him all of that could change, implicitly acknowledging his responsibility for this state of affairs. In return for allowing Juan Carlos to be educated in Spain, Don Juan had hoped to secure some recognition of his claim to the throne, and of his son's status as prince of Asturias. All he obtained were vague promises from Franco, authorising a degree of monarchist propaganda in the press and an amnesty for monarchist dissenters. At this stage, however, the dictator was not interested in controlling the details of Juan Carlos's education; his main concern was that the prince's presence on Spanish soil should contribute to the regime's acceptance by the Western democracies.[27]

As the summer of 1948 drew to a close, Don Juan began to have grave doubts as to whether he should go through with the plan agreed with Franco and send his son to Spain after all. In early October he sent him back to school in Switzerland with Vegas, with the excuse of allowing him to spend some time with his grandmother, Victoria Eugenia, who feared she would see less of him in future. Unable to obtain further concessions from Franco, however, Don Juan recalled his son later that month, and by early November he was ready to travel to Spain.[28]

Juan Carlos first set foot on Spanish soil on 9 November 1948, on a bitterly cold Castilian morning, at the age of ten. He had travelled overnight from Lisbon in a special train driven by a Spanish grandee in a boiler suit, and his journey was cut short at a small station just outside Madrid so as to avoid clashes between monarchist supporters and their antagonists. The young boy was driven straight to the Cerro de los Angeles (the Hill of the Angels), estimated to be the geographical centre of the Iberian peninsula, where he was made to read out the text by which Alfonso XIII had consecrated the nation to the Sacred Heart in 1919. The Francoist monarchists who accompanied him lost no time in explaining that in the early days of the civil war the statue of Christ erected at the site had been 'executed' by Republican militiamen, and had since become a symbol of Franco's victory over the 'reds'. From there he was finally taken to Las Jarillas, the country house that was to be his home for the next two years. On arrival Juan Carlos was greeted by a group of Don Juan's supporters, who had just attended the burial of a monarchist student, Carlos Méndez, who had died while in police custody. It was his first political act as his father's representative in Spain.[29]

Las Jarillas, an estate located some ten miles north of Madrid placed at Don Juan's disposal by the Marquis of Urquijo, was ideal in that it was relatively isolated, but not far from a military establishment whose officers could be called upon to protect Juan Carlos against any possible aggression, and relatively near Franco's residence at El Pardo. The prince was entrusted to a group of carefully selected tutors who enjoyed Don Juan's full confidence, and placed in the company of eight other boys of his age, chosen from amongst Spain's leading aristocratic families. The sole commoner was José Luis Leal, who would become a cabinet minister three decades later. Juan Carlos shared a room with his cousin Carlos de Borbón Dos Sicilias, whose presence attenuated his homesickness. The head tutor was José Garrido, a highly respected liberal pedagogue, who had no difficulty in winning Juan Carlos's trust. His spiritual well-being was left to father Ignacio de Zulueta, a deeply reactionary figure obsessed with court protocol, who made his charges pray for the conversion of the Soviet Union and the victory of the British Conservative Party in the 1950 election. Juan Carlos grew particulary fond of his physical education instructor, Heliodoro Ruiz, who had once taught the founder of Falange, José Antonio Primo de Rivera, and who took it upon himself to transform the prince into a consummate athlete.[30]

During these years it was the Duke of Sotomayor, head of Don Juan's household, who was responsible for deciding who should have access to Juan Carlos, who theoretically acted as his father's representative in Spain. Amongst those who visited Las Jarillas were some of those who would later serve under the future king, notably future prime minister Leopoldo Calvo Sotelo, and the president of the first democratic Congress, Fernando Alvarez de Miranda. One of the prince's favourite vistors was the colourful General Millán Astray, founder of the Spanish Foreign Legion, who had lost an arm and an eye in combat, and who has gone down in history for his dictum 'Long live death! Down with the intelligentsia!'[31]

Juan Carlos's first meeting with the man under whose shadow he was to spend much of his life took place on 24 November, only weeks after his arrival in Spain. Don Juan had been very anxious about his son's first meeting with Franco, and had advised him to listen carefully and say as little as possible without seeming rude. Although Juan Carlos was only a child, he was old enough to realise that he was his father's principal adversary, and he had often heard the adults at Estoril refer to him in less than glowing terms. Franco did his best to ingratiate himself with the young boy and promised to take him pheasant shooting at Aranjuez. During their interview, however, Juan Carlos was distracted by the presence of a mouse under Franco's chair, and paid little attention to his words. Nevertheless he did notice that the Caudillo referred to his father as 'Highness', unlike those who visited him in Estoril, who invariably addressed him as 'Your Majesty'.[32]

Those who shared their time at Las Jarillas with Juan Carlos remember him as a jovial, out-going boy, who preferred the outdoor activities at which he excelled to the more academic persuits imposed on him by his tutors. This contentment may only have been skin deep, however. Back in Estoril for Christmas, Gil Robles had occasion to watch him closely during a visit to Lisbon zoo with his children. 'He is still very much a child in all his charming reactions', he would later write, 'but I find him prematurely serious and even somewhat sad, as though he were aware of the battle being fought all around him. Watching him play in the park and later at home yesterday, I could not help but feel his pain, which is that of a child who knows how to make himself loved. When I think of his future I feel sorry for him. What lies in store for this child who, at the age of ten, is the object of such an acute struggle?'[33]

Franco's public statements during the course of 1949 concerning the future of the monarchy did nothing to allay Don Juan's fears about the consequences of his arrangement with the dictator. In April the count decided against allowing Juan Carlos to attend Franco's annual civil war victory parade through the streets of Madrid. A month later the general's disparaging remarks about Alfonso XIII and his ancestors in his speech at the opening of the Cortes prompted many *Juanistas* to demand that Juan Carlos return to Portugal at once. Don Juan eventually informed the head of state in September that the political climate was incompatible with his son's continued presence at Las Jarillas, to which Franco replied by reminding him that he had promised him nothing, and that it was in the child's best interest – and that of the dynasty as a whole – that he be educated in Spain. Although the Caudillo visited Salazar in Portugal later that month, plans for a second meeting with Don Juan were stillborn. In view of this impasse it was decided – against Victoria Eugenia's wishes – that the child would spend the rest of the academic year at Estoril, assisted in his studies by his tutors from Las Jarillas. Don Juan thereby confirmed Gil Robles's observation to the effect that 'the prince is your only weapon against Franco'.[34]

The winter of 1949–50 was not a happy one at Estoril. In November Juan Carlos lost his maternal grandfather, Carlos de Borbón-Dos Sicilias, who was also his godfather. The child greatly missed the friends he had made at Las Jarillas, and was at a loss to understand why he could not go back to them. To make matters worse for Don Juan, in December 1949 his elder brother, Don Jaime, unexpectedly reasserted his claim to the throne, on the grounds that his renunciation in 1933 had been null and void. This decision inevitably affected Don Jaime's eldest son, Alfonso, who had been mentioned as a potential successor to the throne by a Francoist aristocrat as early as 1947. In the absence of an understanding with Don Juan, Franco was clearly applying pressure on Estoril by encouraging the emergence of other pretenders.

In the belief that he had shown friend and foe alike that he alone dictated his son's future, Don Juan sent Juan Carlos back to Spain in the autumn of 1950, accompanied by his younger brother Alfonso, who had never set foot in the country. Determined to prevent Franco from reasserting his influence, Don Juan had decided to reestablish the school at Las Jarillas in the palace of Miramar, the royal family's summer residence overlooking the magnificent bay of San Sebastián.

Juan Carlos spent four very happy years at Miramar. His tutors, notably Angel López Amo, a law professor who had taught him briefly in Switzerland, were competent and kind-hearted, and he was constantly in the company of a group of hand-picked peers, some of whom he knew from Las Jarillas. His parents did their best to ensure that he was not given special privileges, and at the end of every academic year he underwent the same official oral examination endured by thousands of other Spanish schoolchildren. Juan Carlos was particulary good at science subjects, but also enjoyed history and literature. One of the compulsory subjects he enjoyed least was that entitled 'Formation of the National Spirit', which sought to instruct children in the principles and institutions of the Franco regime. Like so many other boarders of his age, Juan Carlos was often homesick, and always looked forward to the long summer holidays in Portugal.[35]

In July 1951 Don Juan wrote a long letter to Franco in which he urged him to delay the restoration of the monarchy no further. In his reply the general dryly observed that many monarchists, aware of the impossibility of installing a monarchy in Spain that was incompatible with the *Movimiento*, had begun to regard his abdication in his son's favour as the only way of guaranteeing the continuity of the Alfonsist line. With characteristic cruelty Franco reminded the count that his own father had abdicated in his favour for similar reasons, and urged him to follow his example. The dictator went on to admit that the 1945 Lausanne Manifesto had effectively ruled out Don Juan as a suitable candidate and that he had lost all hope of winning him back for his cause. Following this letter the two men did not communicate again until 1954.[36]

In view of Don Juan's attitude, in late 1952 Franco turned to his elder brother Don Jaime, whom he succeeded in convincing of the need to have his son Alfonso educated in Spain under his supervision. Alfonso was initially reluctant to comply with his father's wishes, but eventually agreed to move to Spain to study law at Deusto University. In 1955 he transferred to one of Madrid's most élitist academic institutions, the Centro de Estudios Universitarios (CEU), where he began to associate with many of the country's future leaders.

Even at this early age Juan Carlos was never allowed to forget the threat posed by political events beyond his control. In January 1954, Earl

Mountbatten, who was commander-in-chief of NATO naval forces in the Mediterranean, invited Don Juan, his second cousin, to follow some manoeuvres from a British ship. When this became known in Spain, the Falangist press, always keen to fuel its readers' Anglophobia, launched a vicious attack on Don Juan that threatened to bring the Miramar experiment to a close. Years later, when the prince objected to another similar attack, Franco merely commented 'oh, it's just the way of the press', as if anything could be published in Spain without his consent.[37]

Having passed his official examinations with flying colours, Juan Carlos completed his secondary schooling in June 1954. Although he had no intention of sending his son abroad, at the instigation of Sainz Rodríguez the Count of Barcelona informed Franco that he was thinking of enrolling him at the Catholic University of Louvain, and even sent Gil Robles to Belgium to lend credence to his threat. The purpose of this deceit was to force Franco to agree to a second interview with Don Juan, which the latter hoped to use to his own advantage. As the count had anticipated, Franco came out strongly against the idea of sending Juan Carlos to university, 'however Catholic it may be', promptly presenting his own proposal. The Caudillo intended the prince to spend two years at the Zaragoza military academy, followed by a further year each at the naval and air force academies, after which he would follow a tailor-made two-year course at a Spanish university. Juan Carlos would then embark on a succession of secondments to various ministries, with a view to becoming acquainted with the agricultural, mining and industrial sectors, as well as with the overall workings of the administration. Throughout this entire process the prince would benefit from Franco's direct supervision and guidance. 'I consider it important that the people grow accustomed to seeing the prince with the Caudillo', he wrote to Don Juan, referring to himself in the third person as was his habit, 'so that they may begin to understand what he represents for the nation'.[38]

Over the summer Don Juan submitted Franco's proposal to the members of his privy council, most of whom advised him to accept it. The point of this was to humiliate the dictator by allowing his life-long enemies a say in a matter that was of the utmost importance to him, namely Juan Carlos's future. The count finally replied in September from Tangiers, where the prince had had his appendix removed during a visit to Spanish Morocco. In his letter Don Juan reminded him of his own duties as a father while nevertheless acknowledging that his son's education should be 'Spanish, religious and military'. This did not satisfy Franco, who hastened to inform the count that he intended to educate Juan Carlos in keeping with the regime's political philosophy, while reminding him that 'the monarchy is inviable outside the *Movimiento*'. Discussing this letter with his private secretary, the dictator would later remark that 'if they think I'm trying to turn the prince into a Falangist, so be it'. Don Juan, however, had made it equally clear that he would not allow his son to return to Spain without first seeing the Caudillo again.[39]

The second Franco–Don Juan interview was held on 29 December 1954 at Las Cabezas, a country estate not far from the Portuguese border. The count was deeply moved by the occasion, for he had not set foot in Spain since 1936. True to form, Franco spent much of the meeting reminiscing about his military expoits, barely allowing Don Juan to discuss the matter at hand. At one point in the interview the latter asked him if he would have to abdicate in his son's favour, to which the dictator replied that he was confident that the count would sacrifice himself if necessary in due course. Much to Don Juan's disappointment, the interview only served to reach a basic understanding regarding the second phase of his son's education.[40]

As Franco had hoped, Juan Carlos returned to Spain in mid-January 1955 to prepare for the entrance examination to the Zaragoza military academy. During these months he lived in Madrid, at the state's expense, at the palace of the Dukes of Montellano, under the overall supervision of General Carlos Martínez Campos, Duke of La Torre, a strict though widely respected disciplinarian. His tutors included professor López Amo, the Dominican José Manuel Aguilar, and two military men who were destined to play a crucial role in his life: cavalry officer Nicolás Cotoner, later Marquis of Mondéjar, and artillery officer Alfonso Armada.[41]

Life at the Montellano palace was generally austere and disciplined. Martínez Campos, who worked his pupil hard, insisted that he observe the rules of protocol when addressing his tutors, something the naturally spontaneous Juan Carlos resented. On one occasion the duke refused Juan Carlos permission to attend a wedding in Lisbon so as not to disrupt his work, a decision that earned him Franco's praise. The prince's rigid time-table left little time for entertainment, which may have been a blessing in disguise given his meagre pocket-money. Don Juan had never had much money to spare, and it was often Cotoner who saved the day when it came to buying a new suit.[42]

Juan Carlos's presence in Madrid naturally aroused the hostility of those within the regime who opposed the restoration of the monarchy, notably the more radical sectors of the Falange. Many Spaniards first heard of the young prince in April 1955, as a result of the publication of his first press interview. Later that month a lecture on the European monarchies at Madrid's Ateneo, one of the capital's leading cultural centres, ended in an ugly brawl between Falangists and *Juanistas*, who were unable to prevent the distribution of leaflets ridiculing Juan Carlos. The latter was subsequently booed at a horse show, and was later insulted during a visit to a Falangist summer camp. The Army minister, General Agustín Muñoz Grandes, who was known to favour a regency, barely concealed his hostility to the monarchy, while the Falangist leader Raimundo Fernández Cuesta struggled to impose his authority on the younger members of his organisation. This state of affairs led the mayor of Madrid, the Count of Mayalde, to complain to Franco's private secretary that it was unwise to allow regime apparatchiks to criticise the monarchy if – as Juan Carlos's presence in Madrid suggested – the Caudillo intended to restore it.[43]

At a funeral service attended by Franco in November 1955 for José Antonio Primo de Rivera, an anonymous Falangist shouted: 'We do not want stupid kings!' The dictator, however, was pleased to have the prince with him, and took delight in lecturing him at length on the dangers of falling prey to the aristocracy, and on the need for him to become familiar with the ways and needs of ordinary people, whom he believed to be 'morally healthier, less selfish' and more genuinely patriotic.[44]

Having succesfully completed his qualifying tests, the prince finally entered the Zaragoza military academy in the autumn of 1955, and took the oath to the colours on 15 December. General Muñoz Grandes, who presided over the ceremony, made no reference to his presence in his address to the cadets. On the whole, however, Juan Carlos was well received in the academy, though the defence of his father's good name occasionally led to nocturnal fist-fights with fellow cadets in the indoor riding school, from which he sometimes emerged with a black eye. It was during his years at Zaragoza that Juan Carlos first realised that most officers would never forgive Don Juan for having spoken out against the regime and its founder in the 1940s.[45]

The prince's orderly existence was unexpectedly shattered on 29 March 1956. On leave in Estoril for the Easter holidays, Juan Carlos accidentally shot his younger brother while playing with a revolver, killing him instantly. The official version put about by both the Spanish embassy and Don Juan's household claimed Alfonso had shot himself while cleaning the weapon, and the Madrid authorities became very agitated when an Italian magazine, *Settimo giorno*, printed an account which was far closer to the truth. The prince, aged eighteen at the time, had always been extremely close to Alfonso, a popular, lively fourteen-year-old who had greatly mitigated his loneliness, and was deeply affected by his death. In spite of rumours to the effect that he might renounce his rights and join a friary, within forty-eight hours Juan Carlos was back in uniform. His mother, Doña María de las Mercedes, who was with them when the accident occurred, was sent to a clinic in Germany to recover from a deep depression. To cap it all, Don Jaime, who regarded himself as the head of the Bourbon dynasty, publicly demanded an official enquiry into his nephew's death, thereby incurring Don Juan's wrath. With characteristic lack of tact, Franco later told a senior *Juanista* that 'people do not like princes who are out of luck'. Ironically the revolver in question is said to have been a present from none other than the Caudillo himself.[46]

Juan Carlos's future was to remain uncertain in the extreme for years to come. On the occasion of the first anniversary of Alfonsito's death in 1957, the Count of Ruiseñada considered asking the prince to preside over the unveiling of a bust in his brother's honour. When he informed Franco, the latter suggested that he invite his cousin Alfonso instead, and went on to explain that if Juan Carlos followed in his father's footsteps he would have no option but to find another candidate.[47]

Having completed his stint at Zaragoza in July 1957, Juan Carlos moved on to the naval academy at Marín, in the north-western region of Galicia, and later to the Air Force academy of San Javier, in the south-eastern province of Murcia. As part of his training the prince sailed across the Atlantic in the Spanish Navy's tall ship, the majestic *Juan Sebastián Elcano*, which called at several ports in the United States in May 1958. This coincided with the arrival in America of Don Juan, always a keen sportsman, who had sailed across the Atlantic in his private yacht. In an obvious attempt to reaffirm his preeminence, and with the help of the Spanish ambassador in Washington, the monarchist José María de Areilza, Don Juan dominated most of the events to which Juan Carlos had been invited, much to the State Department's discomfort.[48]

Official thinking on Juan Carlos's future role remained tentative indeed. In March 1959 Franco's alter ego, Carrero Blanco, produced a lengthy report analysing the need for a new constitution, which would eventually be adopted in 1967 as the Organic Law of the State. In this text Carrero still expressed the view that Franco should invite Don Juan to succeed him, on condition that he accept the regime's political philosophy; if he did not, he should be publicly discarded, and the same offer should be made to Juan Carlos, who was already of age. Were the latter to refuse as well, 'we would have to think of someone else, or perhaps a regent'.[49]

Back in Spain the prince remained a controversial figure. In the spring of 1959 he was amongst the officers and men who marched past the Caudillo in the annual military parade held in Madrid to celebrate his victory in the civil war. On the eve of the parade, when Franco was informed that monarchist groups had distributed leaflets urging the capital's inhabitants to show their affection for Don Juan by cheering his son, he merely remarked that 'I will not object if his supporters applaud him'. As expected, minor scuffles broke out on the morning of the parade between members of Carlist, Falangist and *Juanista* youth organisations. In an attempt to ingratiate himself further with the regime's supporters, later that month Juan Carlos laid a laurel wreath at Alicante prison, where the founder of the Falange, Primo de Rivera, had been shot in 1936.[50]

In December 1959 Juan Carlos finally passed out of all three services with the rank of lieutenant. On this occasion the Army minister, General Antonio Barroso, acting with Franco's prior consent, paid tribute to the Spanish royal family and underlined the importance of the prince's future duties. Don Juan had initially intended his son to study at Salamanca University, or at least allowed Martínez Campos to spend several months making the necessary preparations. In late 1959, however, the count unexpectedly changed his mind, possibly at the instigation of Sainz Rodríguez, who appears to have enjoyed playing cat-and-mouse with Franco. This prompted the resignation of Martínez Campos, much to the distress of Juan Carlos, who had spent five years under his tutelage. Don Juan subsequently informed the Caudillo that he preferred his son to take up residence in one of the family's palaces in the north of Spain, preferably Miramar, where he could be taught by professors from a number of different universities. This plan was instantly quashed by Franco, however, who wanted to have the prince closer to hand. As in 1954, the count insisted that he pay the price of another interview before agreeing to his demands.[51]

Don Juan and Franco held their third and final in-depth interview at Las Cabezas on 28 March 1960, not long after Juan Carlos's twenty-second birthday. The two men agreed to replace Martínez Campos with General Juan Castañón de Mena, forming a new household for the prince that was to include Mondéjar and Armada. Additionally, the priest–historian Federico Suárez, a member of *Opus Dei* proposed by Carrero, became his confessor and religious counsellor. It was also decided that the prince's activities would be supervised by a jointly appointed committee, which would in turn select the academic staff responsible for his studies. As on previous occasions, Don Juan left Franco without having obtained any recognition of his right to the throne in return for allowing his son to remain in Spain. In the course of the meeting Don Juan told him that the British prime minister, Harold Macmillan, had recently asked him if it was true that he had secretly abdicated in his son's favour, to which the count had replied that he intended to do no such thing. Later Don Juan insisted that they issue a joint communiqué, threatening not to allow his son back to Spain unless Franco agreed. The latter finally acceded, but subsequently modified the text accepted by his rival without his consent.[52]

Following this encounter Juan Carlos briefly took up residence in the

Casita de Arriba (the Upper Pavilion), a miniscule palace just outside El Escorial, but soon moved to the palace of La Zarzuela, which Franco had begun to renovate for him in 1958. La Zarzuela, originally a hunting lodge once frequented by Carlos III, had the dual advantage of being on the outskirts of Madrid and in the immediate vicinity of the head of state's residence at El Pardo.[53]

With Don Juan's consent, Franco instructed his minister of education to form a committee of academics, who were entrusted with the supervision of Juan Carlos's university studies. The committee was presided by professor Torcuato Fernández-Miranda, whose 'fascinating mind' immediately captivated the young prince. Born in 1915, this diminutive, intensely private intellectual rose rapidly through the ranks of Spanish academia, becoming one of the country's leading political theorists. A deeply religious, conservative man, Fernández-Miranda had never identified with any of the Franco regime's political 'families', but this did not prevent him from occupying senior positions in the Ministry of Education. It was because of his political 'neutrality' that Franco never fully trusted him, to the extent of requesting the prince's military aides, Mondéjar and Armada, to be present during his tutorials to ensure they did not discuss politics. Though hardly a liberal himself, Mondéjar was happy to turn a blind eye.[54]

Colonel Armada, who soon came to resent the prince's excellent relationship with his tutor, would later claim that Fernández-Miranda seemed more interested in showing off his own erudition than in educating his pupil. Juan Carlos, however, does not appear to have shared his opinion. Unlike other tutors, Fernández-Miranda down-played the importance of formal learning and examinations, and encouraged Juan Carlos to think for himself instead. Much to the prince's alarm, the professor often insisted that when he became king he would be left largely to his own devices, like a tightrope walker without a safety net. From then on Fernández-Miranda was to be one of his closest advisers, a little-known fact at the time.[55]

It was also during these months that the prince first met Laureano López Rodó, who was to play a decisive role in the process leading to his appointment as Franco's successor. A professor of administrative law and a prominent member of *Opus Dei*, López Rodó had been drafted into Carrero Blanco's team in 1957 to produce a blueprint for the reorganisation of the Spanish administrative system, and soon became a highly influential figure. In 1962 he was made commissioner of the Development Plan, a post that acquired ministerial rank in 1965 and granted him considerable say in the regime's political life throughout the 1960s. Although Juan Carlos would lean on him heavily in years to come, López Rodó's influence over him was never as great as he liked to think.[56]

In October 1960 Juan Carlos's arrival at Madrid University's law department was greeted with cries of 'Long live King Javier!' and 'Go back to Estoril!' from Carlists and Falangists respectively. The prince remained calm in the face of adversity, and did his best to ensure that his supporters, led by the young monarchist Luis María Anson, did not respond to acts of provocation. With some prompting from El Pardo, the university authorities intervened to quash these incidents, and order was soon restored. As had already happened at the military academies, indifferent and even potentially hostile students were gradually won over by the prince's charm and bonhomie, and by his determination to win their acceptance. As one student – who would later become a cabinet minister – noted with admiration, he even smoked *Celtas*, a very popular brand of cheap black tobacco.[57]

Although the prince's activities were closely watched by the regime, he was occasionally able to mingle with some of its opponents. During a visit to Barcelona in May 1961, Antonio de Senillosa, a liberal Catalan monarchist, offered to introduce him to people not normally invited to official receptions, to which Juan Carlos agreed. The meeting, which was attended by a number of prominent intellectuals, most of whom were hostile to the regime, proved a success. The novelist José Agustín Goytisolo, for one, noted with satisfaction that the prince seemed keener to listen to others than he was to impose his own views.[58]

True to his Bourbon lineage, the prince had shown considerable interest in the opposite sex from an early age. During his Christmas holidays in Portugal in December 1956 Juan Carlos met Olghina de Robilant, an Italian aristrocrat with whom he would remain in touch until 1960.[59] In his early twenties he also frequented the company of Maria Gabriela of Savoy, daughter of the last king of Italy, who had grown up with him in Estoril. Indeed as late as July 1960 the Italian princess was his partner at the wedding of the heir of the Dukes of Württemberg, and they were later seen together during the Olympic Games in Rome. Both these events were also attended by princess Sofía, daughter of King Paul and Queen Frederica of Greece, whom Juan Carlos had first met as a teenager in the summer of 1954, in the course of a famous cruise of the Greek Islands attended by many of Europe's royal families. In 1958 they had danced together at another wedding in Germany, but it was not until June 1961, at the Duke of Kent's wedding, that Juan Carlos began to show serious interest in the Greek princess.

Queen Frederica later admitted that when news of the Spanish prince's advances reached Athens she was at once both 'horrified and delighted'. Her delight owed a great deal to his physical appearance: Juan Carlos was notable for his 'fair curly hair which he personally dislikes but all elderly ladies like myself, simply adore', his 'dark eyes with long lashes', and for being 'tall and athletic'. Additionally, he could 'turn his charm on and off as he likes'. More importantly, 'he is intelligent, has modern ideas and is kind and gentle. He has enough pride to be a real Spaniard, but also enough loving understanding to be able easily to forgive other people's transgressions'. At the same time, however, the Greek monarchs were horrified because he was a Catholic, and they knew that 'before they could get married there would be tremendous discussions on this relatively unimportant subject'. Queen Frederica's delight apparently won the upper hand, and Juan Carlos and his parents were duly invited to spend the summer with the Greek royal family in Corfu. After a very intense court-ship, conducted largely in English, Sofía's engagement to Juan Carlos was formally announced on 13 September 1961 in Lausanne, where his grandmother Victoria Eugenia still lived.[60]

Princess Sofía's childhood had been as unsettled as that of her fiancé. Born in Athens on 2 November 1938, almost exactly three years after the restoration of the monarchy, she and her family had narrowly escaped the German invasion of Greece in April 1941. The next four years were spent in exile in South Africa and Egypt, during which time her father was rarely at home. Following the defeat of Germany, the monarchy was once again put to a referendum, which paved the way for the royal family's return to Athens in September 1946. In the midst of a vicious civil war, Sofía's father succeeded his brother George II as king of Greece in April 1947. After spending several idyllic years at the Tatoi palace on the out-skirts of Athens with her family, in 1951 the twelve-year-old princess, who had been educated in English and had only recently become fluent in Greek, was sent to one of the Kurt Hahn schools, Schloss Salem in Baden-Württemberg. This highly cosmopolitan, coeducational establishment had been taken over by Queen Frederica's brother, prince George of Hanover, whose wife Sophie kept a watchful eye over her young niece. It was during her four years at Salem that Sofía developed an interest in classical music, which was to remain with her for the rest of her life.

On returning to Greece in late 1956 the eighteen-year old Sofía set out to become a children's nurse, and was fully qualified by 1958. During this period she also received private tuition in ancient Greek, literature, history, art and archaeology. With the assistance of her tutor, in 1959 she and her sister Irene published several articles on the excavations they had undertaken in the vicinity of the royal residence at Tatoi. Sofía, as shy and unassuming as she was attractive, led an extremely protected life at the Greek court during these years, and appears to have accepted her parents' authority unquestioningly. Queen Frederica was initially determined to marry her to the crown prince of Norway, who even spent a summer with them in Greece, but Harald had plans of his own and the relationship did not develop.

Although Juan Carlos's choice of a partner was a matter that concerned Franco greatly, Don Juan was careful to exclude him from the proceedings. Indeed the count radioed the news of his son's engagement when the Caudillo was at sea on board the *Azor*, possibly so that the circumstances would discourage him from attempting a lengthy reply. These precautions, which some *Juanistas* deemed excessive, were probably not unjustified. A year earlier, in conversation with one of the prince's tutors, Franco, who was clearly anxious to find a suitable wife for Juan Carlos, had firmly ruled out Sofía and her sister Irene as possible candidates, on the rather curious grounds that their father, King Paul, had once suggested to King Alfonso XIII that the only way to regain his crown was for him to become a freemason. Though anxious to assert his independence, Don Juan did not wish to alienate the dictator unnecessarily, and in late September he not only invited him to the wedding, but offered him the Order of the Golden Fleece as well. With characteristic cruelty, Franco turned it down on the grounds that it was an honour only a reigning monarch could bestow.[61]

Juan Carlos had hoped that his engagement would encourage Franco to clarify his intentions, and even recognise him as Prince of Asturias. This was immediately ruled out by the Caudillo, however, since it would have been tantamount to accepting Don Juan's claim to the throne. On 13 November, in the course of a shoot, Franco simply asked Juan Carlos what he intended to do after the wedding, to which the latter replied that to date he had always obeyed both him and his father. When the Caudillo reminded him that he had come of age, the prince promptly retorted 'I still have a master'.[62]

The engagement was followed by several months of frantic negotiations involving the Vatican, the Greek Orthodox Church, the two royal families, and the Spanish and Greek governments. Madrid demanded a Catholic wedding ceremony, and expected Sofía to embrace her husband's faith beforehand. The Greek authorities, for their part, insisted on an Orthodox ceremony, and refused to allow the princess to convert while still on Greek soil. In January 1962 Juan Carlos and his father visited Pope John XXIII to allay the Vatican's fears, and obtained his authorisation for a double wedding. Much to Queen Frederica's desperation, some conservative Spanish monarchists 'tried to be more Catholic than the Pope', and many remained uneasy at the prospect of a convert one day becoming Queen of Spain.[63]

In early March 1962 Juan Carlos visited Franco to urge him to attend the wedding. The latter declined the invitation, but promised that the Spanish government would be represented by a minister, Admiral Felipe Abárzuza, who would sail to Athens on board the Navy's flagship, the cruiser *Canarias*. Abandoning his legendary reserve, for the first time ever Franco told Juan Carlos explicitly that his chances of reigning were better than his father's, something the prince had suspected since at least 1958. By this stage Juan Carlos was convinced that his father would stand down rather than jeopardise the dynasty, not least because Don Juan had privately assured him that he had no intention of following in the steps of Leopold of Belgium, whose reluctance to abdicate in his son's favour had seriously undermined the monarchy. The Caudillo also reminded him that although he had completed his formal education, there was a still a great deal he needed to learn about his country, in view of which it was essential that he remain in Spain after the wedding. Following this conversation, Franco told his private secretary that Juan Carlos was 'very intelligent, and already surprisingly well-informed'.[64]

The prince's engagement inevitably triggered a fresh wave of speculation as to where he would reside in the future. Already in November, the British ambassador in Madrid, George Labouchere, had been 'assured by some monarchists that the majority of them, supported by Don Juan, are most anxious that after his marriage Don Juan Carlos and his wife should live in Estoril', out of fear that 'should he live in Madrid he will take all the limelight from his father and make it impossible for the latter to come back to Spain to reign'. Labouchere, however, soon concluded that Juan Carlos would not be settling in Portugal, partly on the strength of the evidence provided by 'the Greek ambassador's rather garrulous wife', according to whom the prince had 'protested to her his great affection for General Franco and assured her that the latter treats him like a son'. More importantly, perhaps, in the ambassador's view Queen Frederica was 'hardly the type of lady who would cheerfully allow her daughter to remain exiled from her new country and not at least take her rightful place for some periods of the year in Spain as the wife of the grandson of King Alfonso XIII'. All of which led him to conclude that Franco 'intends now to wait to see whether the immature, if charming, Don Juan Carlos has it in him to attain the calibre to become King of Spain when he reaches the age of thirty in eight years' time'.[65]

The nuptial ceremonies finally held in Athens on 14 May 1962 were transformed into a major political occasion by the more than five thousand Spaniards who travelled to Greece to express their support for Don Juan and the Bourbon dynasty. Although this unprecedented explosion of monarchist feeling alarmed the Francoist authorities, with the partial exception of *Arriba*, the official Falangist newspaper, the Spanish press gave the event extensive coverage, though it subsequently censored news of the honeymoon. Indeed according to the British ambassador in Madrid, 'the wedding brought more publicity to the Spanish Royal Family than at any time since Franco came to power'.[66]

The young couple's enjoyment of their wedding day was marred by several events. On the eve of the wedding the British ambassador in Athens found Juan Carlos 'in rather a gloomy state', which he attributed both to a shoulder injury recently sustained while practising judo with Crown Prince Constantine, and to the pressures exerted on him simultaneously by both his father's entourage and the Spanish authorities. Above all, Juan Carlos was troubled by the fact that, although Franco had granted him the Order of the Grand Collar of Carlos III, the highest decoration he could bestow, his official status in Spain would remain unchanged. Sofía, for her part, had been saddened by the political row that had developed in the Greek parliament over the size of her dowry, which had threatened to disrupt the wedding altogether.[67]

Before embarking on their honeymoon the newlyweds flew to Rome to thank Pope John XXIII for his support, and on to Madrid to pay their respects to Franco. The latter, who was very grateful for their visit, subsequently informed his private secretary that the prince would soon settle in Spain, where he would continue his political apprenticeship. This was Franco's first encounter with Sofía, who had never before set foot on Spanish soil, and who impressed him very favourably.[68]

The couple's five-month honeymoon took them to Montecarlo, Jordan, India, Nepal, Thailand, Japan, the Philippines and finally the United States, where they were received by President John F. Kennedy, even though they were still technically private citizens. On returning to Athens in November 1962, the British ambassador there found Juan Carlos 'infinitely more cheerful, and indeed, almost boisterous'. The prince and princess seemed uncertain as to where they would live, and the former admitted to the ambassador that it was 'rather an embarrassing decision to make'. Sofía, however, was adamant that they should not settle in Estoril, as Don Juan had originally intended.[69] After a brief struggle between the count and Franco, in February 1963 the royal couple finally left Athens for the Iberian peninsula, thereby putting an end to what the Spanish chargé d'affaires described as the 'uneasiness privately expressed by some people at the court' on account of their prolongued stay in Greece. The prince and princess duly took up residence at La Zarzuela palace, where Juan Carlos had already lived briefly as a bachelor, and which was to become their permanent home. This move was widely read as evidence that the prince had a mind of his own after all.[70]

The decision to move to Madrid may also have been influenced by strictly personal considerations. Less than a year after their wedding journalists were already claiming that 'all over Athens there has been talk that the royal pair have not been getting along, and that a separation is possible'. These rumours began to be taken seriously when the Greek politician Elias Bredimas asked a question in parliament about the future of Sofía's dowry were her marriage to fail.[71]

In spite of his son's decision to settle permanently in Madrid, in April Don Juan would still tell the British ambassador that 'at no time has General Franco ever suggested to him or, as far as he knew, to anybody else that Don Juan Carlos might ascend the throne in preference to his father'. The very idea, the count assured him, 'was unthinkable', not least because Juan Carlos was 'too good a son ever to wish to take the place of his father'. Despite this vehemence, Labourchere would later report that 'my guess continues to be that in the long run it is Don Juan Carlos whom the Generalissimo is grooming, albeit in a somewhat half-hearted fashion, for king'.[72]

2 After Franco, Who?

Contrary to what Juan Carlos had hoped, the regime did not immediately modify its treatment of him in the wake of his wedding. On 23 February 1963, after attending the annual requiem mass for Spain's monarchs presided over by Franco at El Escorial, their first public appearance together, Juan Carlos and Sofía were dismayed to discover that state-owned television had failed to mention their presence altogether. General Castañón, who was on good personal terms with Juan Carlos, hastened to inform the minister of information of the prince's disappointment. Manuel Fraga, who had not been noted for his monarchist sympathies in the past, agreed to exert greater control over his subordinates in future, a promise he was not always able to keep. In May, however, Franco invited Juan Carlos to occupy a prominent place during the official funeral for Pope John XXIII.[1]

Franco's already favourable opinion of the young couple was reaffirmed by their move to La Zarzuela. In the spring of 1963 he proudly informed his private secretary that Sofía had made enormous progress with her Spanish, and described her as both clever and charming. He also denied rumours that Juan Carlos was unintelligent and totally under his father's influence, something about which he had seemed less certain in the past, insisting that he was more cultivated and independent than was generally realised. The Caudillo was particularly anxious to prevent the couple from falling under the spell of the idle Madrid aristocracy, thereby distancing themselves from ordinary Spaniards, and urged them to make themselves accessible. The princess needed no prompting in this respect, as she had already decided to dispense with ladies-in-waiting and the like, keeping the entourage at La Zarzuela as small as possible. Indeed on arriving in Spain Sofía had been pleasantly surprised to discover that someone of her rank could lead a relatively normal, anonymous existence.[2]

Juan Carlos remained reluctant to contravene his father's wishes, and continued to hope for a negotiated settlement with Franco that would finally clarify his own position. The christening of his first-born, Elena, held at La Zarzuela in late December 1963, provided him with an ideal excuse to bring them together again, but the Caudillo refused to discuss matters of substance with his arch-rival.[3]

Though clearly fond of Juan Carlos, Franco did not go out of his way to repress the views of those within the regime who resented his presence in Madrid, and even tolerated the proliferation of rival candidates. This was particularly true of Juan Carlos's cousin Alfonso, King Alfonso XIII's eldest grandson, who had begun to question his father's right to abdicate on behalf of his successors. In February 1964 Alfonso surprised observers by sitting next to Juan Carlos at the requiem mass in memory of Spain's monarchs, held at El Escorial. Three months later, however, for the first time Juan Carlos appeared at the dictator's side during the annual civil war victory parade. By this stage Franco was privately admitting that, given Don Juan's hostility to the regime, Juan Carlos was the most suitable successor, as long as he adhered to the regime's principles; if he refused, he could always be replaced by Alfonso, who had publicly embraced the *Movimiento*. The most active champion of Alfonso's cause in government circles was the ubiquitous José Solís, minister-secretary general of the *Movimiento* since 1957.[4]

Juan Carlos was never allowed to forget the hostility his presence aroused in some quarters. Much to Franco's irritation, in May 1963 a group of Carlists greeted the royal couple with cries of 'Viva el Rey Javier!' as they left a Madrid theatre; Sofía later regretted not having replied with a loud 'Viva Franco!' Later that year Don Javier's son changed his name to Carlos Hugo prior to announcing his claim to the Spanish throne. The Caudillo, however, was unimpressed. As he told his private secretary, 'for me the bad thing about the Traditionalists is not their doctrine, which is very good, but their determination to bring a foreign king to our country whom no one knows, who has always lived in France, and for whom the Spanish people feel nothing'. Indeed it was Franco himself who subsequently turned down Carlos Hugo's application for Spanish nationality. To complicate matters further for Juan Carlos, in 1964 his deaf-mute uncle Don Jaime declared himself head of the Bourbon dynasty under the influence of his second wife, a German cabaret singer who had helped him to improve his speech.[5]

The prince was anxious to occupy his time usefully, but knew that Franco would not allow him to pursue his military career. On one occasion, when he requested permission to spend some time with his fellow officers, the dictator curtly retorted: 'Doing what? Going to the bar to play cards?' Unsure as to how to proceed, the prince finally consulted Franco himself, whose sole advice was: 'Let the Spanish people get to know you, Highness'. In view of this, Juan Carlos turned to the minister for public works, General Jorge Vigón, his under-secretary Vicente Mortes, and the ever-solicitous López Rodó, who drew up a plan that was to enable him to obtain first-hand knowledge of key ministries and other state institutions, and to spend time with those who manned them. At the same time Juan Carlos embarked on a systematic tour of Spanish towns and villages.[6]

By and large, Juan Carlos was extremely well received on his visits, which enabled him to become better acquainted with the country and its people, while allowing the latter to familiarise themselves with him in turn. Sometimes, however, those he visited were surprisingly outspoken in their opposition, given the overall absence of political freedom. On one occasion Juan Carlos and the minister of agriculture were pelted with potatoes as they drove through a Castilian village, much to the latter's alarm. Another day, in Valencia, it was the captain-general of the region who received the full impact of the tomatoes intended for the prince. With characteristic bonhomie, Juan Carlos shrugged off these incidents as a mere occupational hazard.[7]

In the absence of official duties which might have tied them down in Madrid, Juan Carlos and Sofía were free to travel far and wide. In August 1965, for example, the prince went on a three-week safari in Mozambique at the invitation of the Portuguese president, Americo Thomaz. Several months later he and his wife embarked on a tour of the US, Japan, Thailand, India, Iran, Lebanon, Jordan and Egypt in the company of the Greek shipping magnate Alex Goulandris. Although they made it abundantly clear that 'they wanted to be left alone', as one Tehran paper put it, the Spanish consulates and embassies abroad closely monitored their progress.[8]

During these years Juan Carlos rarely expressed views of his own, at least in public, a habit that led many to assume he had nothing of interest to say. In his own words, 'at that time, no one, not even I, dared to speak. Self-censorship, prudence, if you'd rather, was the general rule'. The prince knew that his every word and gesture would be relayed to Franco, and was also desperately anxious not to antagonise his father. Juan Carlos was also deterred by an overwhelming sense of uncertainty. 'Personally I couldn't tell how things were going to turn out. I didn't know if I would succeed Franco in his lifetime, or if I would have to wait for his death to become King of Spain. Nor did I know how the country would react to the suggested change'.[9]

By this stage father and son were beginning to diverge in their understanding of Spanish reality. The Stabilisation Plan of 1959 had consolidated Spain's postwar recovery, paving the way for the remarkable socio-economic transformations of the 1960s and early 1970s. The prince was witnessing this silent revolution at first hand, while Don Juan and his closest advisers, who had left the country after the civil war, appeared to be living in the past. The latter were understandably reluctant to accept that Spain had begun to overcome its postwar isolation and was achieving unprecedented levels of prosperity. Indeed during his visits to Estoril, when the prince discussed the new Spain emerging under his eyes, his father would sometimes exclaim: 'Good God!, you're looking at it from

Franco's point of view!' Juan Carlos himself would later acknowledge that their differing viewpoints had become a source of growing tension, as a result of which 'our relations were sometimes difficult'.[10]

In spite of Franco's studied silence, support for Juan Carlos from government ministers became increasingly outspoken in the mid-1960s. At this point the power struggle within the regime was marked by the conflict between those who favoured the institutionalisation of the monarchist formula adopted in 1947 and reaffirmed in 1958, with the adoption of the Law of Fundamental Principles, and those who advocated the eventual appointment of a regent. Amongst the former were Admiral Carrero Blanco, López Rodó, Camilo Alonso Vega and Antonio Oriol, while the latter camp included General Muñoz Grandes (deputy prime minister since 1962), Pedro Nieto Antúnez, and Solís. In November 1965, in an interview for *The Times*, Fraga, the minister of information, who was initially associated with the latter group, became the first government minister to make explicit what many in official circles already said in private, namely that 'it is now increasingly accepted that when General Franco's regime ends, Don Juan Carlos will become King of Spain', adding that those within the political establishment who might wish to prevent this outcome lacked the influence to do so. Fraga's statement, which was censored in Spain by his own ministry, caused an uproar in certain circles, but Franco was unperturbed.[11]

Alarmed by the impact of Fraga's words on Don Juan's entourage, two months later Juan Carlos told *Time* magazine that 'I will never, never accept the crown as long as my father is alive'. In March 1966, however, and much to Don Juan's irritation, he failed to attend a monarchist gathering held at Estoril to commemorate the twenty-fifth anniversary of Alfonso XIII's death. The *Juanistas* had planned to issue a statement in support of the count, to which they intended his son to subscribe. Juan Carlos, anxious not to antagonise Franco, excused himself at the last minute on grounds of ill health, even though he was well enough to visit the Caudillo. Although this incident provoked his first serious clash with his father, the prince continued to hope for a reconciliation that would enable Don Juan to succeed the dictator.[12]

Juan Carlos's reluctance to associate himself publicly with Don Juan was by no means unjustified. Having failed to win substantial concessions from Franco in recent years his father had opted for a more belligerent strategy towards the regime, implemented by a new political secretariat led by Areilza, Count of Motrico. Its aim was to make Don Juan and the monarchy he represented acceptable to democratic, anti-Francoist elements in Spanish society, with a view to preventing a republican backlash after Franco's death. The Count of Motrico, who had recently resigned as Spain's ambassador to Paris out of frustration with the regime's inability to evolve, was the ideal candidate for the task because he was keen to earn democratic credentials by associating himself with the opponents of the master he had once served.[13]

The steady improvement in Juan Carlos's standing at El Pardo did not go unnoticed by his rivals. On the eve of a visit to Catalonia in April 1966, the monarchist daily *Diario de Barcelona* was stoned by a group of youths, who later threatened to petrol-bomb the premises. During the visit itself, Juan Carlos was insulted and pelted with rotten eggs by demonstrators, who distributed leaflets proclaiming 'Neither Don Juan nor Don Juan Carlos'. These acts were carried out by Carlist supporters of Don Javier and his son Carlos Hugo, who were arrested and subsequently released at the prince's request.[14]

Anxious to obtain as complete a view of the Spanish situation as possible, Juan Carlos did his best to sound out some of the more prominent members of the country's political, social and economic élite concerning the future of the monarchy. In late May 1966, for example, he attended a dinner hosted by the prominent lawyer and businessman Joaquín Garrigues-Walker, at which the majority of those present advised him to work with Franco without compromising himself unduly, in the hope of being able to establish a Western-style democracy after his death. One of the regime's numerous intellegence services later informed El Pardo that the prince had expressed a preference for a monarchy such as the British, though he seemed anxious to prevent a proliferation of political parties. This was fully in keeping with a confidential report on the political situation prepared for Juan Carlos a month earlier by Armada, the secretary-general of his household.[15]

By this stage Juan Carlos was beginning to come to terms with the possibility of having to accept Franco's succession plans at his father's expense. In June 1966, during a visit to Barcelona, he unexpectedly asked the mayor, José María Porcioles, 'what advice would you give to a prince?' The mayor hesitantly suggested that he sacrifice his filial devotion for the sake of his country, to which Juan Carlos observed: 'This is very tough, Porcioles, very tough'.[16]

Juan Carlos's prospects improved further in November 1966, when Franco finally submitted the Organic Law of the State to the Cortes, after years of procrastination. The law, which provided the Francoist state with a semblance of a constitution, slightly modified the Law of Succession of 1947, with a view to facilitating the appointment of a king (as opposed to a regent) as Franco's successor. Additionally, it envisaged the future appointment of a *presidente del gobierno* (president of the government, or prime minister), a feature that greatly interested Juan Carlos. When it was put to a referendum in December, the prince hastened to cast his vote, thereby implying that he accepted the provisions for Franco's succession contained in the law. This eagerness to vote – which Don Juan could not bring himself to understand – appears to have been prompted by fears that his cousin Alfonso would attempt to use the referendum to publicise his support for the regime.[17]

In keeping with his decision to vote, during a private visit to the United States in January 1967 Juan Carlos told journalists that he endorsed the *Movimiento* and its principles, underlining that the monarchy would return 'as a continuation' of the existing regime. In July the prince expressed identical views in the course of a meeting with leading *Movimiento* officials in Barcelona. These remarks did not go unnoticed by Franco, who became increasingly outspoken in his preference for Juan Carlos in his conversations with his private secretary during the winter of 1966 and the spring of 1967.[18]

The overwhelmingly favourable referendum results gave the prince's supporters in government circles a new lease of life. In January 1967 López Rodó sent Carrero a lengthy dossier, providing him with fresh arguments with which to convince Franco of the need to appoint Juan Carlos his successor without further delay. The minister compared Franco's role to that of Antonio Cánovas del Castillo, the conservative politician who had restored the monarchy in 1875 in the person of Alfonso XII rather than his mother, Isabel II, who had been overthrown in 1868 and was deemed a liability. López Rodó also reminded the admiral that Alfonso XIII himself had abdicated in his son's favour when he realised he had become an obstacle to the restoration of the monarchy, a gesture he hoped Don Juan might one day emulate.[19]

The prince's cause was further advanced in July 1967 with the dismissal of General Muñoz Grandes, who had been deputy prime minister since 1962. The latter had always fancied himself as a possible regent and successor to Franco, and had done his best to prevent the institutionalisation of the monarchy. Two months later he was succeeded by Admiral Carrero Blanco, one of the prince's staunchest supporters. One of the latter's collaborators, José María Gamazo, was subsequently appointed to liaise between Carrero and La Zarzuela, thereby improving the prince's access to information of all kinds.

At this stage it was still uncertain whether Juan Carlos would agree to become Franco's successor without his father's consent. López Rodó, one of the few genuine monarchists in government circles, was anxious to avoid yet another dynastic dispute, and struggled to find a formula that would enable Don Juan to step down without losing face. Neither Carrero Blanco nor Franco shared his qualms, however, nor did they think it necessary to ease the prince's conscience. As far as Carrero was concerned, the monarchy Juan Carlos would one day embody derived its legitimacy from the Franco regime and the Spanish people, who had endorsed it in the referenda of 1947 and 1966, and not from a military victory, as in 1713, or a mere *pronunciamiento*, as in 1874. Dynastic continuity, in his eyes, was largely irrelevant.[20]

Juan Carlos's position was such that even apparently unconnected external events could prove unsettling. In April 1967 a group of officers staged a successful military coup against the government of King Constantine II, Sofía's younger brother, who had succeeded their father in 1964. The princess happened to be in Athens at the time, and was therefore able to witness these events at first hand. In December, following the failure of an amateurish counter-coup launched at his instigation, Constantine fled into exile, with so little time to make preparations that when Sofía flew to meet him in Rome she took him some of her husband's clothes. The Greek monarch's departure, which came as a great blow to the couple, was greeted with relish by Juan Carlos's opponents, who presented it as evidence of the institution's inherent anachronism.[21]

Constantine's troubles in Greece provided Juan Carlos with much food for thought. When a new, theoretically monarchist constitution was adopted by the Greek military junta in September 1968, it was promptly rejected by Constantine, who declared the referendum null and void. Discussing these events with López Rodó, Juan Carlos observed that it would have repelled him to have to become 'the king of the Colonels', adding that 'they would probably have taken me to the slaughter-house within two years'.[22]

On 5 January 1968 Juan Carlos turned thirty, the minimum age at which he could become king, according to the Law of Succession. Several weeks later, on 30 January, Sofía gave birth to her third child, whom Juan Carlos decided to name Felipe, in honour of the first Spanish Bourbon, though not without first consulting Franco. ('Fernando VII', the dictator argued, 'is still too recent. The Felipes are more ancient'.) The Caudillo's eagerness to know whether Sofía had finally given birth to a male was such that, in his first conversation with Juan Carlos after the event, he forgot to enquire about her condition. The prince was determined that both his father and grandmother would attend Felipe's christening, as he continued to hope that Franco and Don Juan might take advantage of this opportunity to reach an amicable agreement. Juan Carlos would have liked Franco to greet Victoria Eugenia at the airport, but the general declined on the grounds that he did not wish to compromise the state, to which the prince replied that he had long since done so by declaring Spain a kingdom.[23]

In spite of official efforts to downplay her presence, on 7 February 1968

Queen Victoria Eugenia, Alfonso XIII's widow, who had not returned to Spain since her hurried departure in April 1931, was greeted at Madrid airport by an enthusiastic crowd. At the christening held the following day, Franco spoke briefly to Spain's English queen, who seemed reconciled to the fact that only Juan Carlos could guarantee the continuity of the dynasty. As for Don Juan, the head of state did little more than recommend that he visit his recently finished mausoleum at the Valle de los Caidos (Valley of the Fallen) near El Escorial. The Count of Barcelona followed his advice, but also took advantage of his presence in Madrid to hold a number of meetings with regime opponents and dissidents. News of these supposedly secret interviews no doubt strengthened Franco's resolve to bypass the count and appoint his son instead.[24]

By this stage the speculation and uncertainty surrounding Franco's choice of successor were beginning to undermine the regime's political stability. López Rodó informed the general in March 1968 that the mayors of Spain's towns and villages were in a state of total confusion: when they were visited by Juan Carlos they came under pressure from Alonso Vega, the minister of the interior, to ensure that they were good hosts, and were later chided by Solís, the minister for the *Movimiento*, for having gone out of their way; when his cousin Alfonso was their guest, it was Solís who insisted on red-carpet treatment and Alonso Vega who reprimanded them. Not surprisingly the confusion was spreading abroad, to the extent that when Alfonso visited the Philippines early that year the Manila press unanimously described him as 'the pretender to the Spanish throne'. Worse still, some members of the Cortes were beginning to question the prince's right to reside at La Zarzuela at the state's expense, given that he was merely a private citizen.[25]

In spite of Franco's behaviour, Don Juan refused to believe that his son's appointment might be imminent. In an effort to convince him, in May 1968 Juan Carlos took Armada, his household secretary, with him to Estoril. Armada presented the count with a detailed analysis of the political situation, in which he underlined the regime's stability and the weakness of the domestic opposition and concluded that it was increasingly clear that Franco intended to appoint his son soon, at which point Don Juan exclaimed: 'Juanito: if they ask you, you can accept, but I can assure you that will never happen!' Alone with his father, Juan Carlos later complained that it was he who had sent him to Spain in 1948, later preventing him from studying at Salamanca and urging him to remain at La Zarzuela on Franco's terms. Given the role he had played thus far, the prince believed he had no option but to agree to become his successor if he was asked.[26]

By this stage Juan Carlos had long ceased to be a passive recipient of Franco's attentions. This suddenly became clear to an old acquaintance, the maverick lawyer and intermittent *Juanista* Antonio García Trevijano, when Juan Carlos unexpectedly asked him to discover where the loyalties of a senior member of his father's secretariat lay, a request he turned down. In June the prince dutifully attended the annual gathering organised by Don Juan's supporters at Estoril, but on returning to Madrid he urged Franco to appoint a successor without further delay, because he feared he could not long keep his father's advisers at bay. The general, however, was still looking for 'the right psychological moment'. Later that month Juan Carlos gave a speech at a naval celebration in Santander, which his father interpreted as proof of his willingness to accept Franco's offer when it materialised. In July the *New York Times* correspondent in Madrid reported that the prince had recently told two western ambassadors that he was convinced Don Juan would never be king, and was prepared to accept a break with him if necessary. What was more, Juan Carlos was also said to have complained about 'the difficulty in letting the public know he wanted to be king without seeming disloyal to his father'. Fearing an imminent decision on Franco's part, some prominent *Juanistas* tried to make the prince return to Portugal with the count, though without success. Under pressure from his advisers, in October Don Juan sent Juan Carlos a stern letter, obviously intended for eventual publication, in which he reminded him of his duties as son and heir whilst emphasising the importance of the hereditary principle.[27]

It is generally believed that Franco finally took the decision to nominate Juan Carlos in the course of the summer and early autumn of 1968. In September López Rodó advised him to take advantage of the favourable economic climate, while Alonso Vega, one of the general's few surviving personal friends, observed that the Portuguese dictator Antonio Salzar would have been well advised to name a successor before his illness forced him out of office. In a similar vein, the justice minister, Oriol, sought to convince him that the nomination of a successor would improve the regime's faltering relations with Rome, which had deteriorated considerably in the wake of Vatican Council II. Most importantly, on 24 October Carrero Blanco read Franco a detailed dossier in which he advocated Juan Carlos's immediate appointment as successor on the grounds that it would contribute to the consolidation of the regime both at home and abroad, put an end to *Juanista* and Carlist conspiracies for good and allow the prince to prepare himself adequately for his future task.[28]

One of the reasons for Franco's reluctance to name a successor had been his fear of alienating supporters of the regime who might not agree with his choice of candidate. This was particulary true of the Carlists, who had made a decisive contribution to the Nationalist cause during the civil war. By the late 1960s, however, many Francoist Carlists had ceased to recognise the Carlist pretender, Carlos Hugo, who had become increasingly hostile to the regime, and would eventually embrace socialism. This finally allowed Franco to expel the Bourbon-Parma family from Spanish territory in December 1968, without fear of alienating Carlists who continued to support his regime.[29]

Juan Carlos was still under the impact of the letter he had received from Don Juan in October when, several weeks later, the French magazine *Point de Vue* published an article quoting him as having said that 'I will never, never reign in Spain as long as my father lives: he is the king'. Françoise Laot, responsible for the interview, had merely lifted this from the *Time* magazine article published in January 1966, but on this occasion it had far greater impact. When the prince rushed to Franco's side to reassure him of his loyalty he was merely told that 'royal families should not quarrel in the Press'. Juan Carlos and the senior members of his household, Mondéjar and Armada, did their best to prevent the Spanish media from discussing the interview, but as a result of the Press Law introduced by Fraga in 1966, it was politically costly to prevent them from doing so. The information minister himself suggested that Juan Carlos counterattack with his own statement, which duly appeared on 7 January 1969 in the form of a carefully worded interview with the official news agency, EFE. The text was largely compiled by Fraga and Gabriel Elorriaga, a member of his team who acted as La Zarzuela's go-between with the Ministry of Information. In it, the prince spoke of the need to sacrifice individual claims for the sake of the dynasty, and intimated his willingness to endorse the regime's political laws and principles. In his determination to please both legitimists and Francoists, the prince cleverly referred to the future 're-establishment' (*reinstauración*) of the monarchy, and not its restoration (*restauración*) or mere establishment (*instauración*). Unusually for an item concerning Juan Carlos, the interview was carried in all the Spanish media.[30]

The prince's words came as a complete surprise to his father, who had not been consulted beforehand. Don Juan reacted by circulating the letter he had sent Juan Carlos in October 1968 amongst his advisers, but made no reference to the reply he had received in December, which was fully in keeping with the pragmatism of the EFE interview.[31]

Franco was naturally delighted that Juan Carlos had finally pinned his colours to the regime's mast, and when he next saw him on 15 January he not only intimated that he would name him successor within the year, but even implied that he might stand down altogether in the near future. The prince replied that he had sworn to serve his country and was willing to make his acceptance public, adding that he hoped Franco would find a way of informing Don Juan without hurting his feelings unnecessarily. The dictator's elation at the prince's EFE statement was clearly shared by many of his supporters, to the extent that extra staff were required to deal with the flood of congratulatory letters inundating La Zarzuela, including those of some 350 members of the Cortes. Even Carrero Blanco, hardly the emotional type, expressed his warmest approval in a letter to Juan Carlos.[32]

Determined to undermine the impact of the EFE interview, in early March Areilza leaked the news that Juan Carlos would be meeting his father in southern France to coordinate their respective political strategies. The prince had indeed intended to travel to Nice to visit his mother in hospital, but was forced to cancel the visit so as not to play into Areilza's hands.

One of the unforeseen byproducts of Spain's socio-economic transformation and the proliferation of universities that accompanied it was the emergence of a radical student population, which rejected everything the regime stood for. In early 1969 the level of unrest in several universities was such that the authorities decreed a state of emergency. Juan Carlos's opponents in the government sought to delay his nomination by imposing it for a period of six months, but López Rodó and his allies succeeded in limiting it to three.[33]

Franco, who was by this stage the victim of Parkinson's disease, an ailment that is thought to have undermined his resolve, continued to show signs of hesitation. At a nerve-wracking meeting on 10 April, Juan Carlos asked him whether he trusted him, to which Franco replied with a classic 'Why do you ask?' The latter subsequently confided to Carrero that he feared the appointment of a successor would be seen as a desertion and expressed unease as to how the Cortes would react. Indeed at one stage he seemed reluctant to put his decision to the vote at all, but was soon reminded that it required the approval of the Cortes if it was to have the force of law. Franco – who has been described as a 'constituent dictator' – could be remarkably forgetful when it came to implementing his own legislation.[34]

On 15 April 1969, just as Franco was bracing himself to name Juan Carlos his successor, Queen Victoria Eugenia died in Lausanne after a long illness. The prince was very saddened by the loss of his beloved 'Gangan', who had done so much for him as a child, and greatly regretted that she had not lived long enough to see him achieve her life-long ambition. During his brief visit to Lausanne, Juan Carlos had a violent argument with his father, still smarting from the EFE interview, who tried to convince him not to accept Franco's offer when it came.[35]

Determined to put an end to Franco's procrastinations, Carrero returned to the attack with yet another dossier in May, in which he argued that the appointment of a successor would improve the regime's relations with both Washington and the Vatican. In a somewhat unfortunate turn of phrase, he anticipated that this decision would have 'the consoling effect of a tracheotomy'. Later that month, on the eve of his eightieth birthday, General Alonso Vega made one final attempt to sway his old friend. This was apparently successful, and on 29 May Franco finally informed Carrero that Juan Carlos's designation would take place before the summer recess. On 14 June López Rodó duly informed Juan Carlos, who had begun to suspect something was afoot when Franco cancelled a visit to Barcelona earlier in the month. Shortly before leaving for his summer holidays in Estoril, the prince tried to sound out the Caudillo, who merely told him: 'come and see me when you get back, because I shall have something important to tell you'.[36]

Juan Carlos thus travelled to Estoril on 18 June in the belief that Franco was about to make his long-awaited move. The prince wanted to reach an agreement with his father as to how they would both respond to the dictator's offer, but Don Juan refused to believe this was forthcoming and urged his son to stall as long as possible. At one point the count jokingly bet his son five thousand pesetas that nothing would happen. Juan Carlos, however, warned him that if he turned Franco down the crown would be offered to his cousin Alfonso, a possibility Don Juan refused to take seriously. Having failed to convince his father of the need to face up to reality, the prince returned to Spain on 23 June – thereby avoiding the annual meeting organised by Don Juan's supporters – with the conviction that he would have no alternative but to accept Franco's offer when it came.[37]

Juan Carlos did not have to wait long to have his suspicions confirmed. Shortly after returning to Madrid he was visited by Miguel Primo de Rivera, a grandson of the dictator who had served under Alfonso XIII and a nephew of the founder of the Falange, who was of a similar age and shared his reformist aspirations. Primo had driven straight from El Pardo, where Franco had informed him that Juan Carlos's appointment was imminent. The prince was so pleased by the news that the two friends ended up in the swimming pool fully clothed.[38]

On 3 July 1969 Franco informed Carrero that on 17 July he would call a meeting of the Cortes so that they might hear a proposal concerning the succession. Juan Carlos received the news that same afternoon from López

Rodó, who told him the Cortes would meet during the second half of July. The prince, who had not seen Franco in nearly a month, was finally called to El Pardo on 12 July. In his usual nonchalant manner, the general informed him that he intended to seek the approval of the Cortes for his nomination on 22 July. Juan Carlos enquired why he had not been told earlier, particularly since Franco knew he was going to visit Don Juan in Portugal, to which the Caudillo, much given to pious cynicism, replied that he would have had to swear him to secrecy and had not wanted him to have to lie to his own father.[39]

The moment Juan Carlos had been dreading and anticipating for so long had finally arrived. Franco looked him in the eye for several seconds, and asked: 'Well, what's your decision, Highness?' The prince knew that if he turned down his offer the general would seek another candidate, but would never go looking in Estoril. After a brief exchange in which Juan Carlos reiterated his willingness to serve Spain, he formally accepted the offer, at which point Franco half smiled and shook his hand. Franco added that he was not to leave the country without his permission and informed him that he would soon be made an honorary general, a promotion that caused the prince some embarrassment as his contemporaries in the armed forces were still of junior rank.[40]

Chance would have it that Don Juan's political secretariat was due to meet in Estoril on 15 July. Unsure as to how his father would react to his nomination as successor, Juan Carlos waited for the secretariat to disperse before informing him of Franco's offer by means of a letter, which Mondéjar took to Estoril on 16 July. In it the prince explained that he was undertaking 'the biggest sacrifice of my life' in order to secure the return of the monarchy, which he hoped would bring Spain 'many years of peace and prosperity'. On a more personal note, he also assured him of his 'filial devotion and immense affection' and prayed for the unity of the royal family. Later that morning Don Juan also received a personal letter from Franco, who was confident that he would accept the decision with the 'greatness of spirit you inherited from your father Don Alfonso XIII'. Don Juan's state of mind was such that for several days he refused to answer his son's telephone calls; when they finally spoke, on 21 July, he lost his temper and accused him of having witheld the truth during his recent visit to Portugal, something Juan Carlos vehemently denied. The count would later complain bitterly to his closest advisers that he had been deceived by his own son.[41]

On 15 July the prince received Carrero and the president of the Cortes, Antonio Iturmendi, who showed him the text of the bill whereby he would become successor to Franco, 'as king'. Juan Carlos pointed out that it referred to him as Prince of Asturias, which was in blatant contradiction with Franco's decision to bypass his father, and suggested that it be changed to 'Prince Don Juan Carlos de Borbón'. López Rodó was quick to object that this was a name, not a title, in view of which Juan Carlos, at Sofía's suggestion, opted for that of *Príncipe de España* (Prince of Spain). Ironically, Franco was initially reluctant to accept this last-minute modification, but agreed under pressure from his advisers.[42]

Juan Carlos's main concern at this stage was to prevent, or at least defuse, adverse reactions to his nomination. His first step was to invite his cousin Alfonso to witness the swearing-in ceremony, which was due to take place at La Zarzuela. Alfonso not only congratulated him on his appointment, but even sent some of his followers to Paris to convince his father, Don Jaime, who still regarded himself as head of the Bourbon dynasty, not to challenge Franco's decision.[43]

Juan Carlos was particulary wary of reactions in Estoril, where he had a powerful ally in his mother, the Countess of Barcelona, a deeply conservative woman who had long since reconciled herself to Franco's wishes. Once the prince's nomination was finally made public on 17 July, Don Juan's closest advisers, Areilza and Sainz Rodríguez, drew up a manifesto that described Franco's decision as the logical culmination of the process initiated in 1947 with the Law of Succession, which took into account neither the popular will nor the views of the rightful heir to the throne. Don Juan once again described his goal as a Western-style parliamentary monarchy, and appeared to believe this might be achieved by means of 'the peaceful evolution of the existing system'. News of the manifesto, which had been postdated to 19 July at Doña María's insistence so as not to irritate Franco unnecessarily, reached the government in the midst of its annual commemoration of the uprising of 18 July 1936, whereupon it was immediately banned. In spite of its moderate tone, Estoril's response deprived Juan Carlos of his sleep that night, but he was very relieved when his father later disbanded his secretariat and privy council, thereby depriving *Juanistas* of the means with which to further their cause.[44]

Juan Carlos was deeply concerned by the long-term implications of his forthcoming endorsement of the regime's constitution and political principles. Anxious not to be accused of perjury later on, he needed to know whether this act would chain him to the Franco regime for good. Though unclear as to the precise contours of the political system he wished to see established in Spain on his accession to the throne, the prince was already firmly committed to democratic change. He was thus greatly relieved when, in the course of a long interview held on 18 July, his former tutor Fernández-Miranda, an expert in the Francoist political system, reassured him that the constitution he was about to swear to uphold contained mechanisms whereby it could reform itself out of existence. The key, as Fernández-Miranda had often reminded him in the past, was the Law of Succession, which stated that all fundamental laws could be modified or repealed by means of a two-thirds majority in the Cortes and a referendum. In the professor's view, this also included the Law of Fundamental Principles, which described these as 'permanent and immutable'. As Juan Carlos well knew, this interpretation was not unanimously shared by the regime's constitutional experts, hence his apprehension.[45]

Juan Carlos had also consulted another former tutor, the constitutional lawyer Carlos Ollero, who reminded him that the Organic Law only entrusted the armed forces with the 'defence of the institutional system', including its own mechanisms of reform. Ollero was keen to emphasise that there was thus no possible constitutional justification for military opposition to a far-reaching reform process conducted in accordance with the Francoist fundamental laws.[46]

Franco had been justified in fearing that some sectors of the regime would not accept his decision without a struggle. This was particularly true of the *Movimiento* apparatchiks and official trade union leaders, whose figurehead, Solís, regarded Juan Carlos's nomination as a victory for the technocrats led by López Rodó. Solís advocated a secret vote in the Cortes, but at López Rodó's instigation, the attorney general of the Supreme Court, Fernando Herrero Tejedor, arranged a ruling that provided that it be public. At a meeting of Cortes members held on 21 July, his young protegé Adolfo Suárez, who was civil governor of Segovia at the time, distributed a copy of this ruling amongst fellow *procuradores*, in what was probably his first significant service to the future monarch. Earlier Juan Carlos had personally canvassed a number of influential, potentially hostile *procuradores* such as the Falangist José Antonio Girón, who assured him he would obey Franco's wishes.[47]

The government and the Council of the Realm, the seventeen-man advisory body that represented the regime's key institutions, were not officially informed of the Caudillo's decision until 21 July. In the course of an unusually emotional cabinet meeting, Franco justified the nomination of a successor on the grounds that he was almost seventy-seven, and that it was safer to implement the Law of Succession during his lifetime. Additionally, he claimed that during her visit to Madrid the previous year, Victoria Eugenia had implicitly acknowledged the need to sacrifice Don Juan for the sake of the dynasty. Surprisingly, given the nature of the regime, a number of ministers had the courage to speak out in favour of a secret vote in the Cortes, and it was even suggested that this take place in Franco's absence. This prompted an emotional appeal by Alonso Vega, who decided the matter in favour of a public vote, to be taken in Franco's presence.[48]

In his speech to the Cortes on 22 July, Franco went out of his way to emphasise that he was not restoring the institution that had been overthrown in 1931, but rather establishing a 'traditional, Catholic, social and representative monarchy' that was the mature product of the uprising of 18 July 1936. The general had chosen Juan Carlos because of his loyalty to the regime, his military training, and his personal qualities. Franco also acknowledged that the prince belonged to a dynasty 'which ruled in Spain for several centuries', but underlined that the 'monarchy of 18 July' had inherited the fighting spirit of Carlism. Franco went on to justify the monarchy on the somewhat bizarre grounds that, as the northern European democracies had shown, it was perfectly compatible with modern, dynamic societies, though he later added that Spaniards need not look abroad for a suitable model, since the Catholic monarchs had long since provided an excellent one![49]

As had been expected, the Cortes obeyed Franco's wishes, approving Juan Carlos's nomination by 491 votes to 19, with nine abstentions. Those opposing the measure included a handful of *Juanistas*, several Carlists and the odd die-hard Falangist who favoured a regency. Several prominent regime figures who opposed Juan Carlos's nomination stayed away from the Cortes altogether. The prince subsequently thanked Torcuato Luca de Tena, one of the *Juanistas* who had voted against his nomination, for his loyalty to his father. 'History is the way it is', he reminded him, 'and not how we would like it to be'.[50]

The following morning, in a relatively private ceremony held at La Zarzuela, Juan Carlos, wearing his naval uniform, pledged his 'loyalty to His Excellency the Head of State and fidelity to the principles of the *Movimiento Nacional* and the fundamental laws of the realm'. As agreed, his cousin Alfonso acted as witness, in return for which Franco would later appoint him ambassador to Sweden. Juan Carlos was accompanied by Sofía, his daughters Elena and Cristina and his son Felipe, as well as by the head and secretary of his household, Mondéjar and Armada. Don Juan had prevented his mother and two sisters, Pilar and Margarita, from attending the ceremony, but Juan Carlos had secretly received words of encouragment from Doña María de las Mercedes and fully understood that her place was at Estoril; as he confided to one of his advisers, 'my parents' marriage is above everything else'.[51]

Later that day Juan Carlos, dressed in his Army captain's uniform, addressed the Cortes in Franco's presence. As they drove to the Cortes the prince was so nervous that he had to ask the general for permission to smoke in the car. In his speech, written with the assistance of several senior politicians, notably Fernández-Miranda, López Rodó and Silva Muñoz, and polished by Armada and Mondéjar, Juan Carlos sought to reconcile his respect for the past with his determination to preside over an entirely different situation in the future. The prince acknowledged that he was receiving from Franco a political legitimacy born of the military uprising of 18 July 1936, but went on to add that he belonged to the Spanish royal house, and hoped to be a worthy successor of those who bore the crown before him. (Juan Carlos had initially intended to express his filial devotion and affection for his father – 'from whom I have received all that I am' – and even pay tribute to his patriotism, but was advised against it by Franco.) The prince also recognised the regime's achievements in recent years, while insisting that 'the cult of the past should not limit the evolution of a society which is transforming itself at an astounding rate'. Most importantly, perhaps, Juan Carlos believed the monarchy could prove useful as a political system if it proved capable of 'taking root in the authentic life of the Spanish people'.

Princess Sofía, who watched her husband from the public gallery, later admitted to having lost two kilos in the course of the day on account of the excitement. After watching the ceremony on television from the bar of a fishing village near Coimbra, Don Juan telephoned his son to congratulate him on his performance and offer words of encouragement. The prince felt genuinely sorry for his father, who received only fifty telegrams and eighty-three telephone calls in the wake of his appointment, which contrasted sharply with the thousands of congratulatory messages reaching La Zarzuela. Indeed Don Juan was so distraught that he briefly considered the possibility of going to live in Canada, to get out of his son's way. Juan Carlos has acknowledged that the count was 'very cold' towards him for several months, but by Christmas 1969 father and son were back on reasonable terms. In future they would avoid talking politics, in spite of which Don Juan has admitted that 'they were not very pleasant times for us'.[52]

Juan Carlos's appointment as successor finally solved the immediate question 'After Franco, who?', but did not necessarily answer the accompanying query 'After Franco, what?' The Caudillo, Carrero Blanco and many of those who had contributed to his appointment regarded it as a means of guaranteeing the regime's continuity or, as the former declared in December 1969, of ensuring that everything had been '*atado y bien atado*' (tied up and well tied down). At this stage, at least, Franco appears to have harboured no doubts as to the prince's willingness and ability to undertake the task for which he had been chosen.

At the same time there were those in government circles – notably

López Rodó, Fraga and Silva – who were slowly beginning to acknowledge that change was inevitable and even desirable, and were increasingly aware of the need to prepare for a future without Franco. When López Rodó discussed the Portuguese prime minister Marcello Caetano's new slogan ('continuity and renovation') with the prince in the summer of 1969, he found him determined to broaden the regime's base in order to include some of those who had hitherto been excluded. Juan Carlos also wished to meet personalities such as the liberal cardinal Enrique y Tarancón, who was fast becoming a leading figure in the Spanish Church. The prince appears to have been reluctant to contemplate anything more radical at this stage, at least not in the presence of Franco's ministers, however supportive they may have been in the past. Fernández-Miranda, however, would later claim that 'since 1969 Don Juan Carlos knew what he would have to do to establish a monarchy for all, a democratic monarchy'.[53]

Although most Spaniards were indifferent to the monarchy as an institution, Juan Carlos's appointment was generally well received. As one foreign observer noted, 'there are plenty of people in Spain who are not monarchists but who believe that the restoration of the Bourbons would solve the problem of the succession to General Franco'. Indeed even at this early stage, many hoped that Juan Carlos would 'preside over the transition from the anachronistic rule of the Caudillo to something more modern, possibly even something in the liberal-democratic tradition'.[54]

3 Prince of Spain

The impact of Juan Carlos's designation was somewhat undermined by the eruption of the MATESA affair – the most serious financial scandal in the regime's history – in the summer of 1969. The affair, which affected several ministers belonging to the technocrat *Opus Dei* faction, was given substantial media coverage by Fraga and Solís, who thereby hoped to discredit their opponents in government. This prompted Franco to carry out the most sweeping cabinet change in over a decade, inspired by Carrero Blanco and López Rodó, who saw off their major rivals, notably Fernando Castiella, Fraga and Solís. The latter made a desperate last-minute attempt to prevent his removal from office by appealing to Juan Carlos, but the prince was careful to remain above the fray.

Although the October 1969 crisis represented a major victory for those who had done most to wrest Juan Carlos's appointment from Franco, the prince does not appear to have shared their elation. After visiting him in January 1970, journalist Richard Eder reported that Juan Carlos resented 'the fact that the coincidence of timing – the Government was named three months after his own designation – has tied him to it in the public mind', adding that 'unless he can convince his fellow Spaniards that he is more than an appendage to the present government, he considers himself unlikely to outlast it by much'. As far as the prince was concerned, the appointment of his trusted former tutor, Fernández-Miranda, as minister-secretary general of the *Movimiento*, was undoubtedly the most positive outcome of the crisis.[1]

Juan Carlos's designation as Franco's successor clearly strengthened his position, but also put an end to the ambiguities to which he had grown accustomed. His father's supporters, who had watched him with growing suspicion in recent years, were finally free to spurn him as a traitor to the legitimist cause, and ceased to regard him as the rightful prince of Asturias. Don Juan's personal attitude was naturally more understanding, though this did not prevent him from withdrawing the plaque traditionally held by the heir to the throne, which had been in his son's possession since the age of three. In January 1970 the entire royal family gathered at Estoril for the first time since the designation, prompting fresh speculation as to Don Juan's imminent abdication.[2]

As far as the regime's supporters were concerned, it was now possible to express support for Juan Carlos openly without fear of being accused of disloyalty to Franco, but many influential figures remained aloof; as he himself would later explain, 'it was a good idea to be "nice" to me, but not too nice'. The prince thus remained lonely and isolated, uncertain as to whom he could trust.[3]

As had been expected, the organised anti-Francoist opposition rejected Juan Carlos's appointment outright. In December 1969 over three hundred leading professionals, intellectuals and academics – many of whom would play leading roles in the transition to democracy – published a document that condemned the regime's efforts to perpetuate itself by undemocratic means. The exiled PSOE leadership dismissed Juan Carlos as 'a music-hall prince', while the Spanish Communist Party (PCE), the country's largest clandestine organisation, claimed that Franco had deprived monarchists of all hope of ever establishing a democratic monarchy in Spain. The PCE's secretary-general, Santiago Carrillo, dubbed the future monarch 'Juan Carlos the Brief', predicting that his reign would last little over a year.[4]

Juan Carlos himself has described this period as one marked by an overpowering sense of uncertainty, born of the fact that Franco could still go back on his decision and appoint another successor. As he himself put it over two decades later, this was a period 'when it was thought that I would be king, but no one could be absolutely sure of it'. In an environment in which his every gesture was scrutinised and reported, he became increasingly taciturn, with the result that those who barely knew him tended to underestimate him. Eder had assumed the prince would be 'lacking in both wit and gumption', but found him 'better informed, more intelligent and, above all, far more determined' than he had anticipated. In spite of his growing determination, Juan Carlos himself has admitted that he was occasionally tempted to abandon ship, but was prevented from doing so by the knowledege that this was precisely the reaction his enemies sought to provoke. What was more, his father had always taught him that a king had no right to abdicate; though not yet king, Juan Carlos was determined to behave as though he would soon be one.[5]

As was to be expected, his designation induced Juan Carlos to plan ahead in earnest. Eder reported that the prince had begun to let his acquaintances know that 'he does not accept the role apparently chosen for him: that of docile successor' and had 'no intention of presiding over a dictatorship'. The prince, 'aware that Spaniards, who doubt that anyone chosen by General Franco can survive after he goes, have named him Juan Carlos the Brief, . . . insists that only under some form of democracy will he have any real chance of remaining Spain's king'.

During his interview for *The New York Times*, Juan Carlos was careful to underline the distinction between 'the kind of government that Spain may have needed during and after the civil war, and the kind it will need in the future'. Like his father, the prince wished to rule as 'king of all Spaniards', including not only those who had traditionally supported the regime, 'but many of those who have opposed it as well'. Juan Carlos 'does not disavow Franco, but he does not feel himself committed to all of the leader's "political baggage" – fundamental achievements have to be maintained, but Spain is changing and has to change still more'. It would be the prince's role to 'preside over this change, and to represent continuity to a Spanish people that may successively and freely choose conservative, liberal or socialist governments'. In Juan Carlos's own words, 'I am Franco's heir, but I am Spain's heir as well'.

Although the authorities prevented the Spanish media from reproducing this interview, it caused a considerable stir in Francoist political circles. The Spanish ambassador in Washington, who wrote to his minister expressing his concern, observed that if the interview reflected the prince's true intentions, there had been little point in bypassing Don Juan after all. Shortly after the interview saw the light, Juan Carlos told the public works minister, Silva Muñoz, a survivor of the 1969 crisis, that in the future it would be impossible not to govern with political parties, 'but only with two or three'. Not surprisingly the minister left La Zarzuela with the conviction that the interview accurately reflected the future king's views. Aware of the poor impression caused by the Eder interview amongst the more conservative elements of the regime, on 10 February, probably at Fernández-Miranda's suggestion, Juan Carlos presided over a meeting of the *Guardia de Franco*, an association formed by the more reactionary members of the National Council of the *Movimiento*.[6]

During his visit to La Zarzuela – which he described as 'a modest residence with chinz-covered furniture and toys scattered at the door' – Eder detected 'an air of confinement', and was struck by the prince's determination to overcome his dependence on official sources of information by widening his circle of contacts to include foreign journalists, non-regime personalities and even moderate opposition leaders. Weeks later, when the prince asked Silva what line of action he should pursue, the latter encouraged him to see people of different political tendencies, and to refrain from taking any further action for the time being. Juan Carlos complained that this entailed wasting time with people who had little to tell him, but by mid-1970 he was receiving some 120 visitors a month. In order to assist him in this task, the prince employed a new private secretary, Jacobo Cano, a prominent member of the *Asociación Católica Nacional de Propagandistas* (ACNP), a prestigious Catholic lay organisation that was to provide the future democratic regime with many conservative leaders.

Cano's death in a car accident in 1971 would deprive the prince of an extremely useful adviser.

By early 1970 Juan Carlos was indeed beginning to inform himself as to the anti-Francoist opposition's views. In late February he met Areilza, who was highly critical of the new government and the regime as a whole. When the prince duly informed Franco, the latter simply remarked: 'You know how it is, Highness, you can be either prince or private citizen'. A month later, in López Rodó's presence, he expressed interest in a recent statement by Carrillo, who had raised the possibility of reaching an understanding with the future monarch.[7] This inevitably upset the dour *Opus Dei* minister, who warned him against courting the regime's opponents.

Contrary to what he had expected, Juan Carlos's relationship with Franco barely changed in the wake of his designation. As in the past, they continued to address each other as *'Mi General'* and *'Alteza'*; in his absence the prince still referred to him as *'el Generalísimo'*, or simply 'Franco'. The latter initially remained aloof as ever, to the extent that in late March 1970 Juan Carlos complained that he had not seen him for two months. The prince would occasionally telephone him to see what he made of his performance, but Franco would merely reassure him that 'all is well'. When he subsequently told him that he needed his advice, the latter replied that 'Your Highness can manage on his own'. Franco had recently told Carrero that he did not wish to be the prince's mentor, and the admiral himself encouraged him to stand on his own two feet. Carrero visited him once a week, generally on Thursdays, to inform him of the agenda for the forthcoming cabinet meeting, but Juan Carlos would have liked greater contact with Franco. In August 1970 the Caudillo invited him to attend his meetings with individual ministers after the summer, but nothing ever came of it, in spite of the prince's reminders. Franco would occasionally telephone him with enquiries about his official duties, notably his visits abroad, but that was all. By mid-1971 the prince was seeing him once a fortnight, and it was not until 1972 that he succeeded in institutionalising weekly meetings, generally held on Mondays. Between 1969 and his death in 1975, Franco never once set foot in La Zarzuela.[8]

The fact that Juan Carlos had ceased to be a private citizen in order to become the head of state's sworn successor inevitably affected his hitherto casual life-style. Henceforth the prince would have to learn to live with a constant police presence, something he greatly resented at first. When Earl Mountbatten, his second cousin once removed, visited him in 1971, he was surprised to find that heavily armed Civil Guards lined the roads they took at three- or four-hundred yard intervals. The prince explained that there was nothing he could do since this was the procedure laid down by

Franco, but assured him that things would be different when he became king, 'as it was entirely unnecessary and very unpopular with the unfortunate police'.[9]

Juan Carlos was anxious to travel around Spain freely, thereby expressing his concern for the well-being of his fellow countrymen. His brother-in-law Constantine and King Baudouin of Belgium (whose wife Fabiola was a Spanish aristocrat), had often told him that a modern monarch could only survive by ridding himself of the restrictions of court life and establishing direct contact with ordinary citizens, and the former often expressed regret at not having applied this lesson himself. Given Juan Carlos's position, however, this was easier said than done. Ministers often pestered him so that he would attend the opening of public buildings and the like, but were reluctant to allow him to plan his own visits to the provinces. Although these became increasingly frequent, the prince was fully aware of the limitations inherent in such outings. When someone enquired why he did not make a point of visiting more factories, he promptly explained that it would be of little use unless he could tell workers what he wanted to say rather than what government officials expected to hear.[10]

In the wake of his designation, Franco – who had barely left the country since coming to power in 1936 – encouraged Juan Carlos to travel abroad so that foreigners might begin to associate him with the Spain of the future. Given the non-democratic nature of the regime, it was fitting that his first official visit as Franco's successor in October 1969 should have taken him to Iran, a country he would return to in 1971 for the sumptuous celebration of the 2500th anniversary of the Persian monarchy, and again in April 1975.[11] Other than the shah, Franco was also on good terms with autocrats such as Haile Selassie of Ethiopia, whom the prince and princess visited in May 1972, and with Ferdinand Marcos of the Philippines and King Faisal of Saudi Arabia, who received the royal couple in February 1974. In September 1970 Juan Carlos met Pope Paul VI during a visit to the Vatican on the occasion of the proclamation of St Teresa de Jesús as a doctor of the Catholic Church, and in January 1972 the couple visited Japan, where they were officially received by Emperors Hirohito and Nagako.

Though politically conservative, the 1969 government was committed to a policy of economic growth and liberalisation, which demanded ever-closer links with the other European economies and therefore with the EEC. Although Spain had been unsuccessful in its application for membership, submitted in 1962, the EEC was on the verge of agreeing to a preferential trade agreement when Juan Carlos was designated successor and the prince lost no time in visiting Brussels in December 1969 to endorse the government's efforts. The agreement, which was to prove highly favourable to Spanish interests, was finally signed in July 1970.

For obvious geographic, historical and economic reasons, France was Spain's most important partner in Europe and the nation that held the key to its rapprochement with the EEC. Due to the nature of the Franco regime, official visits involving the two countries had never risen above ministerial level. It was thus a considerable breakthrough when Juan Carlos and Sofía were officially received in Paris by President Georges Pompidou in October 1970, a visit they would repeat three years later. The Federal Republic of Germany, another major trading partner, welcomed the prince for the first time in September 1972, in spite of the ruling SPD's traditional hostility to the Franco regime. Indeed President Gustav Heinemann, a social democrat of the old school, was initially highly reluctant to play host to someone he perceived as a fascist dictator's puppet. However, after a long private interview with Juan Carlos, Heinemann told a German journalist he had never been so impressed by a foreign visitor. This was followed by a second official visit to Bonn in October 1974.[12]

In marked contrast, British governments remained reluctant to deal with Franco's successor, partly due to the on-going squabble over Gibraltar. Although Edward Heath's attitude towards the regime during 1970–74 was considerably more accommodating than that of his predecessor, Harold Wilson, he felt unable to make any significant gesture towards the future monarch. The British royal family, however, compensated by inviting their relatives to events such as the Queen Mother's seventieth birthday in June 1970, the Duke of Edinburgh's fiftieth birthday a year later, and Princess Anne's wedding in November 1973. These visits enabled Juan Carlos to consolidate his friendship with Mountbatten, who became one of his staunchest advocates abroad.[13]

Other European governments, notably those of the Benelux and Scandinavian countries, refused to make any distinction between Franco and his successor. As in the case of Britain, Juan Carlos was sometimes able to overcome this official hostility thanks to his personal relationship with some heads of state, such as the king of Belgium. The only country to ignore this tacit northern European veto was Finland, whose president welcomed the prince and princess in June 1975.[14]

Juan Carlos was particularly anxious to win the support of the United States, Spain's major ally since the postwar period. Since 1953 both countries had periodically renewed the agreement whereby Madrid had allowed the United States to set up naval and air force bases on Spanish soil in return for military hardware and financial assistance. The agreement was renewed yet again in the summer of 1970, paving the way for a visit to Madrid in October by President Richard Nixon, who is said to have been impressed by Juan Carlos's aplomb. Back in Washington the president saw Mountbatten, who spoke to him at some length about the need to support his protegé, apparently to good effect. The royal couple were subsequently invited to visit the United States officially in January 1971.[15]

Juan Carlos prepared for this visit with particular care. In order to maximise its impact, he entrusted the lawyer and journalist José Mario Armero with the task of creating a favourable climate in the American media. This required funds that the prince could not provide, in view of which Armero appealed to several Spanish bankers, all of whom turned him down on the grounds that it was unlikely that Juan Carlos would ever reign. Additionally, some no doubt feared that they would be accused of lack of loyalty to Franco if their assistance became public knowledge. Undeterred, Armero travelled to the United States ahead of the royal party, and set about using his professional contacts to the best possible effect.[16]

The week-long visit, which included stops in Washington, California, Texas and Florida, enabled Juan Carlos and Sofía to meet prominent politicians, academics, financiers, industrialists and – significantly – trade unionists. At the launching of Apollo XIV, Juan Carlos recorded a brief televised message in English, which greatly impressed his fellow-countrymen, accustomed as they were to a monolingual head of state. Sofía, for her part, gave her first, highly successful press conference in Washington, which was widely reported in the US media. Nixon is said to have advised Juan Carlos against distancing himself from the regime in public, as his own youthfulness and dynamism were already conveying a positive message to his future subjects.[17]

In spite of this advice, in the course of his visit Juan Carlos made a number of democratising statements, which acknowledged that 'people want more freedoms; the problem is to decide on the timing'. On returning to Madrid he rushed to El Pardo to gauge their impact on Franco. The Caudillo seemed unconcerned, though he did observe that 'there are things you can and ought to say outside Spain and things that you ought not to say inside Spain. It may not be appropriate to repeat here what is said outside. And, at times, it might be better if what is said here is not picked up outside'.[18]

Following this visit and partly at the prince's instigation, Nixon sent Vernon Walters, deputy chief of the CIA, on a secret mission to Spain. The president hoped to persuade Franco to enthrone Juan Carlos during his lifetime, or at least to appoint a strong premier 'who could ensure the transition from Franco's regime to the monarchy'. ('Only you, Mr. President,

are in a powerful enough position to tell him this', Mountbatten had assured him.) Franco informed Walters that the country 'would move some
distance along the road we favoured but not all the way, as Spain was
neither America nor England nor France'. The dictator assured him that
'the succession would be orderly', and insisted that 'there was no alternative to the prince', expressing great confidence in the latter's ability to
handle the situation after his death. 'Tell President Nixon', he concluded,
'that insofar as the order and stability of Spain are concerned, this will be
guaranteed by the timely and orderly measures I am taking'.[19]

Before returning to Washington, Walters met a number of senior army
officers, none of whom believed Franco would place the prince on the
throne before his own death, though they did suspect he might finally
appoint a prime minister. These officers 'made quite clear their support for
the accession of Prince Juan Carlos on Franco's death', and expressed
their belief that 'there would be no disorder or political breakdown in the
nation'.[20]

Though virtually powerless, Juan Carlos naturally sought to influence
events in his favour. Since 1936 Franco had been both head of government and head of state, but the Organic Law of 1967 contemplated the
appointment of a head of government other than the Caudillo. Ever since
his designation, the prince had been anxious to make people understand
that he would only succeed Franco as head of state and not as head of
government, which was best ensured by separating the two posts. Juan
Carlos urged the general to do so as early as May 1970, and repeated his
request in many subsequent interviews, but to no avail. In early 1971 the
prince specifically requested that he appoint Carrero Blanco, who would
shortly celebrate his thirtieth anniversary at Franco's side. Juan Carlos
hardly shared the admiral's plans for the future, but he backed him because
he knew him to be the only candidate acceptable to Franco. What was
more, in January 1970 Carrero had assured him that if he was prime
minister when Franco died, he would immediately tender his resignation
so that the prince could appoint his own man.[21]

Other than the appointment of a premier, Juan Carlos's major goal was
the opening up of the Francoist political system so that the transition to
democracy would prove less traumatic. The Organic Law had envisaged
the possibility of creating political associations, entities whose precise role
remained unclear but which the prince nevertheless supported. Neither
Franco nor Carrero Blanco were convinced, however, and Fernández-
Miranda, responsible for associations as minister-secretary general, soon
grasped it was his task to make haste slowly. In May 1970 he presented
a new draft outline for political associations to the National Council of the

Movimiento, where it lay dormant for three years. In discussing these plans with Juan Carlos in May 1971, Franco rejected the creation of associations on the grounds that they would become political parties, to which the prince observed: 'who can assure me that there will not be political parties in Spain in ten years' time? It would be best to ban one [the Communist Party] now and tolerate the others. You General, could put this matter on the right track'. Franco was unmoved, however, and no significant progress was achieved.[22]

Juan Carlos's designation as successor had created some curious constitutional ambiguities. According to the Organic Law, 'should the head of state be absent from the national territory or in ill health, his duties shall be discharged by the heir to the throne, if there is one and he is over thirty, or otherwise by the Regency Council'. Strictly speaking, Juan Carlos was only Franco's successor, and not the heir to the throne, since the monarchy defined in the law would not formally come into existence until he became king. López Rodó, who detected this anomaly when Franco was briefly indisposed in May 1971, feared that the three-man Regency Council, currently dominated by the president of the Cortes, Alejandro Rodríguez de Valcárcel, might attempt to prevent Juan Carlos from ever becoming king by institutionalising a regency. With Carrero's support, he quickly drew up a bill explicitly granting Juan Carlos the rights and duties attributed to the heir to the throne by the Organic Law, which was adopted in July 1971. The new bill was not without its disadvantages, however, for if Franco became seriously ill but refused to stand down as head of state, the prince could be forced to accept resonsibility for decisions that might jeopardise his future.

This was not the only loophole spotted by Carrero and López Rodó. According to the Organic Law, if Franco died without having appointed a head of government, his successor would have to name one within ten days of his proclamation, in consultation with the Council of the Realm. This meant that, in a matter of a few days, the country would find itself with a new head of government as well as a new head of state. In order to prevent this the admiral and his *éminence grise* proposed that when Franco died the deputy prime minister would automatically become premier, allowing the king ample time in which to decide whether he wished to confirm him in his post or appoint his own man. López Rodó defended this measure on the grounds that it reduced the likelihood of a power vacuum and eliminated the risk of a coup by the Council of the Realm. Given that Carrero Blanco was already deputy premier, the bill, adopted in July 1972, was also clearly intended to perpetuate the admiral's authority after Franco's death.

Indeed the Carrero Blanco–López Rodó tandem left very little to chance. In late 1971, when the composition of the Francoist Cortes came up for renewal, the deputy premier and his men did their best to ensure the presence of a substantial body of *procuradores* sympathetic to the prince's cause and friendly towards their own. With this in mind, López-Rodó suggested that Fernández-Miranda entrust a key post, that of national delegate for the provinces, to a young, up-and-coming politician, Suárez, but the professor failed to follow his advice.

Although the prince was gradually allowed greater freedom of movement both in Spain and abroad, he could not help being associated with the regime in the eyes of the public. From 1969 onwards he dutifully appeared at Franco's side at every major political, military, religious or social event presided by the head of state. By the 1970s many of these events, such as the annual victory parade, had lost much of their political significance and the prince's uniformed presence attracted little attention. Franco, however, also liked him to be at his side on more special occasions. Thus on 17 December 1970 Juan Carlos and Sofía found themselves on the balcony of the Royal Palace, from which Franco addressed tens of thousands of agitated demonstrators who had gathered in protest against foreign reactions to the trial of a dozen members of the Basque terrorist organisation ETA by the Burgos military court. Although the latter passed six death sentences, Franco subsequently issued a pardon. The prince returned to that same balcony in October 1971 to hear the Caudillo – who was celebrating his thirty-fifth anniversary as head of state – announce that he intended to 'remain at the helm', thereby giving the lie to growing rumours of an imminent handover.

Involvement in public events that were covered by state-owned television at least had the advantage of allowing Spaniards to become acquainted with Juan Carlos and Sofía, who were barely known to the general public in 1969. When Mountbatten visited the palace and gardens of Aranjuez with them in October 1971 he was surprised to find that 'wherever we went that day the public in the park gathered in little knots to clap loudly to show their enthusiasm for Juanito and Sophie. When we walked among them they all dashed forward to shake them by the hand and obviously they are very popular'.[23] An opinion poll conducted a few months earlier on behalf of the Ministry of Information reached the same conclusion. According to the latter, the prince was thought to be *simpático* by 68 per cent of those consulted, while 67 per cent held a similar view of princess Sofía.[24]

In November 1971 the government commissioned a second poll, whose results provide some interesting clues as to public attitudes towards Juan Carlos. Given that his designation had taken place in 1969, it is somewhat surprising that only 32 per cent of those polled remembered the date, and that only 22 per cent recalled the circumstances. Nevertheless 76 per cent of those questioned claimed to follow the prince's activities on television, and only 22 per cent expressed no interest in him whatsoever. Significantly, the vast majority of those consulted thought Juan Carlos spent most of his time travelling or attending official functions, while very few believed he intervened in political decision making.

Unfortunately, given that it was conducted in an authoritarian context, the poll does not allow us to reach any firm conclusions as to popular attitudes towards the succession. A majority of those polled, 71 per cent, thought Juan Carlos's appointment as successor was 'important' or 'very important' for Spain's future, while only 13 per cent questioned its significance. Furthermore 51 per cent thought it a positive measure while 22 per cent regarded it as only partially beneficial and 11 per cent as not at all positive. Those who attributed considerable importance to Franco's decision were most likely to regard it as beneficial. However only 24 per cent of those questioned expected things to change for the better under the future king, while 52 per cent anticipated no change and only 8 per cent feared they would change for the worse. Indeed while 29 per cent expected major political changes to take place once Juan Carlos was proclaimed king, as many as 59 per cent doubted this would be the case.

Interestingly, respondents were also asked to identify the politicians who, in their view, could best advise the prince on a daily basis. Twenty-three per cent mentioned Fraga, who was known to 81 per cent of those questioned, while 18 per cent chose López Rodó, who was identified by 69 per cent. The veteran Gil Robles, known to 48 per cent of respondents, was named by 7 per cent, as was fellow-Christian Democrat Joaquín Ruiz Giménez, even though only 34 per cent identified him. Areilza, the 'alegal' opposition leader who saw Juan Carlos most frequently during this period, was favoured by only 3 per cent of those polled, a mere 18 per cent of whom could name him.[25]

Paradoxically, the most serious threats to Juan Carlos's position during this period had their origin within the Franco regime itself. On 20 December 1971 Franco's household announced that his eldest granddaughter, María del Carmen Martínez-Bordiú, was engaged to be married to Alfonso de Borbón, Juan Carlos's first cousin and rival. Franco's wife, the socially ambitious Carmen Polo, who had already succeeded in marrying her only daughter to the Marquis of Villaverde, Cristobal Martínez-Bordiú, was determined to give her granddaughter a royal wedding, insisting that the bridegroom be referred to as Prince Alfonso and addressed as His Royal Highness.

The uneasiness with which news of the wedding was greeted at La

Zarzuela provides a good indication of Juan Carlos's underlying vulnerability. In spite of his objections, the official wedding invitations described his cousin as 'His Royal Highness Prince Alfonso'. What was more, his uncle Don Jaime did not hesitate to bestow the Order of the Golden Fleece on Franco, an honour that the head of the Bourbon dynasty alone could grant. Two days before the wedding Juan Carlos telephoned López Rodó in the small hours to urge him to discourage the Caudillo from wearing the insignia of the Order at the ceremony, which would have caused Don Juan and his followers deep offence. Franco retained a modicum of common sense, however, and never formally accepted the Order.[26]

The fact that Franco succumbed to family pressure and perhaps even his own desire to please his granddaughter does not mean that he seriously contemplated the possibility of her ever becoming queen of Spain. In some ways the wedding actually limited the options available to him, since he could no longer remove Juan Carlos and designate Alfonso without being accused of extreme nepotism.

There is little doubt that some of those opposed to Franco's succession plans, particularly those who sought to undermine the Carrero Blanco–López Rodó tandem, took advantage of the wedding to sow the seeds of confusion. This is best born out by a confidential opinion poll commissioned by the minister of information on 'the forthcoming wedding between Prince [sic] Alfonso de Borbón and María del Carmen Martínez-Bordiú', allegedly intended to ascertain the former's popularity. A large majority of those polled, 89 per cent, were informed of the event, and 76 per cent knew that Alfonso was currently Spanish ambassador to Sweden, but only 47 per cent had heard of him prior to his engagement to Franco's granddaughter. Significantly, 54 per cent believed the wedding could lead Alfonso to occupy positions of responsibility in the future and almost a quarter of those questioned expected Juan Carlos's popularity to suffer as a result.[27]

The nature of the poll suggests that those who commissioned it did not regard Juan Carlos's proclamation as king of Spain a foregone conclusion. One question even sought to discover whether people thought that Alfonso's position as Alfonso XIII's eldest grandson gave him any right to the throne, to which 47 per cent answered affirmatively and 39 per cent negatively. Another pointedly asked whether Alfonso was deemed to meet the requisites necessary to succeed Franco as defined by the Law of Succession, to which 69 per cent replied that he did, while only 15 per cent thought the contrary.

The poll in question openly invited respondents to compare Juan Carlos and Alfonso as candidates to the throne when it asked them to identify the groups and institutions (banks, employers, workers, the Army, Catholic organisations) that might lend them their support. Juan Carlos was thought to enjoy greater support than his cousin amongst all groups, notably the Army, monarchist circles and bankers. In spite of the efforts of Solís and others to popularise Alfonso's figure amongst members of the official trade unions, only 7 per cent of those polled thought he enjoyed their support.

The mere fact that such a study could have been commissioned by a government agency is surprising in itself. The poll may have owed its existence to the growing conflict between the minister of information, Alfredo Sánchez Bella, who was somewhat lukewarm in his support for Juan Carlos, and the newly appointed director of state-owned television, the ever-zealous Suárez, who enjoyed Carrero Blanco's favour. Suárez knew he owed his appointment to Juan Carlos and submitted his resignation when Sánchez-Bella ordered him to provide full live coverage of the forthcoming wedding. At this point Carrero Banco intervened in his defence, and on 8 March 1972 Spanish television finally dedicated less attention to 'the wedding of the year' than might have been expected.[28]

Alfonso himself cultivated a somewhat ambiguous position towards his cousin. When López Rodó visited him in Stockholm in June 1972, he informed him that his acceptance of Franco's decision to name Juan Carlos his successor was conditional on the latter's continued respect for the fundamental principles of the regime. Implicit in this stance was the suggestion that he would not hesitate to offer himself to Franco as a substitute should the Caudillo ever decide that his confidence in the prince was misplaced. Alfonso also seemed anxious to have the existing Law of Succession modified in such a way as to allow him to become next-in-line.

Juan Carlos's difficulties did not end with the wedding, however. In October 1972 his sister Margarita, who was blind from birth, married Doctor Carlos Zurita at Estoril. Don Juan's invitation to Alfonso did not refer him to as His Royal Highness, in view of which he refused to attend. This proved awkward for Zurita, who had asked his colleague Martínez-Bordiú, Alfonso's father-in-law, to act as his *padrino* (best man). When Franco was informed, he flew into a rage and forbade the Spanish ambassador to attend the wedding of his sworn successor's sister.

Shortly afterwards Carrero Blanco unexpectedly informed Juan Carlos that Franco intended to grant Alfonso the title of prince of Borbón. Determined to prevent this, the prince confronted the dictator on his own. Juan Carlos argued that the existence of two princes would confuse public opinion, inevitably creating the impression that they were competing against each other, and that by promoting Alfonso unduly Franco might be accused of favouring his family, something he had succeeded in avoiding to date.

Anxious to appease his cousin, Juan Carlos offered to grant him the title of Duke of Cadiz, a measure to which his father Don Juan had already consented. The prince subsequently described this meeting as one of the worst ordeals he ever experienced, and one that had made him 'sweat inside'. Later that month Franco finally agreed to the concession of the dukedom, thereby putting an end to the dispute. Juan Carlos would later express irritation at the fact that he had been forced to intervene in the crisis himself while others stood idly by.[29]

The above episode demonstrates that Don Juan was willing to come to his son's rescue when needed. Although the former had recently reiterated his claim to the throne and his rejection of Franco's decision to subvert the natural order of succession, father and son met on Spanish soil on several occasions in the course of the year, somewhat to the alarm of the more intransigent *Juanistas*. Indeed the latter's concern was such that in June 1971 Don Juan had been forced to issue a statement in which he assured his followers that he would not allow his affection for his son to interfere with his duties as the rightful heir to the throne.

It was not just the more committed *Juanistas* who were made uneasy by this rapprochement, however. In June 1972 Juan Carlos and Sofía attended the annual gathering at Estoril, at which Don Juan gave another belligerent speech. On returning to Madrid, Juan Carlos apologised to Franco while pointing out that he could not prevent his father from speaking in public. Several weeks later the Spanish ambassador in Lisbon wrote to Franco suggesting that the prince refrain from visiting Estoril altogether. In the course of his daughter Margarita's wedding, Don Juan was careful not to appear too close to his son in public. That same month, however, Franco's personal doctor, the fanatical Falangist Vicente Gil, informed him that there had been talk of a secret pact between father and son at a recent shoot attended by prominent regime politicians. In the ensuing argument the mayor of Madrid, Carlos Arias Navarro, had exclaimed that 'pact or no pact the prince has sworn loyalty to the regime, and he must keep his word; he cannot play with his countrymen'. When Franco was told, his face lit up as he exclaimed: 'Quite right!' Not long after this incident, the Caudillo asked his sister Pilar whether she thought Juan Carlos would look after the Franco family when he was gone, which suggests his confidence in the prince was beginning to waver. Significantly, on several occasions in late 1972 Franco asked the minister for public works not to invite Juan Carlos to the opening of major building projects. In his traditional New Year's Eve address, however, the general once again expressed satisfaction with his choice of successor.[30]

Juan Carlos interpreted several passages in Franco's message to mean that he intended to stand down voluntarily before his health forced him to do so. The prince also believed, however, that he would only feel able to do this once he had appointed a trustworthy head of government. By this stage Juan Carlos was beginning to distinguish between the government that would be called upon to oversee the immediate transition from Francoism to the monarchy, which would presumably be presided by Carrero Blanco and consist largely of experienced politicians, and its successor, which would be dominated by men of his own generation. In January 1973, after meeting a group of journalists from *Pueblo*, the newspaper controlled by the official unions, Juan Carlos would comment that they were wrong to think that the law of July 1972 (mentioned above) would prevent him from appointing his own head of government after his proclamation. This would suggest that the prince was already contemplating the possibility of replacing Carrero Blanco with someone of his own choice shortly after Franco's death.[31]

Juan Carlos grew increasingly frustrated at the government's inability to reach a decision on the long-awaited political associations. Neither Franco nor Carrero approved of them but their only policy was to stall for time. The prince had often told Fernández-Miranda that 'if the associations are genuine I am in favour of them; if not, it is yet another door which closes on me'. In the face of mounting opposition from regime reformists, in November 1972 his mentor was forced to inform the Cortes, in a speech that would earn him a lasting reputation as an unrepentant *continuista*, that the time was not ripe for innovations. Fernández-Miranda was in fact merely obeying Franco, who had told him to 'say no, without saying no'. Unwilling to sanction the birth of associations that he knew to be a mere façade, Fernandez-Miranda preferred to scuttle them altogether but without admitting as much. Aware of his predicament, Juan Carlos had advised him to 'glide without landing'. By this stage the prince had already told his mentor that 'you know as well as I do that when I am king there will be neither a general secretariat nor a *Movimiento-organización*'. In March 1973, when Fernández-Miranda informed him that Franco had apparently agreed to reopen the debate in the National Council, Juan Carlos nevertheless warned him that 'if they do not find a solution, I will be forced to jump out of the aeroplane without a parachute'. Neither Franco nor Carrero were willing to take any risks, however, and the stalemate was unresolved.[32]

Juan Carlos and his entourage spent the first half of 1973 speculating about Carrero Blanco's forthcoming appointment as head of government. In late 1972 the admiral had informed him that he was anxious to appoint ministers of his liking, given that he might well have to work with them

in the future. At that stage the prince was particulary anxious to ensure the
loyalty of the future ministers of the Army, information, and the interior.
His candidate for the latter post was Fernández-Miranda, but he feared that
Arias Navarro would be appointed instead. Juan Carlos also appears to
have been in favour of finding an opening for Fraga, a bitter enemy of the
Carrero Blanco–López Rodó tandem since his fall from favour in 1969, as
well as for Silva, who had left the government in 1970. True to his word,
Carrero Blanco would allow the prince considerable say in the selection
of his future ministers.[33]

On 4 June 1973 Franco informed Juan Carlos that he had finally decided
to appoint Carrero Blanco prime minister, thereby shedding much of the
executive power he had enjoyed since the civil war. Two days later the
admiral showed the prince the list of new ministers. According to López
Rodó, Juan Carlos was extremely pleased with the new cabinet, to the
extent of exclaiming: 'All it needs is the label of "government of La
Zarzuela"'. Most importantly, Fernández-Miranda was kept on as minister
for the *Movimiento* and promoted to the deputy premiership, while López
Rodó was made foreign minister, a development the prince is said to have
described as 'excellent'. Gamazo, the new minister for the presidency, was
a frequent visitor at La Zarzuela, as was the new industry minister, José
María López de Letona. Fernando de Liñan, who had helped Juan Carlos
plan his travels inside Spain, became the new minister of information. The
prince was also on good terms with the Army minister, General Castañón,
who was confirmed in his post. He was probably least happy with the new
minister of the interior, Arias Navarro, who had been imposed on Carrero
by Franco's family circle. Juan Carlos also regretted Carrero's refusal to
appoint Fraga, who subsequently accepted the Spanish embassy in London.[34]

The new government had barely been in office six months when Carrero
Blanco was assassinated by the Basque terrorist organisation ETA on the
morning of 20 December 1973. Shortly after leaving the Jesuit church
where he attended his daily mass, his black Dodge Dart was blown sky-
high by powerful explosives buried in a tunnel dug under a busy sidestreet
in central Madrid, coming to rest in the inner courtyard of a five-storey
building. Carrero Blanco, his driver and a police escort died before they
could be removed from the debris.

ETA's spectacular coup, its most sophisticated ever, took the Francoist
political class entirely by surprise. To this day there are those who maintain
that the organisation could never have planned or executed the assassination without the assistance of a foreign power or the connivance of elements of Spanish state security. Be this as it may, Juan Carlos himself has

admitted that there are many unanswered questions surrounding Carrero's death.[35]

Franco, who had a severe bout of influenza at the time, collapsed when he was informed of his alter ego's assassination, prompting Juan Carlos to preside the official funeral held on 21 December in his stead. This decision caused considerable unease amongst those responsible for his safety but the prince was adamant. There could not have been a more graphic expression of the prince's predicament than the sight of him walking alone behind the admiral's hearse down the middle of Madrid's main avenue, the Paseo de la Castellana, followed at some distance by a motley crowd of official mourners and furious pro-Franco demonstrators.[36]

Carrero Blanco's assassination marked the beginning of the end of the Franco regime. The admiral had been the Caudillo's most trusted adviser since 1941, and had played a decisive role in forming new governments and keeping together the different factions or 'families' that constituted the Francoist coalition. What was more, the general had pinned his hopes for the survival of the regime after his own death firmly on Carrero. The latter's assassination threw the succession plans so carefully worked out over the years into complete disarray. Paradoxically, those who had done most to obtain Juan Carlos's designation as successor were removed from office on the eve of the event they had been anticipating for so long.

Juan Carlos was never on intimate terms with Carrero, but the latter had always shown him respect, which was more than could be said of many other prominent regime figures. As the prince would later confide to Fernández-Miranda, the admiral had sometimes been difficult to deal with but there could be no doubting his personal loyalty. Carrero Blanco was of course a convinced Francoist who would have been totally incompatible with the democratising process subsequently initiated by the future king. Juan Carlos however was always of the opinion that had the admiral still been prime minister at the time of Franco's death, he would have submitted his resignation as soon as it was requested of him, retiring from political life thereafter.[37]

4 The Succession Crisis

The December 1973 crisis and its outcome left Juan Carlos more isolated than ever before. The prince had hoped that Carrero Blanco would be succeeded by his former tutor and trusted adviser, Fernández-Miranda, who handled himself extremely well as acting premier in the aftermath of Carrero's assassination, dissuading both hard-line Francoists and left-wing opponents from taking to the streets. This was no mean feat, since the attack had coincided with the opening of the long-awaited trial of prominent members of the Communist-led Workers' Commissions (CCOO), triggering speculation as to possible 'ultra' reprisals. Fernández-Miranda was not a popular figure, however, and had powerful enemies in the regime's key institutions. Most importantly, Franco, who admired his intellect, had never trusted him as a politician. His own candidate was Admiral Nieto Antúnez, a seventy-six year old former Navy minister and possibly his only surviving friend.[1]

On 22 December Franco informed Nieto that he wished him to succeed Carrero Blanco. Over the next few days, however, the Francoist political class witnessed one of the most remarkable plots in the regime's history, aimed at preventing Nieto's appointment. On Christmas Eve, after a stormy meeting with Franco, Fernández-Miranda realised that he did not enjoy his trust. On 26 December the general went through the motions of consulting Juan Carlos, who suggested that he appoint either his former tutor or Fraga. The following evening a majority of the Council of the Realm came out strongly in favour of Arias Navarro, much to the surprise of Franco, who was reluctant to promote the minister who had failed in his duty to protect Carrero Blanco. By 28 December, however, the Caudillo had succumbed to mounting pressure from members of his inner circle and proceeded to appoint Arias Navarro. Though hardly a great supporter of his, even Nieto Antúnez would have been preferable from the prince's viewpoint. Arias Navarro felt nothing for Juan Carlos or the monarchy and lost no time in proving it.[2]

Anxious to distance himself from Carrero's legacy, Arias appointed twelve new ministers, without even consulting Juan Carlos beforehand. None of the prominent *Juancarlistas* appointed in June 1973 survived the purge and the two men on whom the prince had relied most heavily in recent years, Fernández-Miranda and López Rodó, disappeared from the scene altogether. On 4 January 1974, in the presence of the new government, the former delivered a characteristically disconcerting farewell speech in which he reaffirmed his loyalty to Juan Carlos without once mentioning Franco, only to conclude with a vaguely threatening 'I am not finished; I shall continue'. These words, intended for the prince's benefit as much as for the in-coming government, revealed the depth of Fernández-Miranda's frustration at being deprived of what he believed to be rightfully his. Indeed many orthodox Francoists would later interpret the professor's subsequent contribution to the transition to democracy at Juan Carlos's side as a sophisticated form of revenge.[3] Of the new appointees, the prince was relatively close to the new minister of syndical relations, Alejandro Fernández-Sordo, and had a long-standing – though by no means intimate – relationship with Pio Cabanillas, one of Fraga's former associates, who became minister of information. Juan Carlos was at a loss to explain the premier's motives, to the extent of attributing his choice of ministers to his cousin Alfonso.[4]

Shortly thereafter Arias had the nerve to suggest to Juan Carlos that he form a new political secretariat at La Zarzuela under one of his trusted ministers, Antonio Carro. Arias also warned him that when Franco died he would have to see his visitors at El Pardo and not La Zarzuela, where he had already decided to live as king. Not surprisingly the prince soon concluded that the only policy was to 'smile, rise above petty politicking, not force the pace, and remain on guard'.[5]

Juan Carlos was well aware of the need to bolster his staff at La Zarzuela, but not in the manner intended by Arias. In early 1974 he enlisted the help of José Joaquín Puig de la Bellacasa, a young career diplomat and monarchist of long standing, with the aim of improving relations with the outside world, particularly the media. Puig soon came into conflict with the secretary general of the prince's household, Armada, who regarded him as dangerously liberal.[6]

Arias Navarro's appointment aroused little enthusiasm either in Spain or abroad. The prime minister was known mainly for the severity he had displayed as a military prosecutor in Málaga during the civil war and for his brutality as director general of security under Alonso Vega (1956–65), possibly the regime's most repressive minister of the interior. The regime's supporters, however, preferred to think of him as one of the most competent mayors the nation's capital had ever known.

Arias faced the same basic problem as had bedevilled those in power since the Organic Law was adopted in 1967, namely that of which course political development should take. This was now exacerbated by the related question of whether Franco should stand down in his lifetime in order to facilitate Juan Carlos's future task. The new premier lacked a political programme of his own but he was vaguely aware of the need to offer an alternative to Carrero Blanco's 'immobilism'. Most importantly, he was happy for his trusted collaborators, notably the minister for the presidency, Carro, to take the initiative. According to the latter, Franco had settled the important succession issue, 'but he had failed to foresee how power would be exercised effectively in the future, a matter which should not be left to the monarch, but rather to the Spanish people'.[7]

Arias took everyone by surprise with his first major speech to the Cortes on 12 February 1974, in which he promised a genuine 'opening up' of the regime in a given period of time. This decision was justified with the argument that the national consensus, which had hitherto found expression 'by way of consent', would in future express itself 'by way of participation' in the political process. More specifically, Arias promised to regulate the right of political association, to reform the syndical system and to provide for the direct election of mayors and other senior officials.[8]

Franco was of course shown the speech before it was delivered and had merely counselled Arias to 'be prudent'. Interestingly, the only paragraph vetoed by the dictator made reference to the imminent proclamation of Juan Carlos's son, Felipe, as Prince of Asturias. Due to the anomalies inherent in an elective monarchy such as Franco's, according to the legislation then in force, Felipe's rights as successor would only come into being after his father's proclamation. Juan Carlos had been anxious to have his son recognised as next-in-line ever since 1969, particulary in the wake of his cousin's marriage to Franco's granddaughter, even if it meant antagonising Don Juan and his supporters.[9]

The shock-waves from the explosion that deprived Franco of his alter ego were also felt at Villa Giralda, the Count of Barcelona's residence at Estoril. Unlike other opposition groups, the PCE had consistently rejected the possibility of establishing a democratic monarchy under Don Juan. In the wake of Carrero's assassination, however, Carrillo came to the conclusion that, as well as applying pressure on the regime 'from below', by means of strikes and demonstrations, it was advisable to erect 'political obstacles' in Juan Carlos's path. More specifically, he intended to exploit the conflict that would presumably erupt after Franco's death between Don Juan, who had committed himself to the establishment of a Western-style constitutional monarchy, and his son, who had sworn to uphold the regime's fundamental principles. Carrillo hoped Don Juan would challenge his son openly and place himself at the head of a broad, Communist-led anti-regime coalition – the *Junta Democrática* – which would step into the vacuum left by Franco after his death, form a provisional government, and call a plebiscite on the monarchy. With this in mind, Carrillo duly enlisted the support of Rafael Calvo Serrer, a former Francoist *Juanista* who had turned against the regime, and the indefatigable García Trevijano, who enjoyed ready access to Estoril.[10]

In early 1974 Don Juan travelled to Paris to meet Carrillo's go-between, Teodulfo Lagunero, who assured him that the Communists would accept a Western-style parlimentary monarchy in return for their legalisation. In return for agreeing to lead their coalition, García Trevijano and Calvo Serer subsequently offered him the possibility of becoming regent after Franco's death, until a plebiscite settled the institutional issue for good. Increasingly influenced by developments in Portugal, the count was rapidly reaching the conclusion that his son's fate would be not unlike that of Caetano, and was sorely tempted by the offer, to the extent that García Trevijano left Estoril in the belief that he had successfully enlisted his support. Juan Carlos was duly informed of these visits by his mother and he was later heard to exclaim that the opposition were brainwashing Don Juan. The latter had recently written to him urging him to visit him in Estoril but Juan Carlos replied that he was unable to travel for security reasons. Shortly afterwards the Countess of Barcelona sent her son news of Don Juan's enthusiasm for General Spinola's efforts in Portugal, openly admitting that she was 'petrified'. Nevertheless, after a decisive conversation with his son in Palma on 9 June, Don Juan finally refused to endorse the manifesto prepared for him, which was due to appear as an article in *Le Monde*. Instead, on 22 June the count presided over a large gathering of moderate opposition leaders, who assembled at Estoril to hear him reaffirm his commitment to a democratic monarchy, though without mentioning his son. Don Juan thereby incurred the wrath of Carrillo and his allies, who proceeded to launch their *Junta Democrática* without him.[11]

The tense calm prevailing at La Zarzuela since Carrero Blanco's death was unexpectedly shattered on 9 July 1974 when an aide telephoned to inform Juan Carlos that Franco had been taken to hospital. Puig de la Bellacasa, who was with him at the palace of La Quinta near La Zarzuela, where the prince saw some of his visitors, recalls having seen him lean heavily on a writing table that had once belonged to Alfonso XII, stunned by the news. In spite of his age, Franco's health had been reasonably good and Juan Carlos had not expected to face a crisis of this nature so soon.[12]

Three days earlier Franco had begun to complain of a swelling in his right foot, which was quickly seen as evidence of a blood clot in a vein. Before entering hospital the Caudillo had instructed Arias and Rodríguez de Valcárcel to draw up the decree by which Juan Carlos would assume the functions of head of state in keeping with Article 11 of the Organic Law. The prince, however, strongly opposed this measure, both out of deference to Franco and out of fear of being held responsible for acts over which he had little control. Juan Carlos wanted the dictator either to stand down for good or not at all, and on 11 July he begged him not to sign the decree, assuring him that he was in no hurry to replace him.[13] Franco suffered a major relapse on 19 July, however, in view of which Juan Carlos reluctantly agreed to become acting head of state. The prince was immediately requested to sign a joint Declaration of Principles with the United States, intended to pave the way for yet another renewal of the Spanish–American agreement of 1953, which President Nixon endorsed simultaneously from California by means of a satellite link-up.

The summer of 1974 was undoubtedly one of the most trying moments of Juan Carlos's political career. As was to be expected given the nature of the regime, Franco's illness triggered intense speculation concerning the country's political future. Some reformists, including government ministers such as Cabanillas, openly favoured an irreversible transfer of power that could only be achieved by proclaiming Juan Carlos King of Spain. This infuriated hard-line elements such as the new minister for the *Movimiento*, José Utrera Molina, who found an ally in Franco's son-in-law, the Marquis of Villaverde, the self-proclaimed champion of the general's family's interests. Arias, for his part, was simply consumed with guilt and irresolution.

Much of this speculation was rendered futile by Franco's surprising recovery, which enabled him to leave hospital on 30 July. On 9 August the prince chaired his first cabinet meeting ever, which was held at El Pardo, rather than La Zarzuela. In the course of the meeting Juan Carlos made his feelings clear when he described his period as acting head of state as 'necessarily brief'. By 17 August Franco was well enough to travel north to Meirás, his summer residence in Galicia, in view of which Juan Carlos joined his family at Marivent palace in Palma de Majorca.[14]

Juan Carlos took advantage of his predicament to transmit the idea that his proclamation as king would open the way to substantial political change. Alfonso Osorio, one of the younger members of the Cortes, was on holiday in Santander when he heard a French news bulletin claim that he and other reformists had been called by the prince to discuss the political situation. On making enquiries in Madrid, he was subsequently informed that the news had been leaked by La Zarzuela. The purpose of the exercise was to give the impression that Juan Carlos was already busy planning the future with the help of young politicians who had little in common with those currently in power. The prince also inspired an article by the reformist pressure-group *Tácito*, which criticised the decision to make him temporary head of state.[15]

While some ministers did their utmost to bring about Juan Carlos's proclamation, others worked equally hard to prevent it. In late August, Utrera Molina, the minister whom Franco had seen most often during his illness, warned him against some of his fellow ministers' plans to force his retirement. The Caudillo reassured Utrera that he would soon resume complete control, and would never tolerate the dismantling of the *Movimiento*'s institutions, currently being contemplated by the government. The minister also informed Franco that 'certain well-placed members of the administration . . . amongst them several ministers' had been seen at La Zarzuela, as if this constituted evidence of disloyal behaviour.[16]

On 27 August Juan Carlos travelled to Galicia to visit Franco, who was making good progress. In view of his condition the prince urged him to resume his powers as soon as possible, arguing that Spaniards should not be given the impression that there were two heads of state. Franco seemed unconcerned, however, and merely complimented him for his performance to date. After chairing a cabinet meeting on 30 August, Juan Carlos returned to Palma with the distinct impression that Villaverde was conspiring to restore his father-in-law to office as soon as possible.[17]

On 1 September Franco unexpectedly telephoned Juan Carlos in Majorca to inform him that he had decided to resume his powers the following day. For once the prince lost his temper and reproached him for not having informed him of his intentions in person during his recent visit, but received no explanation. Franco's decision was probably prompted by reports that Don Juan had interrupted a cruise and returned to Estoril on hearing of his illness, remaining in frequent communication with his son thereafter. The dictator's inner circle interpreted this as evidence of a conspiracy and urged him to resume office at once, much to his daughter's distress.

Puig de la Bellacasa, who was on duty at Marivent that day, heard Juan Carlos swear that he would never stand in for Franco again. President Valery Giscard d'Estaing, whom he had recently met at a shoot in France, subsequently advised him not to surrender his powers unless he was proclaimed king at once, but Juan Carlos knew better than to burn his boats and returned to Madrid to await developments. Given the rapid deterioration of the Spanish economy as a result of the international oil crisis and the growing conflict with Morocco over the Spanish Sahara, the prince was relieved to free himself of the burdens of office. When Franco returned to Madrid on 9 September, Juan Carlos stayed away from the airport in order to underline his growing detachment.[18]

If Juan Carlos had ever expected the Arias government to initiate a significant liberalisation of the Francoist political system, he was soon disappointed. The enthusiasm initially aroused by the so-called 'spirit of 12 February' in reformist circles had begun to wane that same month as a result of the house arrest imposed on the bishop of Bilbao, Monsignor Añoveros, who had defended the use of the Basque language from the pulpit. In early March the government agreed to the execution of a young Catalan anarchist, Salvador Puig Antich, accused of murdering a policeman. In June Juan Carlos had been dismayed by the dismissal of the liberal chief of the general staff, Lieutenant-General Manuel Díez Alegría, on his return from a mysterious visit to Romania.[19] To cap it all, in late October Franco ordered Arias to dismiss Cabanillas for allowing the publication of an interview with the newly elected secretary-general of the illegal Spanish Socialist Party (PSOE), Felipe González. This triggered the resignation of a number of senior officials, something unprecedented in the regime's history.[20]

Juan Carlos's impatience with those intent on obstructing political change increased in the light of events in Portugal following the military coup of 25 April 1974. Unusually for a Spaniard, Juan Carlos spoke Portuguese well and had many Portuguese friends, some of whom turned to him for help when they fell foul of the new military authorities. Above all, the Portuguese crisis revealed what could happen when an authoritarian regime refused to evolve, preventing the more moderate sectors of society from organising themselves politically. Discussing these events with Osorio in July, Juan Carlos expressed interest in the future existence of 'a powerful, broad-based political force which would support the succession and provide leadership during the transition'. Three months later the prince urged López Rodó to discuss Spain's political future with other leading politicians such as Fernández-Miranda, Fraga and Areilza, and to give the meetings publicity. 'It is necessary to organise the right', Juan Carlos concluded, 'and we will have to incorporate the left'.[21]

Juan Carlos's plans necessarily required official recognition of the right of political association, but he was soon to be disappointed. The Statute of Associations finally adopted by a decree law in December 1974 legalised associations and envisaged their participation in future elections, but also granted the *Movimiento*'s National Council full veto powers. This rendered it unacceptable not only to the anti-Francoist opposition but also to many within the regime who wished to begin to move towards a Western-style democracy.

In spite of its limitations, Juan Carlos was in favour of making the most of the statute. In late December he took advantage of a private visit to London to urge Fraga to re-enter the political arena. Fraga had been made ambassador to Britain by the Carrero government in order to remove him from Madrid, where his campaign for political reform had acquired considerable momentum. By late 1974 his prestige was such that the statute's future was widely believed to be in his hands.[22]

On returning from London, Juan Carlos encouraged Osorio to form a broad-based political association that would bring together elements within the regime willing to contribute to the gradual but sincere democratisation of political institutions necessary for the future monarchy's legitimation. More specifically, Juan Carlos believed the success of the operation required an understanding between Areilza, Fraga and Silva Muñoz, all of whom had defended reformist positions in the past.[23]

Fraga was reluctant to form an association of this nature without first ascertaining the government's committment to a democratisation of the political system, however limited. In January 1975 he presented his conditions to the Arias government, including the election of a lower house by universal suffrage, free trade unions and the right to strike. Fraga's plans were deemed too ambitious, however, and when they were brought to Franco's attention he is said to have inquired: 'And what country did you say this was for?' The prince's unholy alliance of reformist prima donnas was thus stillborn.[24]

Juan Carlos had long been aware of the need to take into account the anti-Francoist opposition, and his first priority was to inform himself fully as to their strategy and demands. In order to do so he enlisted the help of a childhood friend, Nicolás Franco, the dictator's nephew, whose father had been Spanish ambassador in Lisbon. In the course of 1974 the prince's envoy canvassed a large number of prominent opposition leaders and questioned them in particular about their attitude towards the future monarchy. However Franco's meeting with Carrillo in Paris, which was promptly detected by the regime's agents, was not a success, and in late 1974, in a widely circulated interview with two prominent French intellectuals, the Communist leader declared without hesitation that 'Juan Carlos will be the regime's perpetuator. What is more, he has discredited himself in the eyes of the Spanish people by selling his father down the river for the sake of the crown; not even the monarchists will forgive him for it'.[25]

In view of the PCE's continued hostility, Juan Carlos redoubled his efforts to establish contact with the Communist leadership. The prince knew that Don Juan had been in touch with Carrillo in early 1974, but could not seek his help in this matter. Instead he turned to the president of Romania, Nicolae Ceaucescu, whom he had briefly met in Tehran in 1971 during the sumptuous commemoration of the foundation of the Persian dynasty, and who had boasted of his friendship with the Spanish Communist leader. In the autumn of 1975 he duly sent his friend and confidant, Manolo Prado y Colón de Carvajal, to Bucharest to see Ceaucescu, who was informed of the prince's determination to bring democracy to Spain and legalise the PCE in due course. In the interim, Juan Carlos hoped Carrillo would not reject the monarchy outright and would refrain from damaging personal attacks. Ceaucescu later relayed this message to Carrillo in person, and a Romanian diplomat was subsequently sent to Madrid with his reply. According to Juan Carlos, his message was simple: 'Carrillo will not move his little finger until you are king. After that you will have to agree on a period of time, not too long a one, within which to make your promise of legalisation good'. The prince's assurances did not fully suc- ceed in dispelling Carrillo's fears that a supposedly temporary exclusion might well become permanent, but the mere fact that Juan Carlos had gone to such lengths to communicate with him augured well for the future. Nevertheless, in an interview with Oriana Fallaci published in October 1975, the Communist leader would still refer to the future monarch as 'a puppet whom Franco manipulates at will, a poor devil incapable of any dignity or political sense'.[26]

Juan Carlos was also anxious to establish links with the various Socialist groups that were beginning to emerge in Spanish society after years of relative inactivity. In public at least, the new PSOE leadership elected at the Congress held in the Parisian suburb of Suresnes in October 1974 was consistently hostile to the future monarchy. According to their official publication, *El Socialista*, in Spain it had always been 'impossible not to identify the monarchy with authoritarianism', which was why the popu- lation had 'clearly said no to the monarchy' on 14 April 1931. Contrary to what some monarchists claimed, during the civil war the monarchy had been far from impartial, participating fully in the struggle against 'the working class, the intelligentsia, democracy, and liberty'. Clearly unim- pressed by Don Juan's efforts to distance himself from the regime, in the PSOE's view the monarchy had 'backed dictatorship and repression from the very first day', and it was therefore futile to expect it to bring about the restoration of democracy. As far as the Socialists were concerned, Juan Carlos's monarchy could therefore represent nothing but the continuity of the Franco regime. For fifteen years the prince had 'been at the dictatorship's complete disposal', never raising his voice against the repression, corruption, and injustice it had engendered, and he should therefore be regarded as 'an accessory to the crimes committed on behalf of the *Movimiento*'. Since 1969 he had done little more than travel abroad and carry out 'demagogic visits' to Spanish towns and villages, usually in the wake of a natural disaster. The rest of his time had been taken up by the armed forces and the Franco family, 'with which he identifies more closely than his own'. Juan Carlos's monarchy would thus be another Francoist institution, in view of which the only option left to decent Spaniards was to 'fight against it with the same strength and vigour with which we have fought the dictatorship'.[27]

In spite of the above, the PSOE was already showing evidence of considerable pragmatism. The party programme adopted in October 1974 advocated a *ruptura democrática* (democratic break) and the formation of a provisional government, but made no reference to a plebiscite on the institutional question. Indeed the term 'republic' only appeared once, in the context of the PSOE's aim to create 'a federal republic of nationalities of the Spanish state'. Furthermore González – who had consistently declined to meet Don Juan, whose 'dark biography' he criticised at Suresnes – refused to join Carrillo's *Junta Democrática*, not least because he thought it unlikely that the count would ever represent a viable alternative to Juan Carlos. As he would later explain, in family conflicts such as this there is always a mother who eventually restores common sense.[28]

At this stage the PSOE leadership did not have direct access to La Zarzuela and therefore lacked reliable evidence of the prince's democratising intentions. Juan Carlos was forced to use roundabout methods to communicate with the party, and his messages thereby lost much of their credibility. Luis Yáñez, responsible for the PSOE's external relations, was approached by an expert in international law who did not belong to the party but sympathised with their cause, Juan Antonio Carrillo, in whom Juan Carlos had confided his plans for a democratic future. Similarly Luis Solana, who was close to the PSOE leadership, occasionally visited Juan Carlos at La Zarzuela, taking care not to remove his motorcycle helmet until he was indoors so as to avoid recognition by the palace guards. According to González, however, the information gleaned from these contacts did not significantly influence the PSOE's strategy.[29]

In spite of this lack of communication, the prince soon realised that the renovated PSOE was a force to be reckoned with and did his best to remove obstacles from their path. In October 1975, when Yáñez was arrested for having criticised the regime during a visit to Sweden, Juan Carlos intervened at the request of the German ambassador, his friend the aristocrat Georg von Lilenfeld, to obtain his release. A month later, at Willy Brandt's request, the prince was instrumental in obtaining a passport for González – who had had it withdrawn by Franco's police – so that he could attend the SPD party conference at Manheim. By this stage the PSOE had already formed its own *Plataforma de Convergencia Democrática* in response to the PCE's efforts to impose its will on the entire anti-Francoist opposition.[30]

The PSOE was not the only Socialist party Juan Carlos had to reckon with. Its main rival, the largely middle-class *Partido Socialista Popular* (PSP), was led by professor Enrique Tierno Galván, who had publicly endorsed the restoration of a democratic monarchy under Don Juan as early as 1959, and had occasionally attended subsequent *Juanista* gatherings.

True to this position, the PSP's 1974 programme asserted that 'though republican, the party will accept that form of government which brings and sustains democracy in Spain'. Although the PSP joined the PCE-dominated *Junta Democrática* in mid-1974, it was to prove consistently pragmatic in its attitude to Juan Carlos. Amongst those who secretly visited La Zarzuela during 1974 with Puig de la Bellacasa's assistance was fellow diplomat Fernando Morán, Tierno Galván's right-hand man.[31]

The prince also courted the Christian Democratic parties led by Gil Robles and Ruiz Giménez, both of whom had supported Franco in the past. Gil Robles had abandoned the *Juanista* camp in the early 1960s, whilst Ruiz Giménez, Franco's education minister in the 1950s, was indifferent to the institutional question. With characteristic pragmatism, in 1974 a position paper published by the latter's party, *Izquierda Democrática*, observed that when Franco died Juan Carlos should be given the benefit of the doubt, on the grounds that 'if the monarchy tries to evolve it will come into contradiction with the Francoist system', in view of which 'we should not render such a process inviable by adopting irreversible attitudes'. The party also acknowleged the need for the monarchy to be 'ratified by the people in some way', but did not insist on a plebiscite. In August 1974 Don Juan himself informed *Izquierda Democrática*'s leaders that his son was becoming increasingly aware of the need to legitimise the crown democratically.[32]

In spite of growing evidence of the prince's democratising intentions, Franco was reluctant to admit he had made a mistake. In December 1974 Utrera Molina openly warned him that 'he very much doubted his successor was sincerely committed to projects which might represent the regime's continuity'. Franco, deeply shocked by this accusation, replied: 'that is not true and what you are saying is very serious. . . . I know that when I die nothing will be the same but there are oaths which bind and principles which must remain'. The general tried to convince his minister that existing institutions would perform what was expected of them, and that if they failed Spain would once again succumb to 'fragmentation and discord'.[33]

In public at least, Franco's confidence in the prince remained intact to the very end. In his traditional New Year's Eve address, which was to be his last, the Caudillo paid tribute to Juan Carlos's behaviour during the summer crisis, praising 'his personal qualities, his political prudence, his training, and above all, his high sense of duty', which had confirmed 'the hopes vested in him'. Several weeks earlier, however, Franco had remarked in private that, of its own accord, the monarchy would obtain less than 10 per cent support in a plebiscite.[34]

In an attempt to regain the political initiative, in March 1975 Arias reshuffled his cabinet, replacing Utrera with Herrero Tejedor, a former vice-secretary general of the *Movimiento*. It was under Herrero that Suárez had first become involved in politics in his native Avila, and it was his former mentor who once again rescued him from oblivion by appointing him vice-secretary general of the *Movimiento*. According to Armada, this was very well received at La Zarzuela, for Suárez 'had always been a good friend and his affection for the prince was plain for all to see'. Several months earlier the prince had asked Suárez to draw up a report on the reforms that would have to be undertaken after Franco's death. Suárez had left La Quinta palace under the firm conviction that 'the future was in my hands', and was deeply disappointed to discover that Herrero Tejedor, amongst others, had been entrusted with an identical task. According to Suárez, his report contained the broad outline of the reform programme he would eventually implement as premier.[35]

Herrero Tejedor was determined to make the most of the Statute of Associations, however inadequate. In April he offered Fraga the possibility of leading an association that would enjoy full government backing, but was turned down. Undeterred he set about the formation of his own association with the help of *Movimiento* officials throughout the country. The fruit of his labours was the Unión del Pueblo Español (UDPE), which he was barely able to launch before his tragic death in a road accident in June 1975.

Herrero is said to have hoped to become Juan Carlos's first prime minister, and according to Armada his name was often raised at La Zarzuela, 'thinking of the future'. Suárez, however, has no evidence that the prince ever thought of his mentor for this post, nor did he ever have the impression that Herrero expected to occupy it. His death seriously endangered Suárez's own career, since the new minister for the *Movimiento*, the veteran Solís, refused to confirm him in his post. By way of consolation Solís nevertheless allowed Suárez to take over UDPE, already well on its way to becoming an association for those who favoured the regime's continuity. Suárez appears to have been motivated by opportunism rather than ideology and UDPE proved a useful platform from which to pursue his political ambition. More importantly, his efforts on the prince's behalf had not gone unnoticed. Shortly after Herrero's death Juan Carlos asked Anson, editor of *Blanco y Negro* magazine, to look after Suárez, who was 'one of the few trustworthy men I have in that sector [the *Movimiento*]'. Several weeks later the magazine unexpectedly proclaimed Suárez 'politician of the month'. In October, the prince told a German journalist, Michael Vermehren, that he expected Suárez to prove very useful in the near future.[36]

Juan Carlos had long since concluded that Franco would never stand down unless he trusted his government, a requisite that had clearly been lacking since Carrero's death. In February 1975 he asked López Rodó to convince him to retire, which the latter attempted without success. Three months later, when Franco informed him that the legislative life of the Cortes was to be extended another three months, the prince asked: 'And what if, in the meantime, something happens to you and I am landed with a constituent Cortes?', to which the general dryly replied that 'nothing will happen'. In June, Juan Carlos confided in Fraga that 'the wait is getting too long' and that he 'thought about it a great deal'.[37]

The prince could only lose sight of developments in Estoril at his own peril. In March, during a visit to London, Don Juan told Fraga what he wanted to hear, namely that the succession process was irreversible, and he seemed anxious not to be regarded as an impediment. Shortly afterwards he urged José Luis de Vilallonga, the *Junta Democrática* representative in Paris, to 'help the prince in every way you can'. In June, however, and in the presence of numerous moderate opposition leaders, Don Juan defiantly described the monarchy embodied by him as the only institution capable of guaranteeing a peaceful transition to democracy and a lasting national reconciliation. He also asserted that Franco's succession plans 'cannot contribute to the democratic change which national interest and the Spanish people are demanding unequivocally because they were conceived with the purpose of guaranteeing the regime's continuity', thereby placing his son in an extremely awkward position. At the same time, however, he was willing to modify his stance if 'those who are really in a position to change the course of the state convince themselves that they must do so to enable the Spanish people to recover its sovereignty at long last', thus leaving open the possibility of a democratising process initiated by Juan Carlos.[38]

Don Juan subsequently received a letter from Mountbatten enquiring as to 'why he had made that very odd public speech which had so embarrassed his son'. By way of reply, the count explained that 'if only Franco had not taken back power after his illness all would have been well. But now he was an old senile man holding on to power and it was going to be very difficult for his son to take over under the aegis of an ailing dictator'. Consequently he had 'thought it was much better that he should make an anouncement showing that he was perfectly ready to rally the Democratic parties away from the Dictatorship, which he would not have had to do if Franco hadn't messed things up'. This would suggest that, as late as mid-1975, Don Juan had still not given up hope of becoming king if his son's card failed.[39]

As a result of this statement the Arias government declared Don Juan *persona non grata* on Spanish soil without even bothering to inform Juan

Carlos beforehand. Armada, hardly a sympathiser of Don Juan, would later recall that 'the prince was naturally very distressed by this insult to his father'. Juan Carlos had recently requested his son Felipe's official recognition as his heir and was almost relieved to hear that the general had turned him down.[40]

The final months of Franco's life were to prove extremely trying for Juan Carlos. In August 1975 the government adopted an anti-terrorist decree that imposed the death penalty for terrorists and their accomplices in the event of their activities resulting in the death of policemen or other public servants. By the end of the month eleven death sentences were pending, three for ETA activists and eight for members of FRAP, a miniscule Marxist–Leninist terrorist organisation formed in 1973. The Arias government came under severe international pressure but nevertheless sent five of the eleven to their deaths on 27 September. Both Juan Carlos and his father were amongst those who pleaded for clemency, but Franco did not even reply to Don Juan's request.[41]

The executions were greeted with indignation and violence on the streets of many European cities, while in the Basque provinces strikes and demonstrations continued well into the following month. On 1 October the Plaza de Oriente in Madrid was once again taken over by tens of thousands of Franco supporters, who gathered in defiance of international public opinion. Juan Carlos, who stood next to a senile and teary-eyed Caudillo whose voice was barely audible above the din, looked unusually stern. This was to be his last major public appearance at Franco's side.[42]

Like many Spanish conservatives, the prince appears to have believed in the existence of an international campaign instigated by the extreme left and masterminded by Moscow with a view to destabilising the country. Juan Carlos was particulary critical of the hypocrisy of those in the West who hastened to condemn the Spanish government for executing terrorists convicted for murdering policemen but remained silent in the face of repeated atrocities in the East, and was deeply incensed by the affrontery of those Eastern bloc governments that had joined the wave of condemnations.[43]

Fortunately for the prince the end was in sight. Franco fell ill during the *Día de la Hispanidad* celebrations on 12 October and suffered a heart attack in his sleep three days later. In spite of his condition, he insisted on presiding a cabinet meeting on 17 October, which was dedicated to the Saharan crisis. The International Court of Justice had recently ruled in favour of the territory's self-determination, prompting King Hassan of Morocco to announce the imminent, allegedly peaceful occupation of the Spanish Sahara by tens of thousands of unarmed civilians, including women and children, in what came to be known as the 'Green March'. Two days later Franco suffered a second heart attack but felt well enough to see the prince the following day. Juan Carlos refused to contemplate another interim arrangement and wanted power to be handed over only if the decision was irreversible. He also suggested that Franco appoint Fernández-Miranda president of the Cortes when Valcárcel's term expired on 26 November, but to no avail.[44]

On 20 October Juan Carlos finally unburdened himself to Fernández-Miranda and informed him that he wanted him to be his first prime minister. 'Nobody', he told him, 'has ever spoken to me the way you do, or kept his own counsel like you do'. Fernández-Miranda's appointment, however, required Arias's removal, and Juan Carlos was by no means certain of being able to achieve this. Two days later he invited his former tutor to decide which institution he wished to preside over after Franco's death, the government or the Cortes (and the Council of the Realm). Fernández-Miranda's reply was characteristically cunning. 'As a political man, which I am, I would like to head your new government but I can be a great deal more use to you as president of the Cortes'. His explanation was as simple as it was convincing: it was the Cortes that would have to carry out the reform of the Francoist constitution, and the Council of the Realm that would appoint a new prime minister. What was more, Fernández-Miranda very much doubted the existing Council – which had vetoed him in December 1973, when it chose Arias – would ever agree to his appointment as head of the government. At this point Juan Carlos seemed resigned to the impossibility of removing both Arias and Valcárcel at once, in view of which he would concentrate on replacing the latter.[45]

In the wake of this conversation Fernández-Miranda confided to his diary that, although he clearly enjoyed the prince's trust and esteem, Juan Carlos also 'feared' him and was somewhat 'uncomfortable' in his presence because he knew him to be intellectually superior. Several days later he would add: 'he accepts me as a counsellor, but would not stand my tutelage'.[46]

Franco's condition deteriorated further on 23 October, in view of which his son-in-law urged Arias to enforce a temporary transfer of power. The Marquis of Villaverde had intended Juan Carlos to face Arias and Franco's doctors at El Pardo in the hope of convincing him to become acting head of state again, but the prince refused to attend. Instead he informed Arias and Valcárcel that he would only become head of state if it was for good. That same day Franco was informed of Juan Carlos's recent contacts with members of the opposition, but was too ill to care.[47]

On 25 October Juan Carlos invited Mondéjar and Armada to lunch to discuss the political situation. Hitherto Armada had been very keen to keep Arias on, because a change of prime minister would imply too sharp a break with the Franco regime. On this occasion, however, he seemed in favour of replacing Arias with Fernández-Miranda and reappointing Valcárcel president of the Cortes. This greatly surprised the prince's former tutor, who knew that Armada had often told Juan Carlos that he was no doubt an excellent academic but useless as a politician. It subsequently dawned on Fernández-Miranda that Armada was backing him in the prince's presence because he knew the Council of the Realm would never agree to his appointment; once the attempt had failed, Juan Carlos would not be able to make him president of the Cortes either, and he would lose all possibility of influencing events. Not surprisingly, two days later Armada took offence when Juan Carlos instructed him to discuss his proclamation speech with Fernández-Miranda.[48]

On 30 October, after yet another relapse, Franco himself instructed that Article 11 of the Organic Law be enforced and Juan Carlos take up the duties of head of state. Arias and Valcárcel duly informed the prince of the decision and appealed to his patriotism and sense of duty to obtain his consent. In view of the Saharan crisis, Juan Carlos finally acceded, even though he was unable to obtain assurances from them that the decision would not be reversed.[49]

The following day, at a meeting of the National Defence Junta which Juan Carlos presided at La Zarzuela (and not at El Pardo, as Arias had intended), the prince raised the possibility of a morale-boosting visit to El Aaiún, the capital of the Spanish Sahara, where several thousand officers and men were stationed. Arias and several of his ministers advised him against the visit on the grounds that it might interfere with the negotiations then under way, but both the Army minister and the chief of the general staff were in favour. The prince, 'full of determination and excitement', also consulted Armada, who expressed his support, as well as Sofía, who was of the opinion that 'a general must stand by his troops'. Only the head of his household, Mondéjar, opposed the idea at La Zarzuela, to the extent of accusing Armada of irresponsible behaviour.[50]

True to his word, on 2 November Juan Carlos landed his own aircraft at El Aaiún, where he spent the day in the company of the garrison stationed there, whom he assured that 'we shall do whatever is necessary so that our glorious Army may preserve its prestige and honour intact'. On returning to Madrid, Sofía, who was celebrating her thirty-eighth birthday, was heard to remark that her husband's gesture was the best present she could have hoped for. Don Juan, one of the first to learn of the visit, was overcome with joy and fatherly pride. Both in the Sahara and in Spain itself, the prince's visit caused an excellent impression in military circles. Indeed several dozen officers of the élite Brunete armoured division stationed near Madrid, led by General Jaime Milans del Bosch, drove to the airport on the spur of the moment to congratulate the prince in person. In Armada's view, Juan Carlos had simply followed his instinct, and had reacted 'like an Army officer'.[51]

The prince, who prided himself on knowing the armed forces well, had grown increasingly alarmed at the growing signs of unrest within the officer corps. In early November 1975 Juan Carlos privately expressed concern at the fact that the entrance exam to the Military Academy was run by teaching staff from Zaragoza University, many of whom were thought to be Marxists. Influenced by events in Portugal, in 1975 a group of young left-wing officers – mostly in the Army – had formed a clandestine *Unión Militar Democrática* (UMD) with a view to preventing regime hard-liners from using the armed forces to resist the *ruptura* advocated by the opposition. Juan Carlos, who publicly described these officers as 'a few misguided people, influenced by foreign propaganda', saw them as a threat to the institution's internal unity and feared they would provoke precisely the type of military intervention they supposedly wished to prevent.[52]

In late July 1975, nine of the UMD's leaders had been arrested, amongst them one of the prince's former instructors at the Academy. Later that year the UMD formally rejected the imposition of a monarchy, and demanded a plebiscite or a vote on the institutional issue by a future constituent assembly. 'It is not that we reject the prince as an individual', the UMD declared, 'indeed the vast majority of us feel affection for him as a result of his presence at the military academies. What we reject is that his legitimacy as king should originate in the existing regime'.[53]

Juan Carlos had hoped his presence in El Aaiún would contribute to establish him – both in Spain and abroad – as an independent figure capable of acting of his own accord, free from Franco's tutelage. His visit was indeed given ample coverage by the international press and he was privately congratulated by several heads of state, including King Hassan of Morocco, whose aggressive expansionist policies had provoked the crisis in the first place. According to a poll specially commissioned by the government, the visit appears to have had a far wider appeal than expected. Indeed 85 per cent of those polled knew of the visit, and of these 76 per cent were satisfied or very satisfied with the prince's action, while only 20 per cent claimed indifference. Whether Arias liked it or not, Juan Carlos's gamble had clearly paid off.[54]

The prince's decision was no doubt also influenced by his burning desire to be recognised as a worthy commander-in-chief by his fellow officers. Juan Carlos was relatively confident of being able to enlist their support, 'because I had been designated by Franco, and in the Army Franco's decisions were not debated'. What was more, he was personally known to many officers of his generation as a result of his military training in the three service academies and had taken good care to nurture these relationships ever since.[55]

According to the journalist Arnaud de Borchgrave, who spoke to him at length in late October, Juan Carlos was anxious to dispel the notion that the armed forces were holding him hostage and that he would be forced to respond to their political demands. In his opinion, this view was based on a misreading of their role under Franco, and of the extent of their power and autonomy. Juan Carlos was firmly convinced that the vast majority of his officers 'have no desire to get involved in politics' and were mainly concerned with the creation of modern, professional, technologically minded armed forces.[56]

In keeping with this spirit, on 12 November the prince met the three military ministers to reiterate his faith in them, in return for which he expected their unqualified loyalty and support. He also informed them that, in an attempt to dissuade Don Juan from issuing a belligerent statement on Franco's death, he was sending Díez Alegría to remind him that the armed forces would stand by the legally appointed successor. In 1968 Díez Alegría had been involved in a plot to restore Don Juan to the throne should Franco die without having named a successor, and the prince hoped his views would still carry some weight with his father. The military ministers, for their part, expressed their deep concern over events in the Spanish Sahara.[57]

This meeting was to have grave, unforeseen consequences. When Arias was informed on 13 November that his military ministers were meeting the prince behind his back, he flew into a rage and submitted his resignation. Juan Carlos would later recall having felt 'as though the floor had collapsed from under my feet'. With Franco on his deathbed and the Saharan crisis unresolved, the premier's resignation left him in 'a totally precarious situation', to the extent that 'when he told me he was going home, I was unable to hold back my tears. I think I cried with impotence'. After much pleading and a visit from Mondéjar, Arias finally withdrew his resignation two days later. This incident greatly undermined the prince's position while reinforcing that of Arias, who had the impudence to boast to Mondéjar that he could bring Franco's body temperature down to 33° if he wished, thereby prolonging the crisis.[58]

At the height of this confrontation Juan Carlos briefly thought of replacing

Arias with Fernández-Miranda once again, but soon recognised that the post of president of the Cortes suited him far better. Indeed he even admitted to his mentor that, in spite of having been together for fifteen years, it was likely that they would fall out if he ever became prime minister due to the very nature of the post. This was something Juan Carlos would rather not contemplate at a time when he badly needed him at his side.[59]

Juan Carlos became increasingly apprehensive about his own future during Franco's agony. Indeed at one point he is said to have remarked to Fernández-Miranda that he half expected to see the Civil Guard driving up to La Zarzuela to arrest him. The prince knew there were very few committed monarchists on whom he could rely, and most of them would rather have supported his father. In spite of his contact with opposition groups, it was as yet unclear how they would behave once Franco was no longer on the scene. More generally, it was difficult to predict the reaction of Spaniards at large, even though his travels had led him to believe that 'while rural and small town areas might accept the monarchy without much trouble, the farther up the social scale you went the more openly doubtful people were'.[60]

Above all, Juan Carlos was anxious as to how he would begin to effect political change. His only source of comfort in this regard was Fernández-Miranda, who reasured him that 'it will be easier than you think'. In the professor's view, 'when people see there is a king in Franco's place they will understand that things can't go on in the same way as before; they won't need to have everything explained to them'.[61]

Franco's condition remained critical but stable until the evening of 3 November, when he suffered a severe haemorrhage, which forced his doctors to carry out a life-or-death operation in the sick bay of the guard house at El Pardo. As his condition continued to deteriorate he was taken to hospital, where he underwent a second operation. On 14 November a further massive haemorrhage forced a third and final operation, from which he never recovered. He died of heart failure in the early hours of 20 November 1975, having lost consciousness two days earlier.

In his political will, read out by a tearful Arias on national television, Franco asked Spaniards to 'surround the future king of Spain, Don Juan Carlos de Borbón, with the same affection and loyalty that you have offered me, and ... grant him at all times the same support and collaboration that I have had from you'. Significantly, the text made no mention of the *Movimiento* or its institutions, and merely emphasised the importance of maintaining 'the unity of all the lands of Spain'. Indeed Franco's parting request to Juan Carlos had been that he do his utmost to 'preserve the unity of Spain'.[62]

Juan Carlos had not been close to Franco, who was never known for his ability to establish intimate relationships with fellow human beings. Nevertheless he had enjoyed as good a working relationship as was possible with the wily Galician. In spite of his treatment of Don Juan and the suffering he had inflicted on his family, the prince could not help respecting Franco, a sentiment that was no doubt mutual. Indeed some of those closest to the Caudillo have often claimed that he regarded the prince as the son he had never had. Be this as it may, Juan Carlos believes he was one of the few people who generally spoke his mind in the dictator's presence, partly because he felt he had little to lose. At worst, Franco could have sent him back to Estoril with his father, an outcome he sometimes secretly wished for.[63]

In Juan Carlos's view, in spite of Franco's boast that everything had been 'tied up and well tied down', he was 'too intelligent to think that things would remain as they were after his death'. At most, 'what the general meant with these words was that he was leaving behind him the structures the country required'. Only some elements of the status quo, such as the capitalist economy and the unity of Spain, could be expected to remain in place. On several occasions in the past, when the prince had asked him for advice, Franco had replied that it would be of little use to him, since the political context would be very different when he became king.[64]

Juan Carlos was finally proclaimed King of Spain on 22 November 1975 in the presence of the assembled Cortes. Dressed in Army uniform, he swore to 'obey and make others obey the fundamental laws of the kingdom, and to remain loyal to the principles which inform the *Movimiento Nacional*'. Juan Carlos greatly resented this oath, because he knew that 'even if I swore to uphold them, the Francoist principles could not remain in force, since that amounted to admitting that the regime remained in place'. As in 1969, Fernández-Miranda was by his side to reassure him: 'Swear to maintain the principles of the *Movimiento*, and at a later date we will change them legally, one by one'.[65]

Juan Carlos set great store by his proclamation speech, which he largely wrote himself, with some help from Fernández-Miranda and others. In it he announced the beginning of 'a new phase in Spanish history', which would be characterised by 'an effective consensus based on national harmony'. Juan Carlos spoke of the need for 'radical improvements' and referred to 'the participation of all in decision-making at every level, in the media, in education, and in the control of the national wealth'. He also acknowledged 'the diversity of peoples which make up the sacred unity of Spain' and expressed his intention of becoming 'king of all at once and of

each in his culture, his history and his tradition'. Although he paid tribute
to the armed forces and the Catholic Church, he made no mention of the
Movimiento or its institutions.[66]

Juan Carlos acknowledged that he derived his legitimacy from the
fundamental laws and the referenda of 1947 and 1966, but also justified
his proclamation on the grounds of historical tradition, a view neither
orthodox Francoists nor monarchist legitimists would have shared. More
significantly, perhaps, he was bold enough to attribute his own sense of
duty to his father's example, an observation that was greeted with indifference by the Cortes. In the dictator's absence, he was thus finally free
to make amends for his enforced silence of July 1969.

Following his proclamation Juan Carlos addressed his first message to
the armed forces as their commander-in-chief. The king acknowledged
their role in 'safeguarding and guaranteeing compliance with the fundamental laws', which he described as 'a faithful reflection of the will of our
people'. In language clearly intended to appeal to the more conservative
officers, he referred to the Spanish flag as a 'symbol of our virtues and our
race', which he would defend from 'the enemies of the *Patria*', a sentiment
that echoed Franco's will to the effect that he forgave his enemies but
hoped and believed he had had none 'who were not also enemies of Spain'.[67]

In marked contrast to his son, whose early public statements were necessarily cautious, Don Juan could afford to speak his mind freely. In mid-
November Calvo Serer and García Trevijano had returned to Estoril in the
hope of convincing Don Juan to declare war on Juan Carlos, but were
turned away for good. Nevertheless, and in spite of his son's efforts, the
Count of Barcelona issued a statement that not only described Franco as
an absolute ruler, but paid tribute to those who had fought on the Republican side during the civil war 'for what they thought was best for their
country'. Don Juan continued to defend a monarchy that would contribute
to a long-overdue national reconciliation, social justice, the consolidation
of a genuine democracy and Spain's full integration in Europe. Juan Carlos
no doubt shared these goals himself by this stage, but was nevertheless
irritated with his father for undermining his own position at such a critical
juncture.[68]

One of Juan Carlos's most urgent tasks at the time of Franco's death
was to win international support for his cause. The United States and the
major European powers had been following events in Spain with growing
apprehension in the wake of the Portuguese revolution. While the former
was primarily concerned with geostrategic considerations and in particular
the need to guarantee continued access to its military bases on Spanish
soil, the latter, notably Germany, hoped to make a substantial contribution

to a process of gradual, peaceful democratisation. The US administration did not allow the September 1975 executions to stand in the way of its short-term goals, and signed a decisive pre-agreement securing continued use of its bases the following month. The major European countries, however, withdrew their ambassadors in protest, and the EEC suspended its talks with Spain.

In spite of this highly unfavourable climate, Juan Carlos was determined that his reign should start on a different footing. In early November he secretly dispatched his friend Prado y Colón de Carvajal to Washington, to enlist the support of Secretary of State Henry Kissinger. The latter had promised that President Gerald Ford – who had visited Madrid in May, much to the democratic opposition's chagrin – would attend the investiture if he could, and would be represented by the vice-president if not. Kissinger was anxious to press on with the renegotiation of the bases agreement and was determined to visit Madrid in December, but Juan Carlos's envoy requested that he wait for a new government to take office. The prince was unhappy with the document signed in October and wanted the United States to raise the bases agreement to the rank of a full treaty, which required the approval of the Senate, thereby acknowledging the change of regime.[69]

Juan Carlos also sent his personal emissary to visit President Giscard d'Estaing, with whom he had established a good rapport. Several months before Franco's death, Giscard had asked Don Juan about the future of the monarchy in his son's hands, to which the latter had replied that 'the Monarchy will turn out to be how I have always described it to you; whether it is he or I who embodies it is irrelevant, but you must support it, for it alone will prevent another civil war'. Whether or not this conversation predisposed him favourably, Giscard agreed to attend the investiture, in return for which Prado promised him a private breakfast with Juan Carlos. This no doubt encouraged the German president, Walter Scheel, to follow suit.[70]

With the assistance of the ever-willing Mountbatten, who was on close terms with the British Prime Minister, Wilson, Juan Carlos was also able to secure the presence of the Duke of Edinburgh. Mountbatten had failed to arrange a secret meeting between his protegé and Wilson, and although the latter avoided any direct commitment, he was well-disposed towards Juan Carlos. 'I recognise, even if it cannot be put bluntly in public', he informed President Ford in December, 'that King Juan Carlos has a very hard row to hoe. So we shall encourage him privately to move as fast as possible, but try to avoid public condemnation when we can, if the pace is slower than public expectation here may demand'.[71]

The only prominent members of the international community to attend Franco's funeral on 23 November were Vice-President Nelson Rockerfeller, Imelda Marcos and General Augusto Pinochet. Four days later the king's investiture at the Church of the Jerónimos was attended by representatives of all the major democracies, amongst them President Giscard, President Scheel and the Duke of Edinburgh.[72] The contrast between the two ceremonies could not have been more explicit, nor more intentional.

On the day of his investiture Juan Carlos shared the limelight with the archbishop of Madrid, Tarancón, who solemnly declared that 'the Church does not want any type of privilege; it merely wants the freedom which it proclaims for all'. Tarancón also hoped that Juan Carlos would succeed in reigning as 'king of all Spaniards', and wished that in future 'legal and political structures might offer the opportunity for all to participate freely'. These words were not well received in conservative circles, but far from taking offence Juan Carlos is said to have thanked him warmly for his support.[73]

The king's early efforts to distance himself from the regime without antagonising its supporters failed to impress the democratic opposition. Carrillo described Juan Carlos as 'nothing more than the representative of Francoism beyond the dictator's open grave', and the Communist weekly *Mundo Obrero* greeted his proclamation with the headline: 'No to an imposed king'. In the PSOE's view his speech to the Cortes had been 'empty, . . . without structure, composed of brief paragraphs aimed at appeasing different sectors of the regime and without any reference to the democratisation of political institutions'. The entire ceremony had 'merely provided fresh evidence of the political vacuum which surrounds the figure of an imposed monarch'. In the Socialists' view, 'the Francoist clan surrounding Juan Carlos intends to use him as a liberalising front in order to obtain the support of foreign governments', but 'the people will not be fooled by the substitution of the yoke-and-arrows [the Falangist symbol] with a crown'. Nevertheless, on the eve of Franco's death the former Communist leader Fernando Claudín was surprised to discover that González did not exclude the possibility of a democratising process inspired by Juan Carlos. Several days later Areilza found the young Socialist leader similarly well-disposed towards the future monarch. Although they could not admit as much in public, the more far-sighted opposition leaders were beginning to give Juan Carlos the benefit of the doubt.[74]

5 After Franco, What?

Shortly before his investiture Juan Carlos told a foreign journalist that his overriding goal was 'the restoration of real democracy', by which he understood the establishment of a Western-style parliamentary monarchy. The king's reasons for advocating such a system of government were at once simple and complex. The period since Carrero Blanco's assassination had given him a realistic foretaste of what was in store for him as king of a Francoist monarchy and it was a prospect he did not relish. Although the situation after Franco's death was different in that he had inherited some of his powers, Juan Carlos could still be held hostage by the government, the Cortes and the Council of the Realm, institutions over which he had relatively little control. His first goal was therefore to become genuinely independent of the executive and legislative institutions of the country, something that could only be achieved in the context of a fully democratic parliamentary monarchy.[1]

Additionally, Juan Carlos had become increasingly aware of the growing demand for democratic change emanating from broad sectors of Spanish society. This was something he readily perceived in his tours of the country and in his countless interviews with Spaniards of all kinds, as well as from the increasingly outspoken press. Furthermore his frequent visits abroad and his contact with foreign statesmen had led him to conclude that, socio-economically, Spain was a country not unlike its Western European neighbours and was therefore capable of sustaining a democratic system of government.

Juan Carlos also advocated a democratic solution for Spain because it was the natural option for a country already highly integrated in the Western sphere of influence. Thus in October 1975 Borchgrave found him 'eager to join the ranks of the Western alliance and to link Spain's efforts with Western Europe's democracies in what he views as the most important endeavour of the age – the unification of the European continent'. Later, in his proclamation speech to the Cortes, Juan Carlos emphasised that 'we Spaniards are Europeans', adding that 'Europe must take Spain into account'. Given the EC's refusal to have authoritarian regimes in its midst, this amounted to an endorsement of sweeping political change.

At this stage the king did not have a blueprint for democratisation, though he was determined to 'act legally and constitutionally under all and any circumstances', as Fernández-Miranda had always advised him. Juan Carlos believed it was the government that should take the political initiative, without involving him unnecessarily in its decisions; at most he would 'counsel it and orient its thrust and its action'. In keeping with this aim, he would abstain from presiding cabinet meetings except on special occasions.[2]

The king's immediate concern was to secure Fernández-Miranda's appointment as president of the Cortes and the Council of the Realm. This was essential, as these two bodies would determine the government's legislative activity and the selection of a future premier respectively. His former tutor's appointment was by no means a foregone conclusion, however, not least because the out-going president, Valcárcel, who enjoyed the full support of the Council, intended to stand for reelection. On 27 November Juan Carlos duly convinced Valcárcel to withdraw his candidature by insinuating the offer of a ministerial post in the new government.

The following day the king sought Arias's support in winning over the more recalcitrant members of the Council of the Realm. Arias, who had assumed the king would attempt to remove him, read this as evidence of his own confirmation and immediately offered his enthusiastic collaboration. With the Saharan crisis and his own investiture behind him, however, Juan Carlos was in a considerably stronger position than before, and he intentionally delayed Arias's ratification, thereby linking his continuity in office to Fernández-Miranda's appointment. Leaving nothing to chance, Juan Carlos also canvassed several councillors himself, amongst them Antonio Oriol, one of the Franco regime's most influential figures, and two of its younger members, Primo de Rivera and Enrique de la Mata.[3]

After an extremely tense session, the longest in its history, on 1 December 1975 the Council of the Realm finally presented the king with a *terna* (or list of three candidates), from which he immediately selected Fernández-Miranda. Two days later, at his swearing-in ceremony, the Machiavellian professor declared, largely for the benefit of Juan Carlos, that 'I feel absolutely responsible for my entire past. I am loyal to it, but it does not tie me down'.[4]

Although the Council of the Realm had obeyed the king's wishes on the understanding that Arias would remain in office, Juan Carlos was sorely tempted to appoint his own prime minister after all. In November he had briefly considered the candidature of López de Letona, a former minister of industry and distinguished technocrat, in what came to be known as the 'Lolita operation'. The latter, however, appeared to be masterminded by Fernández-Miranda's rivals, and was stillborn.[5] The king also entertained the possibility of appointing another former minister, Castiella, who had been summarily dismissed by Carrero Blanco in 1969 after dominating Spanish foreign policy for over a decade.

On 3 December Juan Carlos called the newly appointed president of the Cortes to La Zarzuela to discuss Arias's possible replacement in the presence of Armada and Mondéjar. The members of the king's household, particularly Armada, spoke out in favour of Arias, whilst Fernández-Miranda acted as the devil's advocate, reminding them of the premier's attitude towards Juan Carlos in the past. In the end, however, even the professor admitted it was unlikely that a Council of the Realm that had so recently appointed him at Arias's insistence would agree to his replacement several days later. When Fernández-Miranda had left, Armada turned to Juan Carlos in triumph and said: 'Didn't I tell you, Your Majesty, that Torcuato was not invincible?' The king said nothing, but thought to himself: 'We will see in the long-run. This man does not know Torcuato'.[6]

To his amazement Juan Carlos soon discovered that Arias had no intention of submitting his resignation, not even as a matter of courtesy, and sent Fernández-Miranda to prod him, without any success. In view of this, on 4 December the king finally decided to confirm him in his post so that observers would assume Arias had submitted his resignation beforehand. Much to his irritation, however, the following day's newspapers made no reference whatsoever to his ratification. In despair Juan Carlos telephoned Arias in the middle of a cabinet meeting, only to have him explain that it had simply slipped his mind. Adding insult to injury, on returning to the cabinet table the latter promptly announced the king's ratification. Arias thereby sought to remind Juan Carlos that he owed his five-year appointment to Franco, and regarded his confirmation as a mere formality.[7]

Contrary to what Juan Carlos had feared, in return for his confirmation Arias proved willing to allow La Zarzuela to play a full role in the appointment of his new government. Determined to compensate for the poor impression caused by Arias's confirmation both at home and abroad, the king aimed to enlist the reformist troika formed by Areilza, Fraga and Silva Muñoz, which he had failed to unite earlier in the year. At the same time he wished to see a number of younger, less well-known faces sitting around the cabinet table. Fernández-Miranda, who expected nothing from a government presided by Arias, preferred not to intervene at all.[8]

Fraga had been acting like a premier-designate for some months. In the autumn of 1975 he had stepped up his reformist campaign, which aimed to convince those in power and public opinion at large that only his programme and leadership could save Spain from the extremes of stagnation and revolution. On leaving his post as ambassador to London, the impetuous Galician visited Juan Carlos on 20 November with a blue-print for reform not unlike that rejected by Arias earlier in the year. At La Zarzuela, Fraga obtained the impression that the king's inner circle favoured a cautious approach and seemed anxious to win time.[9]

Arias was still annoyed with Fraga for having rejected the 1974 Statute of Associations and he initially intended to give him a non-political portfolio, such as that of minister of education. When his candidate for the ministry of the interior failed him, however, Arias offered the post to Fraga, who was also made deputy premier for political affairs at the king's suggestion.[10]

Areilza, one of Spain's most attractive political figures, had also regarded himself as a potential future prime minister, to the extent that in early December he even discussed the reforms he intended to carry out with Ollero, the leading monarchist constitutionalist. In spite of his earlier association with Don Juan, the Count of Motrico had visited Juan Carlos on fifteen occasions since 1969 and liked to think that he enjoyed his confidence. Areilza would later attribute his failure to obtain the premiership to a mysterious dossier compiled by hard-line elements in order to discredit him with the king. The mere fact that he gave credence to this interpretation, however, suggests that his relations with Juan Carlos were not as intimate as he liked to claim. It was nevertheless largely at the king's insistence that Arias finally offered him the Foreign Ministry.[11]

At the king's request a cabinet post was also offered to Silva Muñoz, but the latter insisted on drawing up a plan of action with Areilza and Fraga beforehand, in view of which Arias withdrew his offer. Juan Carlos tried to compensate for his absence with the appointment of another reformist, Antonio Garrigues, as minister of justice. During their honeymoon tour of the United States in 1962, Garrigues, who was then ambassador in Washington, had greeted Juan Carlos and Sofía as future heads of state, a gesture they greatly appreciated. More importantly, his recent press statements were fully in tune with the king's own thinking. On the eve of the dictator's death, Garrigues had boldly declared that 'Juan Carlos is the successor to Franco, not to Francoism' and predicted that 'Francoism will die with Franco'.[12]

Looking back at the early months of his reign almost two decades later, Juan Carlos would recall that in order to face the imponderables, dangers and hopes posed by the post-Franco era with success, he required 'young people, with a vision of the world their elders dared not entertain. Under Francoism, absolute power was wielded by an old man. And I, the newcomer, was a young man with an almost physical need to surround myself with others of my age'.[13]

This need was readily apparent from the composition of the new government. Thus it was Juan Carlos who suggested that Osorio be appointed minister of the presidency, a position that should have enabled him to watch Arias closely had the latter not removed him almost immediately to an adjoining building. This did not deter Osorio, who recalled having heard Juan Carlos frequently remark that 'the prime minister who does whatever has to be done will be chosen from amongst the members of my first cabinet'. Juan Carlos also intervened in the appointment of Osorio's under-secretary, Colonel Sabino Fernández Campo, who was being trained with a view to occupying positions of responsibility in the royal household in the near future. Armada, who had suggested his name to the king, was getting ready to succeed Mondéjar as head of the household, and was anxious to have a second-in-command of his own making.[14]

Suárez was another of the king's young protegés. In order to secure his appointment, Fernández-Miranda first had to convince Arias to move Solís – the last government minister personally appointed by Franco – to the Ministry of Labour, thereby freeing the *Movimiento* portfolio for Suárez. In spite of the decisive role played by the president of the Cortes in his promotion, the new minister never doubted it was ultimately inspired by Juan Carlos himself. Suárez would subsequently become Fernández-Miranda's major source of information on the activities of the Arias government.[15]

Juan Carlos had first met Suárez briefly when he was head of television programming, and got to know him well during his stint as governor of Segovia. The 1969 crisis had swept Suárez to the pinnacle of the Spanish radio and television organisation, an appointment he rightly attributed to Juan Carlos's influence. Thereafter he had taken it upon himself to improve the prince's public image, a task that earned him his gratitude and even friendship. The more senior Francoist politicians tended to overwhelm Juan Carlos with their bookish knowledge and statesmanlike posturings, and to make him uncomfortably aware of his intellectual shortcomings. In marked contrast, charming, self-made Suárez, who was six years his junior, was a fun-loving, unpretentious companion with whom he felt very much at ease.[16]

When Carrero Blanco formed his government in June 1973, Suárez had been disappointed not to become vice-secretary general of the *Movimiento* under Fernández-Miranda. In spite of this, when the latter fell from favour in the wake of Carrero's assassination, Suárez, who had detected his influence over Juan Carlos, continued to court him assiduously. The young politician from Avila finally became vice-secretary general under Herrero Tejedor in March 1975, but the latter's unexpected death briefly truncated his political career. Arias had toyed with the idea of replacing Herrero Tejedor with Suárez, but Franco insisted on having Solís, who had already occupied the post for much of the 1960s.

The king was also responsible for the appointment of Rodolfo Martín Villa, the youngest member of the cabinet, who had enjoyed a meteoric political career, first in the official students' union and later in the regime's labour organisation. At the time of Franco's death, Martín Villa was governor of Barcelona, a post from which he had contributed to dedramatising Catalan political life by means of gestures such as the de facto acceptance of the Catalan flag. On a recent visit to Barcelona by Juan Carlos and Sofía, the governor had gone out of his way to enable them to meet a broad cross-section of Catalan society, including many who were critical of the regime, a gesture that had not gone unnoticed at La Zarzuela.[17]

Other members of the so-called 'prince's generation' to join the Arias government were Calvo Sotelo (public works), Carlos Pérez Bricio (industry), and Virgilio Oñate (agriculture). Calvo Sotelo had been a *Juanista* in his youth, to the extent of having been one of the coffin-bearers at Alfonso's burial in 1956. Don Juan eventually invited him to join his privy council, but Calvo Sotelo turned down the offer, and by 1969 he was regarded as a staunch *Juancarlista*. Pérez Bricio was a promising young politician with ready access to La Zarzuela, while Oñate was a follower of Silva Muñoz.[18]

The king was particularly anxious to enjoy the full support of the military ministers. Many observers were disappointed by Arias's failure to appoint the then military governor of Ceuta, Manuel Gutiérrez Mellado, widely regarded as a liberal on account of his long-standing association with Díez Alegría. Juan Carlos had indeed referred to him in conversation with a German journalist in October 1975 as someone whose services would soon be required. Gutiérrez Mellado, who had not yet been promoted to the rank of full general, would later attribute his failure to reach the cabinet to a smear campaign masterminded by hard-liners who sought to discredit him in the eyes of the king by presenting him as the spiritual father of the UMD. Instead Arias created a new deputy premiership for defence affairs, which he entrusted to General Fernando de Santiago y Díaz de Mendívil, a notorious reactionary recently returned from the Sahara, and placed him in charge of fellow ministers Gabriel Pita da Veiga (Navy), Félix Alvarez Arenas (Army) and Carlos Franco Iribarnegaray (Air Force).[19]

Juan Carlos was soon made aware of Arias's inability to control his own government. By mid-January 1976 the latter had already been to La Zarzuela with a newspaper cutting describing a secret meeting of notorious hard-liners recently attended by General Santiago, threatening to resign in protest at what he saw as a conspiracy to dislodge him. Senior Army officers, including the military ministers, became increasingly uneasy at the sight of strikers and demonstrators taking to the streets on an unprecedented scale, but Juan Carlos knew that their views were not widely shared by officers of his own generation.[20]

The views of the more senior officers were clearly taken into account when the ten UMD leaders arrested in mid-1975 were court-martialled and expelled from the armed forces in March 1976. Gutiérrez Mellado, who was not without sympathy for the UMD's professional goals, had feared that if the sentences were unduly severe, 'at least five hundred officers would turn republican overnight'. The Communists, who followed events in the armed forces very closely, were quick to accuse the king of sacrificing his fellow officers for the sake of appeasing his hard-line ministers. Impressed by events in Portugal, Juan Carlos had indeed feared that the UMD might feed on the frustration of officers recently evacuated from the Sahara. Indeed the king favoured Spanish membership of NATO precisely because he hoped it would provide the armed forces with new interests and objectives, thereby reducing the likelihood of intervention in domestic affairs.[21]

Within weeks of coming to power the second Arias government faced a formidable array of challenges that it was ill-equipped to deal with. Partly due to its predecessor's failure to face up to the consequences of the 1973 oil crisis, by this stage the Spanish economy was in deep recession. This manifested itself in a sharp increase in both inflation and unemployment, which partly explains the spectacular increase in strikes registered in early 1976. To make matters worse, in November 1975 the out-going government had imposed an unpopular wage freeze, and in February its successor devalued the peseta. These strikes, which brought Madrid's industrial belt to a stand-still and later extended to Barcelona and elsewhere, soon became politicised by growing demands for the creation of truly representative trade unions and the right to strike without fear of reprisals.

The government also faced demands for the release of all political prisoners and the immediate return of political exiles. On 25 November 1975 the out-going government had granted a limited pardon to mark Juan Carlos's proclamation, which the justice minister had broadened in scope at the king's insistence. The pardon excluded those convicted for terrorist activity, who constituted the largest category of what the democratic opposition described as political prisoners. The pro-amnesty campaign thus continued to gather momentum throughout 1976, notably in Catalonia and the Basque country, where it was fuelled by an increasingly radicalised nationalist community. In these regions of Spain the demand for political freedom was invariably accompanied by requests for a statute of autonomy, if not the right to national self-determination.

The government's response to these challenges was far from satisfactory. Its anti-inflationary measures could not be enforced without a degree of collaboration from industrial workers, who were unlikely to agree to them without first being allowed to elect their own representatives. This required the complete transformation of the regime's labour institutions, which the government hoped to address once it had tackled the prickly subject of political reform. Similarly the concession of a general amnesty was ruled out on the grounds that it would be interpreted as a sign of weakness, and that it required a prior reform of the penal code. As to the demands of the regions, the government claimed that the establishment of a new political framework should take priority. In other words, none of these pressing issues could be tackled without first reforming the Francoist constitution.

The Arias government's programme, presented to the Cortes on 28 January, disappointed Juan Carlos and exasperated Fernández-Miranda. The premier claimed his aim was to 'shift Franco's responsibility onto the nation as a whole, onto its politicians, its institutions and its citizens' and described his goal as 'an arbitrating monarchy' not unlike those of Western Europe. Arias announced the creation of a bicameral Cortes, though without specifying how it would be elected or what powers it would enjoy. (Earlier, in an interview with a foreign journalist, he had promised the election of a lower chamber by universal suffrage by 1977.) More encouragingly, he admitted that the 1974 Statute of Associations had failed to achieve its goals and was to be replaced with new legislation, but rather spoiled the effect by emphasising the exclusion of advocates of 'terrorist violence', promoters of 'any form of anarchy', those who 'threaten the sacred unity of the *Patria*' and those advocating 'Communism and the dictatorship of the single party'. (In the above-mentioned interview Arias had promised that four or five political parties would be functioning normally within two years.) The latter was particulary ironic given that Arias had technically succeeded Franco as head of the *Movimiento*, about whose future he was extremely vague. Finally Arias promised new legislation regulating the right of assembly and public demonstration and the reform of the 1966 Press Law. Although the government had recently faced the most serious wave of strikes in Spain's history, the prime minister failed to address this issue altogether.[22]

Fernández-Miranda had long held the view that the only genuinely reformist option available to Juan Carlos was to submit a law to the Francoist Cortes paving the way for the election of a democratic constituent assembly. This evidently entailed the modification of a number of fundamental laws, and therefore required the endorsement of two thirds of the Cortes and a referendum. Fraga, who largely inspired the government's proposals, feared that the Francoist Cortes would never accept such a frontal attack on the fundamental laws, and therefore sought ways of developing the latter's democratic potential to the full without actually replacing them.[23]

The task of transforming Arias's vague promises into concrete proposals was entrusted to a joint committee of cabinet ministers and members of the National Council. This committee was the brainchild of Suárez, who thereby sought to ingratiate himself with Fernández-Miranda, who had created a similar body in 1973 to study the right of political association. Fully aware of what an excellent time-wasting device the earlier committee had proved to be, the president of the Cortes readily agreed to its creation.[24]

At the first meeting of the joint committee on 11 February, Arias unexpectedly declared that 'what I want is to continue Francoism. And as long as I am here or still in political life, I'll never be anything but a strict perpetuator of Francoism in all its aspects and I will fight against the enemies of Spain who have begun to dare to raise their heads'. During the next three months the twenty-one man committee spent nine endless evenings finding excuses to water down the government's already rather limited proposals. Juan Carlos was kept fully informed of the committee's deliberations by Fernández-Miranda, as well as by some of the younger ministers anxious to prove their loyalty, notably Suárez. In the professor's opinion the committee was doomed from the outset because it 'ignored the king's true position and concerns'.[25]

Juan Carlos grew increasingly impatient at the government's lack of progress. At the suggestion of its president, Fernández-Miranda, on 2 March he addressed a meeting of the Council of the Realm for the first time, with the intention of winning its members over to his cause. At the same time Juan Carlos took this opportunity to warn the Francoist political class, and the Cortes in particular, that 'the king's will cannot be supplanted nor qualified'. More specifically, he reminded them of his power to submit major bills directly to the nation in times of crisis, such as when 'certain minorities present themselves, unjustifiably, as the expression of the will of the people'. Fernández-Miranda's text originally included a reference to the king's power to dismiss the head of the government, which Juan Carlos preferred not to include in the final version out of fear of antagonising Arias unnecessarily.[26]

Arias presented the fruit of the joint committee's labours in a televised speech to the nation on 28 April. True to form, he succeeded in presenting its proposals in the least favourable light possible. The novelty of a lower chamber elected by universal suffrage was greatly undermined by describing its future members as 'representatives of the family'. In discussing the future Senate, Arias was silent about its composition or method of election but specified it would inherit the role of the National Council of the *Movimiento*. Similarly, the new Law of Association was announced without mentioning political parties by name. Worse still, in language reminiscent of Carrero Blanco, he warned his audience that 'international communism has not forgotten its defeat on our soil, and . . . avidly seeks the moment of revenge'. Furthermore, the future electoral law was justified on the grounds that it would enable voters to distinguish between groups with real social support and those that were 'nothing more than pretentious initials condemned to ridicule and oblivion'. Arias once again failed to address the reform of the official labour organisation, while castigating those responsible for the loss of fifty million working hours in the first two months of 1976, which he described as 'an act of treason'. Given the overall tone of the speech it is hardly surprising that the promise of a referendum on constitutional reforms in October and of local and general elections in early 1977 should have gone virtually unheeded.

Juan Carlos was deeply irritated with this performance, not least because Arias had failed to send him a copy of his speech before recording it. The king was also annoyed with some of his ministers, who showed no hesitation in criticising Arias in La Zarzuela but lacked the courage to stand up to him at cabinet meetings. Worse still, by this stage he was having to intervene directly in government affairs to compensate for the latter's inexplicable apathy. Aware of Martín Villa's increasingly desperate efforts to improve labour relations, for example, on 2 May he publicly declared that syndical freedoms 'must parallel the principles of freedom and representation in the political sphere'.[27]

Juan Carlos also sought to compensate for his government's lack of progress by establishing direct contact with his fellow countrymen. Aware of the relative indifference with which his investiture had been greeted in certain regions, he decided that his first official visit within the country should be to Catalonia. In his conversation with Borchgrave in October 1975, Juan Carlos had conceded that Spain was suffering from over-centralisation and had advocated greater autonomy for its regions, provinces and cities. A month later, in his proclamation speech to the Cortes, he had promised the recognition, 'within the unity of the kingdom and of the state, of regional peculiarities as an expression of the diversity of peoples which make up the sacred reality that is Spain'. The government, however, had been content to set up a committee to study the creation of a special administrative status for several provinces, a proposal that was met with derision by the Catalan opposition.

On the eve of the king's visit, Fraga authorised the governor of Barcelona to explore the possibility of arranging a private meeting for Juan Carlos

with Catalan opposition leaders. This was later discarded in view of the
governor's reluctance to discriminate against those whom the Arias government was currently excluding from the political process, such as
the Communist leader Antonio Gutierrez.[28]

The high-point of Juan Carlos's visit to Catalonia in February 1976 was
undoubtedly the official reception at the Tinell palace, one-time residence
of the kings of Aragon. Much to the surprise and delight of his immediate
audience, in the midst of his televised speech Juan Carlos switched from
Castilian to Catalan, a language those in power had not spoken in public
for almost forty years. According to the governor of Barcelona, who was
at his side, 'when he finished the king was intensely happy, for he had
understood the impact his words had achieved'. During the second day of
his visit Juan Carlos saw Cardinal Jubany, a leading figure of the Catalan
church, and later visited Montserrat, the monastery traditionally regarded
as the seat of Catalan Catholic culture.[29]

The government had originally advised the king against this visit, on
account of the region's acute industrial strife. Juan Carlos nevertheless
insisted on visiting the Baix Llobregat, an area noted for its heavy industry, which had recently experienced a general strike. In Cornellá he promised an audience consisting of several thousand industrial workers that
'all your rights will be recognised and enforced', while at the same time
urging them to fulfil their responsibilities, since 'social justice, which we
are determined to see established in Spain, is a combination of rights and
duties, and you cannot have one without the other'. The king's brave
performance failed to impress the Catalan Communists, however, who
condemned the visit in strong terms.[30]

Encouraged by the success of his Catalan visit, Juan Carlos continued
to seek greater direct contact with the man in the street. In April the king
and queen visited Andalusia, and a month later they toured the Asturias
region. According to a poll commissioned by the government in the wake
of their Andalusian tour, 81 per cent of those consulted regarded this
direct contact between the monarch and his subjects as either positive or
very positive, while only 10 per cent questioned its value. The king, for
his part, is said to have been 'pleased and impressed' by the enthusiastic
public welcome awarded him.[31]

Not everyone was so positive about these visits, however. Areilza, who
felt that Juan Carlos's speeches on these occasions were 'charming and
paternalistic, but little more', nevertheless feared that the government might
attempt to 'live off the oxygen provided by the popular enthusiasm aroused
by the monarch'. Other observers were alarmed by the political continuity implicit in the nature of these visits. Provincial governors, *Movimiento*

officials and city mayors continued to provide free food and transport in order to guarantee large, enthusiastic crowds, and arranged the display of placards and banners. As one editorialist observed in the wake of the Asturias tour, 'the king is not Franco, and the habits and behaviour which surrounded the former head of state must change in relation to the sovereign'. Some ministers were quietly contributing to this end already. In Seville the royal visit coincided with a severe water shortage, and Fraga instructed the mayor that existing restrictions should also apply to the royal residence, as he knew the king would want to be treated 'like any other Sevillian'.[32]

As in the past, political developments in Madrid continued to have a direct bearing on Juan Carlos's relationship with Don Juan. The king had hoped to convince his father to renounce his title to the throne in his favour shortly after his proclamation in the Cortes, a ceremony that greatly impressed the count. The latter was initially willing to comply with his son's wishes, and in late November 1975 he instructed Antonio Fontán, a liberal monarchist who acted as their go-between, to inform Juan Carlos that he should henceforth regard himself as the *de facto* head of the dynasty and rightful king of Spain. When Fontán told Juan Carlos, he seemed moved but not surprised. The king had in fact instigated leading members of other European royal families, amongst them Mountbatten, to encourage Don Juan to take this step, and the latter began to plan a formal renunciation on board the destroyer that he hoped would bring back King Alfonso XIII's remains from Italy. Some leading *Juanistas*, notably Sainz Rodríguez, believed he should not renounce his rights until there was unequivocal evidence of Juan Carlos's willingness and ability to embark on a process leading to the establishment of a constitutional monarchy. In December 1975, however, in a letter to his loyal adviser, Don Juan recognised that if his son failed it was unlikely he would be able to do much for the monarchy himself. When López Rodó visited the count in Lausanne in late April, he expressed grave doubts as to the viability of the Arias reform but seemed anxious not to undermine his son's efforts. Earlier the king had asked the former minister to reassure his father as to the monarchy's future.[33]

During the early months of his reign Juan Carlos was obsessed with the need to convince the democratic opposition both of his democratising intentions and of the viability of a far-reaching transformation of the political system compatible with the letter of the Francoist constitution. Most opposition groups were initially of the view that such an operation was either unfeasible, or would fail to satisfy their minimum requirements, and therefore regarded his efforts as futile and misguided.

The king's attitude towards the Communist Party at this stage was intentionally ambiguous. His early public statements about Communism were those of a typical mid-1970s cold-warrior, but this may have been due to the fact that they were addressed to an American audience. Thus in late 1975 *Newsweek* reported that in Juan Carlos's view the transition could not be undertaken in collaboration with the Communists, whose political philosophy he considered totally alien to the concept of democracy, even though they increasingly paid lip service to it. Juan Carlos had watched developments in Portugal closely and had been alarmed by the role of Cunhal's Communist Party. Although he did not rule out the possibility of allowing the Spanish Communists to become part of the legal opposition to the government, he was initially in favour of postponing this until a stable democracy had been established. 'Spain', he told *Newsweek*, 'cannot build a viable democracy with non-democrats'.[34]

Juan Carlos was particularly anxious to obtain the monarchy's acceptance by the PSOE, the party that was internationally acknowledged as the legitimate representative of Spanish socialism. In the wake of his investiture the king succeeded in establishing contact with González via the Duke of Arión, one of his most trusted friends, who sought to convince the Socialists of his democratising intentions. In public, however, the party remained deeply sceptical as to the chances of a democratisating process inspired by Juan Carlos. On 8 December 1975 the police had broken up a Socialist demonstration attended by party leaders intent on commemorating the fiftieth anniversary of the death of their founder, Pablo Iglesias. This led *El Socialista* to conclude that in spite of 'attempts to create a liberal image for the king in order to obtain foreign support' nothing had changed since May Day 1975, the previous occasion when a similar event had met the same end. In view of this 'accurate proof of the king's intentions', the PSOE concluded it should reject the advice of those who demanded 'a truce for the liberal king', and go on the offensive. Unbeknown to *El Socialista*, Juan Carlos had turned livid when he was informed that the government had suspended a press conference at which González was due to address foreign journalists in Madrid.[35]

In more restricted circles, the PSOE was somewhat less belligerent. In December 1975 Yáñez, one of the party's better-known leaders, specified that the PSOE's attitude towards the monarch would depend on whether he attempted to perpetuate the Franco regime or even carry out a limited reform, or whether he contributed to the establishment of a genuine democracy. Yáñez was reasonably confident that Juan Carlos would do the latter because only a democratic solution could save the monarchy, though he admitted that even this might not be sufficient to guarantee its survival.[36]

The Christian Democrats, widely regarded as key players in Spain's immediate political future, adopted a consistently pragmatic attitude towards the new king. In January 1976, at their first illegal though tolerated party conference, the groups that made up the Christian Democratic Team of the Spanish State advocated the election of a constituent asembly and the creation of 'provisional executive institutions', but stopped short of demanding a plebiscite to determine the institutional question. True to this pragmatism, in late February Ruiz Giménez told Areilza that he was willing to visit Juan Carlos on behalf of the moderate opposition and submit their programme to him in the hope that he would agree to their legalisation.[37]

Ironically, some of those who had been extolling the virtues of a Western-style parliamentary monarchy the longest also proved to be amongst the most reluctant to accept Juan Carlos. Shortly after the king's investiture, Joaquín Satrústegui, leader of the liberal-monarchist Unión Española, had even advocated that he abdicate at once in Don Juan's favour. Satrústegui was of the view that in order to save the monarchy the constituent Cortes demanded by the opposition should be convoked by Don Juan rather than his son.[38]

In early 1976 the *Junta* and the *Plataforma* came under growing pressure to come together in a single opposition platform. The issue that kept them apart was precisely the attitude they should adopt towards the king and the government. While the *Junta*, and more specifically the Communists, continued to demand the formation of a provisional government, the *Plataforma*, and in particular the Socialists and the Christian Democrats, were reluctant to accept this as the cornerstone of their programme. In spite of this, in March the two organisations finally agreed to form a new body, *Coordinación Democrática*, which demanded the opening of a constituent period that would lead to a decision on the form of the state 'by means of a popular vote based on universal suffrage'. Implictly, this 'popular vote' did not have to take the form of a plebiscite; it could also refer to elections leading to the formation of a constituent assembly, or to a referendum on a future constitution. Furthermore, instead of the provisional government hitherto advocated by the *Junta*, *Coordinación Democrática* demanded the formation of 'coalition-type organs of executive power', a formula vague enough to include even a future government appointed by the king.[39]

Juan Carlos figured very prominently in the debates leading to the creation of *Coordinación Democrática*. While the PSOE's spokesman, Enrique Múgica, favoured a pragmatic, non-belligerent approach, the self-appointed representative of the more radical groups, García Trevijano, seemed intent on placing the monarch at the centre of the political debate. Múgica felt there was nothing to be gained by attacking Juan Carlos personally, a view that gradually imposed itself in opposition circles.[40]

Juan Carlos was not at all pleased with the Arias government's handling of the opposition. In late March 1976 Fraga arrested a number of left-wing *Coordinación Democrática* leaders as they were about to launch their first manifesto from García Trevijano's office. Much to the king's irritation, at a cabinet meeting chaired by him during his Andalusian tour, Fraga announced that he would hold them hostage in prison in order to guarantee a peaceful May Day. Juan Carlos subsequently endured the humiliation of receiving a telegram from the president of the European Parliament demanding the release of these and other political prisoners, much as Franco might have done several years earlier.[41]

Arias's refusal to meet even the most moderate opposition leaders prompted Juan Carlos to see them himself. Given the government's strategy, he could not publicly meet representatives of parties belonging to *Coordinación Democrática* because it included the Communists. He therefore began by meeting independent figures such as the constitutional expert Ollero, and moderate opposition leaders such as the Social Democrat Antonio García López.

In early April Ruiz Giménez's *Izquierda Democrática* had been through a turbulent party conference that had resulted in the departure of many of its members, amongst them the monarchists Alvarez de Miranda and Iñigo Cavero, who later formed their own party. This schism was partly motivated by their opposition to membership of *Coordinación Democrática* on the grounds that it implied an excessively close association with the Communists and their strategy of mass mobilisation. Shortly thereafter they visited Juan Carlos to express their opposition to the Arias government's programme, which they knew to be unacceptable to all those in favour of a genuine democratisation.[42]

In early May Juan Carlos also saw the veteran Gil Robles, whose sons he had befriended as a child in Portugal. Like the Christian Democrats who had preceded him to La Zarzuela, Gil Robles had decided to keep his own group, the *Federación Popular Democrática*, out of *Coordinación Democrática* on account of the Communists' presence. In his view, the solution to the exisiting stalemate between government and opposition lay in the formation of a 'politically and morally independent' executive, which would call a referendum aimed at providing the king with a clear mandate, thereby paving the way for the election of a constituent assembly.[43] Gil Robles realised that an open-ended constituent process of this nature might endanger the monarchy, but he was confident that if the operation was successful the majority of the population would continue to place their trust in 'a head of state who, in order to overcome an extremely difficult situation, accepted certain exceptional powers for a limited period of time and with the specific purpose of bringing democracy to Spain, and later complied with a fundamental law drawn up by a freely elected assembly'. Instead of waiting for the opposition to impose a constituent process on him, in Gil Robles's view the king should launch it himself by appealing to the people, thereby becoming the driving force behind the democratising process. In the veteran leader's mind there was no doubt that 'the responsible left' would collaborate in such a process. Gil Robles had indeed been authorised to speak on behalf of moderate Basque nationalism as represented by the PNV, whose leaders were willing to present their arguments to the king in person.[44]

Areilza formally embraced Gil Robles's plan in the course of a dinner-meeting hosted by the *Siglo XXI* Club on 10 May. The count spoke of the need to reach a 'national pact' between government and opposition under the auspices of the king with a view to advancing towards a new democratic constitution. According to his plan, Juan Carlos – whom he had recently described as '*el motor del cambio*' (the engine of change) – would invite leading opposition leaders to agree to a blueprint for the democratising process, which would then be negotiated with those in power. What Areilza failed to explain was how Gil Robles's plan and the 'national pact' could be made compatible with the need to respect the regime's fundamental laws, upon which the king's own legitimacy still rested.[45]

Unable to meet prominent Socialist leaders himself, Juan Carlos encouraged others to do so on his behalf. In early April he urged Suárez to see González, but the latter refused to meet someone who occupied the post of secretary-general of the *Movimiento*. The king therefore turned to Osorio, who was promptly told that the PSOE would only talk to Fraga, because in the party's view 'it was Fraga who was in power'.[46]

In mid-April Fraga had allowed the Socialist trade union, the as yet illegal *Unión General de Trabajadores* (UGT), to hold its thirtieth congress in Madrid, a decision he had only consulted with the king. Indeed Fraga would later claim that Juan Carlos was 'one of the few people who seemed pleased when I told him about it'. This paved the way for a meeting between the minister and the PSOE's secretary general, finally held on 30 April. Fraga's main concern was that González should accept Juan Carlos and the monarchy, which the PSOE refused to do at this stage. At one point in the interview the minister lost his temper and exclaimed: 'Remember I represent power and you are nothing', to which the Socialist leader, ten years his junior, calmly replied that 'in a few years' time you will depend on me much more than I will on you'. Six years later it was indeed González who would became prime minister, whilst Fraga swallowed his pride as leader of the opposition.[47]

Fraga claims to have come away from the interview with the impression that 'the Socialists were full of empty talk, and not even the institutional question posed insuperable problems'. Some of his more conservative cabinet colleagues would later accuse him of having negotiated a secret deal with González, presumably so as to undermine his standing with the king. In his secret talks with PSOE leaders, one member of Fraga's team, José Manuel Otero Novas, even suggested that they recognise the monarchy on a temporary basis on the understanding that they could revise their position when they came to power. Otero realised it would be difficult for them to go back on such a decision, but so did Socialist party leaders, who remained reluctant to commit themselves.[48]

Fraga's optimism was not entirely misplaced, however. In late May González publicly declared that 'the Spanish monarchy is not necessarily incompatible with democratic freedoms ... if the king is capable of assimilating and adapting to this historic process, the monarchy will survive'. According to Otero, who was in constant communication with Socialist leaders, by the spring of 1976 the PSOE 'still said no, but began to toe the line'. The leader of the other major Socialist party, Tierno Galván, was even willing to negotiate directly with the monarch.[49]

In spite of the government's poor showing, by this stage even the Communists were becoming more accommodating. On 2 April Carrillo – who had been living secretly in Madrid since February – told journalists in Paris that 'if by a miracle the king should agree to consult the people ... we would not be an obstacle'. A month later, *Mundo Obrero*, which held Juan Carlos responsible for his government's shortcomings, reluctantly admitted the possibility that he might break with the Francoists 'in a moment of courage', and seek the support of democratic opinion. This would not guarantee the monarchy's future because 'the democratic solution requires that the institutional question be put to the people sooner or later', but 'only a king capable of running this risk would be in a position to hope for the democratic legitimation of the monarchy'. In the Communists' view, even though he might thereby place the crown at risk, unless Juan Carlos opted clearly for the democratic solution his fate would resemble that of his brother-in-law Constantine. *Mundo Obrero* concluded by warning that the king's apparent passivity threatened to convince public opinion that 'a democratic *ruptura* inevitably requires the proclamation of a republic', a statement that must have surprised party members accustomed to regarding this as a basic tenet of their programme.[50]

The PCE's attitude betrayed a growing sense of alarm at the prospect of the king and the government reaching an understanding with the non-Communist opposition. In public the Communists dismissed Juan Carlos's interviews with moderate opposition leaders as nothing but 'empty gestures', but in private they were seen as a serious threat to opposition unity and evidence of an attempt to exclude them from the process.[51]

Juan Carlos still appeared to harbour grave misgivings about the Communists when *Newsweek* revisited him in mid-April. An avid reader of the foreign as well as the Spanish press, the king was well aware of growing international pressure in favour of their legalisation, but remained sceptical as to their commitment to democratic principles. Surprisingly he even appears to have lent credence to sightings of bands of well-armed Communist exiles hiding in Portugal. Borchgrave thus left La Zarzuela under the impression that the PCE would not be legalised until a sturdy democratic structure had been erected in Spain.[52]

The PCE's legalisation was to remain the litmus test of the government's democratising intentions. In May the European Parliament reminded the Spanish government that 'the legal existence of Communist parties is a characteristic which is common to our Western democracies, and in the nine countries of our Community Communist parties are recognised as lawful organisations'. A month later Fraga himself admitted to the *New York Times* that the Communists' eventual legalisation was inevitable. This enfuriated Admiral Pita da Veiga, who demanded a public disclaimer without success, in view of which he took his complaint to La Zarzuela, where the king did his best to appease him. The Navy minister would subsequently warn Osorio that the PCE's legalisation would be very badly received by the armed forces, to the extent of endangering the monarchy itself. Ironically Fraga's statement also alarmed the Communists, who feared the rest of the opposition would agree to take part in the elections currently envisaged by the government on the understanding that the PCE would be legalised at a later date. This fear appears to have influenced Communist strategy, and by June PCE leaders were secretly offering to suspend their campaign against the crown in return for their legalisation.[53]

Juan Carlos knew that much of this discussion would remain academic unless the government succeeded in forcing its reform bills through the exisiting political institutions. In late May the government enjoyed its first triumph when the Cortes passed a bill regulating the right of assembly and demonstration, which removed existing restrictions on private meetings and lifted many of those affecting public gatherings. The government faced a more serious challenge when the Law of Association was debated in the Cortes on 9 June. Although it was initially assumed that Fraga would defend it, Arias, who resented his protagonism, asked Osorio instead. The latter declined the offer but suggested, in consultation with Fernández-Miranda and the king, that Suárez be given a chance to prove himself.

Suárez's speech was a superb combination of ambiguity and pragmatism. The recognition of basic political rights such as that of association was presented not as a break with the Francoist past, but rather as the culmination of a forty-year process of national reconstruction. According to Suárez, under Franco Spaniards had known peace, social justice, and cultural and material progress; the time had finally come for them to enjoy full political rights as well. The bill was defended on the grounds that the de facto existence of political parties could no longer be ignored and should be regulated so as to isolate those unwilling to play the democratic game. In the shorter term, it was hoped it would facilitate the dialogue between government and opposition.

This speech was to have a lasting impact on Suárez's career. Shortly before he was due to speak Juan Carlos telephoned him from Burgos, where he was following some military manoeuvres, to wish him luck. 'You simply cannot imagine', he later confided in him, 'how much easier this makes things for me'. Not long afterwards the king told a former minister that 'it was about time someone said these things'. Even Armada, traditionally wary of reformist statements, admitted that Suárez had 'caused an excellent impression; he spoke well, and transmitted security'. Several days later Juan Carlos jokingly told Osorio, who had recently lectured on the role of the monarchy, that 'Suárez and you have been copying me'.[54]

The king's elation was short-lived, however. The bill had gone through the Cortes virtually unchallenged because it left the definition of what constituted illicit association to a new article in the penal code. When the latter came up for debate that same afternoon, the Cortes forced the government to take the bill back, rendering its earlier victory meaningless. Two days later the government's constitutional reforms ran aground in the National Council. Shortly afterwards Juan Carlos admitted to López Rodó that 'the government lacks the support of the Cortes, and Fraga is unravelling'.[55]

Unable to speak his mind freely, Juan Carlos took advantage of his official visit to the United States in early June, on his first trip abroad as king of Spain, to clarify his intentions further. In keeping with his wishes, in January the two countries had signed a new Treaty of Friendship and Cooperation, which inaugurated a more balanced bilateral relationship. In a carefully prepared speech to Congress delivered in excellent English, Juan Carlos gave assurances that the monarchy would ensure 'the orderly access to power of distinct political alternatives in accordance with the

freely-expressed will of the people'. As intended, this espousal of liberal democratic principles, his most explicit to date, caused an excellent
impression both in Spain and abroad.[56]

Areilza, who masterminded the visit, was less than happy about Juan
Carlos's performance at a subsequent press conference, which was undermined by 'childish suggestions made by members of the king's inner circle
to be used when faced with "dangerous" arguments'. Fortunately, however,
'his spontaneity was much more valid'.[57]

Before landing in the United States, in late May Juan Carlos had briefly
visited Santo Domingo, thereby becoming the first Spanish monarch – and
indeed the first Spanish head of state – ever to visit the lands claimed
on behalf of Queen Isabella almost five centuries earlier. This was the
king's first opportunity to express his almost obsessive commitment to the
improvement of relations between Spain and its former colonies, which
was to become one of the hallmarks of his reign. Significantly, amongst
those who congratulated the king for his success in Washington was General
JorgeVidela of Argentina, a gesture which pleased the former, even if he
was a military dictator.[58]

The success of his American tour boosted Juan Carlos's self-confidence
and strengthened his resolve to face up to the failure of the Arias government
at home. The king had begun to discuss Arias's replacement with Fernández-
Miranda and some of his ministers in mid-March, and in April he told
Newsweek that the premier was 'an unmitigated disaster'. Juan Carlos had
done his best to influence Arias, but when he confronted him he merely
answered 'Yes, your Majesty', and proceeded to do nothing, or even the
opposite of what the king had intended. His attitude was such that in April
Juan Carlos confided to Fernández-Miranda that 'I think he sometimes
believes he is stronger than I am and that deep down he does not recognise
me as king'. Arias did not always bother to return his calls, and on one
occasion ten days elapsed without him visiting La Zarzuela. Worse still,
Juan Carlos suspected that his telephone conversations were being intercepted by the intelligence service, which was accountable only to Arias.
In Borchgrave's view, what worried the king most was that 'Arias's policies
– or non-policies – were polarising Spanish politics, by turning both right
and left against the government'. This was also perceived by Don Juan,
who saw his son in Madrid on 21 May to urge him to rid himself of Arias
before it was too late.[59]

Juan Carlos knew that the only solution to his problems was Arias's
replacement, but he was unsure as to how to bring it about. If the latter
refused to submit his resignation, the king could only dismiss him with the
full support of the Council of the Realm, and although Fernández-Miranda

was rapidly imposing his authority its members could still react unfavourably. Additionally, the king lacked the support of his own household, as neither Armada nor Mondéjar believed Arias should be replaced against his will. Consumed with doubt, the king spent many a sleepless night roaming the empty rooms of La Zarzuela like a ghost. Lack of sleep made him increasingly irritable, to the extent of shouting at Sofía in the presence of his aides, prompting the queen to burst into tears.[60]

Aware of the king's predicament, Suárez and Osorio visited Arias on 5 May in an attempt to make him modify his attitude. When they pointed out that he had never shown Juan Carlos his speeches in advance, the premier promptly replied that the king had never shown him his. Arias resented the latter's talks with opposition figures, and claimed that he telephoned provincial governors to give them orders without the government's permission. At one point he even compared his difficulties in talking to Juan Carlos to his inability to engage in conversation with five-year-old children; after five minutes he simply had nothing to say to him![61]

The king's decision to dismiss Arias has sometimes been attributed to pressure exerted on Juan Carlos (or him) by the Ford administration during his visit in June. This interpretation seems totally unfounded, however. When Kissinger visited Madrid in January 1976 to sign the new treaty, his main concern had been that Spain should not follow in Portugal's footsteps, advising Areilza to 'go slowly'. Five months later in Washington, the secretary of state assured both Areilza and the king that the administration would understand if the Communists were legalised, but would also be quite happy to see the decision postponed several years. In the State Department's words, 'it would be absurd to make the legalisation of a party dedicated to authoritarian principles a litmus test as to whether or not democratisation is taking place'. Given this attitude, it seems unlikely that Juan Carlos would have come under American pressure to move more swiftly towards democracy.[62]

In spite of the obvious need to rid himself of Arias, Juan Carlos seemed paralysed by doubt. Indeed when López Rodó visited him on 11 June he seemed uncertain as to whether the time was ripe for a change of government. Some of those closest to him were at a loss to explain his hesitant behaviour, to the extent that one minister, Pérez Bricio, concluded that it was in some way connected to the existence of compromising recordings of telephone conversations between Juan Carlos and his father. Others, such as Puig de la Bellacasa, who had been removed from La Zarzuela in early 1976 by Armada, who regarded him as a dangerously liberal influence on the monarch, attributed the delay to the fact that it was important that Arias's replacement should not be seen as a concession to pressure from below.[63]

The need to replace Arias at the first possible opportunity forced Juan Carlos to think of a substitute. The obvious candidate was Fernández-Miranda, but as the latter reminded him in early April, having appointed him president of the Cortes it was impossible to make him chief executive without prompting accusations of 'rasputinism'. Fernández-Miranda's integrity was such that he did not hesitate to turn down the most sought-after political post in the land out of fear of unduly compromising the king. Instead he set out to find the ideal candidate on Juan Carlos's behalf.[64]

According to the president of the Cortes, in April 1976 the king's own candidates, in order of preference, were Areilza, Fraga, López de Letona, Pérez Bricio, Silva, López Bravo and, finally, Suárez. In spite of his obvious affection for him, Juan Carlos initially regarded the young *Movimiento* minister as being excessively 'green behind the ears'. Fernández-Miranda, however, greatly valued both his 'availability' and his willingness to allow himself to be guided from above, and consequently set about convincing the king that he was the best choice available.[65]

Areilza always fancied his chances of becoming prime minister, and his hopes were no doubt raised by the king's habit of criticising Fraga and Arias in his presence. At a personal level, their relations were always good, even if the count was closer to Don Juan's generation than his son's. Determined to improve his standing at La Zarzuela, on 15 April Areilza visited Fernández-Miranda, who delighted him by explaining his reasons for not wanting to replace Arias himself. Juan Carlos subsequently informed Areilza that, in Fernández-Miranda's view, neither he nor Fraga would be accepted by the Council of the Realm, but the president of the Cortes later assured him that he was still the king's favourite. In early May Juan Carlos went out of his way to prevent Areilza from resigning in disgust at Arias's performance.[66]

In Fernández-Miranda's view there were far too many obstacles in Areilza's path. Above all, the more conservative members of the Francoist political class had never trusted him and it was unlikely the Council of the Realm would include him in a list of candidates unless the king exercised his full authority, something that was best avoided. Indeed some of the count's most dedicated opponents were in La Zarzuela itself. Early in the year, when the foreign minister publicly declared that Carrillo was a Spaniard like any other and was therefore entitled to a passport, Armada had urged the king to have him expelled from the government at once. Juan Carlos did not share his sense of outrage, but was not always on the same wavelength as the count. Indeed after a particulary disconcerting talk in April, Areilza had concluded that 'either the king is preparing some vast Bourbon move to change the government at will, or he feels safe in the "bunker" with his army men and personal "ultras" '.[67]

Additionally, Areilza clearly had a mind of his own, as his disagreement with Juan Carlos over the question of Church–state relations had revealed. Traditionally, Spanish monarchs had enjoyed a say in the appointment of bishops, a prerogative that Franco had perpetuated and the Church had come to resent in the wake of Vatican Council II. When Areilza first raised this issue in January, the king – who had defined himself as 'profoundly Catholic' and had expressed his 'most respectful consideration for the Church' in his proclamation speech – seemed reluctant to let the Vatican have its way. In April, just as an agreement with the Holy See had begun to seem possible, Juan Carlos surprised Areilza by asking him whether they were not in fact granting everything in return for nothing, thereby running the risk of antagonising the more conservative sectors of the clergy. The king reminded his minister that Franco had refused to allow the Pope to visit Santiago de Compostela out of fear that he might publicly demand his renunciation of this 'right of presentation', to which Areilza replied that this was precisely what should differentiate the monarch's attitude from that of his predecessor.[68]

Fraga was possibly more acceptable to conservative elements within the regime and even the royal household, but it was difficult to think of someone who had less in common with the king than he. The minister, who was sixteen years his senior, did not wear his considerable intellectual prowess and erudition lightly, a trait that did little to endear him to Juan Carlos. Significantly, in spite of the many difficulties he faced during his term as minister of the interior, Juan Carlos rarely proferred words of encouragement. In the king's view, Fraga's heavy-handed response to the admittedly daunting wave of strikes and demonstrations that had marked the first five months of his reign had been counterproductive. Otero Novas, for his part, had deduced his minister was not a serious contender from the fact that Juan Carlos occasionally used him as a go-between rather than speak to Fraga in person. Fraga himself knew his chances to be slim due to his long-standing rivalry with Fernández-Miranda and later attributed the outcome of the crisis to the fact that 'while I had to spend almost twenty-four hours a day answering the telephone, Fernández-Miranda had all day to prepare his next conversation with the king'.[69]

In an attempt to discover where he stood with Juan Carlos, in one of his frequent visits to La Zarzuela Suárez had suggested that he replace Arias with Fernández-Miranda. When the latter was informed, he invited Suárez to dinner on 8 March to explain his reasons for not wanting the post, and at one point he suddenly asked: 'And why not you?' To Fernández-Miranda's amazement, Suárez did not even bother to feign surprise, thereby revealing his secret ambition. Since Christmas 1975 the young *Movimiento* minister had cultivated the professor assiduously, never taking a decision without consulting him beforehand. In his own words, during this period 'Fernández-Miranda observed my every movement, as though he were examining me'. Suárez came to the conclusion that the king wanted a prime minister of his own generation, without too much experience, and without an excessively distinguished academic or professional record. Most importantly, he needed someone who had served the regime, but who was not automatically associated with any of its political 'families'.[70]

Osorio had first detected Juan Carlos's interest in Suárez in early March, as a result of the Vitoria crisis. Fraga had gone to Germany, leaving Suárez behind as acting minister of the interior, when the police opened fire on a group of strikers who had gathered in a church in the Basque city of Vitoria, killing several workers. Suárez immediately took control of the situation, and spent the next thirty-six hours seeking to prevent the violence from escalating. On the afternoon of 5 March the king, who was described by a visiting journalist as being 'deeply concerned' by these events, asked Osorio whether Suárez had performed 'as well as he says he has', to which the minister loyally replied in the affirmative.[71]

Suárez had been preparing his candidature with consummate skill. His task was made easier by the fact that, given the nature of the *Movimiento*'s general secretariat, he was virtually a minister without portfolio, or, in the words of Martín Villa, 'the only full-time politician in the government'. Once he had correctly identified Fernández-Miranda as the king's *éminence grise*, he set about consolidating his position in the *Movimiento* structure. It was this that led him to seek – and obtain – his appointment as one of the National Council's *Cuarenta de Ayete*, an exclusive group formerly appointed by the head of state. Suárez knew his chances of being included in the Council of the Realm's *terna* would depend on his standing amongst some of the regime's most conservative figures, and acted accordingly.[72]

Juan Carlos finally chose Suárez because he was 'young and modern, and ambitious enough to want to be the man who dealt with the period we were going through'. He was the ideal candidate 'because his roots lay in Francoism and he couldn't be suspected of wishing to introduce excessively radical changes'. Fernández-Miranda, for his part, always assumed he would make a 'very obedient and very disciplined' premier. Years later the professor would explain that 'in our conversations with him we saw that he absorbed our suggestions and developed them at once. The things which he said had to be done were nothing more than a final version of what we had outlined and suggested should be done. I had never before seen such capacity for absorption. The man was a veritable sponge'.[73]

Suárez was always of the opinion that it was ultimately Fernández-Miranda who convinced the king that he was Arias's ideal replacement and not vice-versa. The young politican had left nothing to chance, however, and when it came to pleasing the monarch his zeal was unlimited. On the eve of Juan Carlos's visit to the United States, *Cambio 16*, Spain's most widely read political magazine, published a caricature of Juan Carlos in evening dress, dancing against a New York skyline. Both Fraga and Areilza found this treatment of the head of state refreshing, but Suárez appeared to take offence and urged Arias to have the issue banned. Whether or not this behaviour pleased Juan Carlos, by June he had made up his mind, as Suárez soon realised. In the course of that year's cup final, the king, observing the contrast between the veteran president of Real Madrid and the youthful president of Real Zaragoza, pointed out to him that young presidents were more agreeable. With characteristic audacity Suárez replied: 'the trouble is the older ones refuse to stand down'.[74]

The decision to dismiss Arias had already been taken by the time the king left for the United States in June, but it was the intervention of the military ministers that forced him to implement it in early July. In late June Pérez Bricio informed Juan Carlos that General Santiago intended to send him a letter demanding Arias's resignation on account of his weakness in the face of the opposition. Amongst others, the king consulted Suárez, who identified two possible options: he could either dismiss Arias before he received the letter, or remove Santiago and allow the premier to stay on for several months, so that his critics would not think they had forced his hand. After further soul-searching Juan Carlos opted for the former course of action.[75]

The date of Arias's dismissal was also determined by other, more subtle considerations. Since January Fernández-Miranda had instituted fortnightly meetings of the Council of the Realm, the body responsible for nominating a new prime minister. Under Franco the Council had only met to ratify crucial decisions involving the head of state, and was therefore closely watched. Once they became frequent, however, these meetings ceased to be of interest, allowing Fernández-Miranda to submit matters of the utmost importance without causing a stir. As its president had intended, most members of the Council were unaware of Arias's dismissal when they assembled for their fortnightly meeting on 1 July.[76]

Juan Carlos spent the morning of 1 July at the Royal Palace, greeting the new ambassadors from the Sudan, Cameroon, Argentina and Irak. When they had left, he turned to Areilza and exclaimed: 'This cannot go on any longer, for fear of losing everything. A monarch's office is sometimes an uncomfortable one. I had to take a difficult decision and have finally done so. I will carry it out at once, surprising everyone'. Minutes later he received Arias in a small study that once belonged to Alfonso XIII.[77]

According to Arias, the king's distressed manner and his reluctance to initiate the conversation immediately alerted him as to his predicament, in view of which he promptly submitted his resignation. Juan Carlos thanked him profusely for his services to the monarchy, in return for which he would be granted the title of Marquis of Arias Navarro. In Martin Villa's words, when he informed his ministers of this interview that afternoon he 'tried to show respect for the king's decision without quite achieving his purpose'. Arias himself compared his meeting with Juan Carlos to the often-cited occasion in 1909 when Alfonso XIII summoned his prime minister, Maura, only to greet him with an embrace and the words: 'Thank you, don Antonio, for your patriotic gesture. What do you think of Moret as your successor?'[78]

At the Council of the Realm meeting held later in the day, Fernández-Miranda did not propose any specific candidates and instead suggested that they discuss the future premier's ideal profile. His aim at this point was to ensure that Suárez's name was included without fellow councillors detecting his interest. After several meetings, on 3 July each councillor selected three candidates, producing a total of thirty-two names. Amongst others, these included nine ministers, fourteen former ministers (including Ruiz Giménez) and two generals, whose names were removed at the objection of the military councillors present. When Fraga's name came up for discussion, one of the generals present accused him of having reached an understanding with the Communists, and it was promptly dropped from the list. Areilza's name met a similar fate shortly afterwards. At the end of the meeting Fernández-Miranda was left with three names: Silva Muñoz, with 15 votes, López Bravo, with 14, and Suárez, with 12. Virtually all those present assumed the king would choose between the first two candidates, and regarded the young *Movimiento* apparatchik as a mere fill-in.[79]

On his way to La Zarzuela the professor told journalists that 'I am in a position to offer the king what he has asked me for'. Fernández-Miranda said this so as to strengthen Suárez's standing in the eyes of public opinion by presenting him as Juan Carlos's royal nominee, but in view of the unfavourable reaction he was forced to issue a disclaimer, underlining the Council's independence. In Suárez's opinion, it was his mentor's only serious slip-up during the entire process.[80]

The king later called Silva Muñoz to congratulate him for having been included in the Council's *terna*, and explained that it had been very painful for him to have to make a choice in the knowledge that, whatever the outcome, he would be disappointing two loyal friends. Juan Carlos also assured him that the new government would only be in office between eight months and a year, until democratic elections could be held, a prediction which was to prove remarkably accurate.[81]

On learning of Arias's dismissal – which Juan Carlos allowed him to announce as a resignation – Suárez had decided not to go on holiday with his family as planned. Alone in the sweltering heat of his Madrid flat, he had begun to have serious doubts when the telephone rang. 'What are you doing?' asked the king casually. 'What do you think I'm doing?' came the reply. 'Would you like to come for coffee?' As he drove to La Zarzuela at break-neck speed, Suárez began to fear he would not be made prime minister after all, and might be asked to become minister of the interior instead, a job he thought he could do well. On entering the king's office Suárez was surprised not to see Juan Carlos, who, ever the practical joker, was watching him from behind a partition. 'Adolfo, I want to ask you a favour', the king finally said as he emerged. 'Please agree to become my prime minister'. To this, an overjoyed Suárez exclaimed: 'And about time too!'[82]

6 In the Driving Seat at Last

In his first in-depth conversation with the king as prime minister, held on 5 July 1976, Suárez requested that he be kept in power for a minimum of three months, after which time he would resign if he had failed to make substantial progress. Juan Carlos admitted that he was used to leaning heavily on two main props, Fernández-Miranda and Armada, and advised him to seek his own. The young premier was determined to go it alone, however, and expressed the hope that the king would adopt a less prominent profile, allowing him to bear full responsibility for political affairs. Even at this early stage Suárez claims to have made it clear that a successful reform operation would leave the monarch virtually powerless.[1]

Having finally succeeded in appointing a prime minister of his choice, the king's immediate concern was the formation of a suitable cabinet. Juan Carlos was initially of the view that it was best to have Areilza and Fraga in the government, not least because they could prove formidable opponents if excluded. He also asked Suárez to keep Arias's military ministers, to which the former agreed with some reluctance and not without first warning him that he would not hesitate to remove them if they stood in his way.[2]

The king duly telephoned Fraga on the night of 3 July to urge him to stay on as deputy premier, but the latter had already decided not to serve under Suárez. Juan Carlos tried again the following morning, but to no avail. Fraga's wife, who overheard this second conversation, later reprimanded him for having been 'excessively blunt'. Months later Fraga would tell Suárez: 'I will never forgive you for having retired me ten years before my time'.[3]

In spite of having seen far more of him than of Fraga during the preceding months, Juan Carlos did not plead with Areilza himself, leaving this task to Suárez. When the latter telephoned Areilza at home on the afternoon of his appointment he was informed that 'the prime minister is resting'. The foreign minister had been so confident of succeeding Arias that he had even offered cabinet posts to some of his friends and was therefore understandably reluctant to serve under Suárez. The latter was in fact greatly relieved to be able to form his own team without interference from some of his more senior former colleagues, who had always looked down on him.[4]

Suárez's political friends were largely *Movimiento* apparatchicks whose appointment would have disconcerted public opinion at home and abroad, in view of which the king was forced to exert his own influence in enlisting the collaboration of potential ministers. Most of those approached had long since been identified as promising young men by Cano, Juan Carlos's private secretary in the early 1970s, which partly explains the presence of so many prominent ACNP members amongst them. The list included Marcelino Oreja (foreign affairs), Eduardo Carriles (treasury), De la Mata (syndical relations), Andrés Reguera Guajardo (information), Calvo Sotelo (public works), Landelino Lavilla (justice) and Osorio (presidency). In many cases Juan Carlos spoke to them personally to ensure they would not turn Suárez down. Oreja recalls that the king's telephone call woke up his wife, who almost hung up on whom she assumed was a practical joker. In many ways it is thus Suárez's July 1976 cabinet, and not its predecessor, that should be regarded as the first government of the monarchy.[5]

In an attempt to counteract the hostility that had greeted his appointment, on 6 July Suárez went on the offensive with a televised speech in which he promised he would govern in accordance with the wishes of the majority of the population, which he assumed were in line with the monarch's 'express wish to attain a modern democracy for Spain'. The new government's long-term goal was encapsulated in the hope that 'future governments may be the result of the free will of the majority of Spaniards', while the opposition was offered 'respect' and 'the possibility of collaboration'.[6]

The opposition was initially at a loss to interpret the outcome of the July crisis. Carrillo, who was unwilling to 'forget the king's responsibility for this mess', initially accepted the interpretation first put forward by the newly launched *El País* to the effect that Suárez's appointment represented a victory for the hard-line sectors of the regime. The PCE's executive committee was of the opinion that the new government's imminent failure would bring with it 'the erosion of the man who has formed it in his own image, namely Juan Carlos de Borbón', and foresaw that during the Suárez government's brief existence the popularity of the republican option would increase dramatically since 'today, in the eyes of the country, the monarchy is a symbol of continuity'. The PSOE, considerably more perspicacious in its analysis, took heart in the appointment of someone 'without a relevant political past, who comes from the *Movimiento* and knows it so well that he may be the ideal architect to demolish the institutions'. The Socialists nevertheless warned that unless Suárez made real progress towards democracy, there would be a major crisis, whose first victim would be the monarchy.[7]

At this point Suárez's only source of support and legitimacy was the king himself. With Fernández-Miranda's assistance, Juan Carlos had exerted all the influence he could muster in obtaining his appointment; henceforth his prestige and personal authority would depend largely on the new government's performance. In spite of Suárez's wishes the king could not help associating both himself and the monarchy with the task at hand. This commitment was made explicit in his first address to the new cabinet, in which he urged them to undertake 'the necessary evolution towards new social and political structures' while respecting 'the essential values which constitute the *raison d'être* of our nation'. Juan Carlos also spoke of the need to 'become fully acquainted with the aspirations of the Spanish people' in order to succeed in finding adequate channels for them, urging his ministers to 'act without fear'.[8]

Juan Carlos's support for his government was expressed in other, less public ways as well. Aware of the lack of enthusiasm with which his appointment had been greeted abroad, Suárez was anxious to carry out a lightning visit to a major European capital so as to begin to acquire foreign credentials. At Osorio's suggestion the latter approached the king, who in turn spoke to Giscard d'Estaing. On 13 July Suárez landed in Paris for a brief session with Prime Minister Jacques Chirac, thereby obtaining a much-needed photo opportunity.[9]

Suárez himself has admitted that his appointment could have cost Juan Carlos his crown. Indeed a close childhood friend of the king telephoned him shortly after the event to tell him that 'you have just thrown the monarchy out of the window', and Juan Carlos himself would later admit that 'I did not realise one could suffer so much'. Arias's removal had been greeted with satisfaction both by regime reformists and the opposition, but this soon turned to bitter disappointment. While in November 1975 politicised Spaniards had assumed Juan Carlos had been forced to keep Arias on against his will, in July 1976 they held him fully responsible for the choice of a successor.[10]

Determined to prove his critics wrong, Suárez put his ministers to work at once. At this stage he intended 'the first thirty or forty days of my government to be a continual surprise, by taking steps never attempted in the past'. The government's programme, issued on 16 July, unequivocally stated that 'popular sovereignty resides in the people', and promised to work for 'the establishment of a democratic political system based on the guarantee of civil rights and freedoms, on equal opportunities for democratic groups, and the acceptance of genuine pluralism'. More explicitly, the government looked forward to 'the emergence of majorities which will in future determine the composition of representative institutions and of the government of the nation', the first indication that future governments would be accountable to a democratically elected Cortes. Finally, Suárez promised a referendum on constitutional reform, and general elections before 30 June 1977.[11]

In spite of Suárez's efforts, the democratic opposition's public reaction to his programme was hostile. On 21 July *Coordinación Democrática* declared the government unfit to meet the nation's genuine needs and demanded the formation of 'a government of broad democratic consensus' capable of opening a constituent period and holding a plebiscite on the institutional issue. As in the past, the platform insisted on 'the impossibility of advancing towards democracy from within the system and the political institutions inherited from Francoism', and described the innovative style and content of Suárez's programme in terms of the need that 'even a reactionary government such as this' felt to appease the opposition.[12]

The appointment of a premier respectful of La Zarzuela's wishes allowed the king to put forward a proposal for a second pardon, which was announced by the government after a cabinet meeting chaired by Juan Carlos on 30 July. Earlier in the month *Coordinación Democrática* and a host of smaller organisations had staged a pro-amnesty week in which some one million people were said to have taken part. The government's decree did not fully satisfy the opposition, however, and still left some 145 Basque activists in prison, most of them ETA sympathisers.

On making this measure public, the justice minister referred to 'the amnesty which the government has proposed to the king and which his majesty has deigned to grant', thereby attributing the decision openly to the monarch. This was not without its dangers given the public criticism it would attract, but the government had no alternative but to rely on the king's prestige and authority. Foreign Minister Oreja made this explicit when he told journalists in mid-July that 'the king is the engine of change and Adolfo Suárez is the executor'.[13]

The king's influence was similarly in evidence in other spheres. Shortly before the new government was sworn in on 8 July, Juan Carlos had requested Oreja's advice as to how to achieve a significant foreign policy coup. The latter, a Christian Democrat who had emerged as a major reformist figure within the regime's ranks, urged him to act at once to improve relations with the Vatican. Having freed himself from Arias's tutelage, the king duly sent Mondéjar to Rome with a personal message for the Pope, relinquishing his say in the appointment of Spanish bishops. After signing an agreement to this effect with the Vatican in late July, it was Oreja's turn to travel to Rome for a highly emotional audience with Pope Paul VI, who urged him to inform Juan Carlos that his democratising endeavours enjoyed the blessings of the Catholic Church.[14]

On 3 August Juan Carlos left Madrid for his annual holiday in Palma de Majorca, where he met Don Juan, leaving Fernández-Miranda and Suárez behind to work on the details of the constitutional reform. True to his avowed intention of establishing a dialogue with the opposition, the latter took advantage of the summer recess to meet the major non-Communist opposition leaders in an attempt to convince them of his intentions. His aim was to 'get to know their views', and if possible, 'transmit confidence'. Above all, he wanted them to know that 'they were about to achieve their fundamental goals', though at first 'they refused to believe it'.[15]

Suárez met the Socialist leader González for the first time on 10 August 1976. The former obtained the impression that the PSOE's immediate goal was the establishment of a Western-style democracy, but was relatively unconcerned as to exactly how this was brought about. Suárez's main concern was that the Socialists should accept the monarchy, something they had hitherto refused to contemplate without first submitting the matter to the vote. In Suárez's view, a referendum of this nature would have entailed a break with the very laws and institutions that had allowed Juan Carlos to become king and would have dashed all hope of undertaking a reform process from within the exisiting constitutional system. What was more, at this stage Suárez feared the republican option would prove more popular.[16]

Otero Novas, who had left Fraga in order to join Suárez, later came to the conclusion that it was in the course of this meeting that González began to reconsider his position towards the monarchy. Be this as it may, the PSOE's public attitude remained sceptical, if not openly critical. In late August González warned his supporters against the danger of taking part in a provisional government under the king, whether it was a 'government of national concentration', as proposed by Tierno Galván, or a 'government of national reconciliation', as advocated by the Communists. In his view a 'decidedly republican' party such as his own should not legitimise the monarchy indirectly with its presence in a government of this nature. Several days earlier, whilst sailing off the Majorcan coast, Juan Carlos had told a future cabinet minister that 'I have to support a moderate form of Socialism'.[17]

During the summer of 1976, both Juan Carlos and his prime minister began to face up to the inevitability of the Communist Party's legalisation, though they were far from certain as to how this might be achieved. On 14 July the Cortes had finally approved the reform of the penal code, though not without first forcing the government to accept an amendment that excluded the legalisation of groups 'subjected to an international discipline which seek the establishment of a totalitarian system', in clear reference to the Communists. In August Suárez declared that the PCE would not be legalised in the course of 1976, and subsequently dismissed the Spanish ambassador in Paris for agreeing to see Carrillo.[18]

Anxious to establish a direct line of communication with La Zarzuela, in early August the PCE's secretary general announced he would gladly meet Juan Carlos in person. Carrillo then approached one of the king's friends, Armero, who had already acted as middle-man when Franco's nephew sounded out the Communist leader on Juan Carlos's behalf in 1974. With the king's consent Suárez instructed Armero to visit Carrillo in order to obtain a clearer idea of his intentions. Above all the prime minister wished the PCE to accept that some elements of the Francoist heritage – namely the monarchy, Spain's national unity and the integrity of the armed forces – were not subject to negotiation. In keeping with what other, less prominent Communist leaders had been telling Otero Novas since the spring, Carrillo assured Armero that the PCE would accept the monarchy as long as it proved compatible with a genuine democracy.[19]

Given his exceptional constitutional position, political analysts scrutinised Juan Carlos's every move in search of clues to the government's intentions. In mid-August he was paid a courtesy visit in Palma by Alexander Haig, who was not only NATO's supreme commander but also commander of all US forces in Europe. Several days later Juan Carlos triggered further speculation by boarding one of the US Navy's nuclear-powered aircraft carriers, the *Nimitz*, off the coast of Majorca. In view of the democratic opposition's hostility to the presence of US troops on Spanish soil and the Ford administration's interest in bringing Spain into NATO, these gestures were perhaps ill-advised. On the other hand they appear to have prompted Carrillo to announce that his party would not object to US bases on Spanish soil if a democratically elected government agreed to keep them.

The king interrupted his summer holidays on three occasions to discuss the government's plans for constitutional reform with Suárez and Fernández-Miranda in Madrid. The premier was initially uncertain as to which course to take and turned to his mentor for assistance. Suárez and Fernández-Miranda met on several occasions between 17 and 20 August, after which the latter locked himself up in his mountain retreat for the weekend. On returning to the capital on 23 August he gave Suárez the decisive blueprint for the reforms that were later carried out, with the words: 'here you have this, which has no father'. The following day the prime minister submitted it to his cabinet, without mentioning Fernández-Miranda's contribution. On 26 August Juan Carlos saw them both simultaneously and formally endorsed the project, which was later perfected by a number of ministers and government experts.[20]

The legal text that was to make the transition to democracy possible – the Law for Political Reform – was made public on 10 September. The text, brilliant in its simplicitly, provided for the election of a two-chamber Cortes, consisting of a 350-strong Congress of Deputies and a Senate representing the 'territorial entities', up to a fifth of whose members would be nominated by the king. (This proviso gave *procuradores* hoping to return to the Cortes as royal nominees a powerful motive for endorsing the government's wishes.) The bill also established that subsequent constitutional reforms could be initiated by both the government and the new Congress, from where bills would pass to the Senate; in case of disagreement the Congress's views would prevail. According to the Francoist constitution, neither the king nor the government could dissolve the existing Cortes, but this was unnecessary since its term was due to expire in June 1977, the date set for the future elections. The difficulty lay in the fact that, since the bill affected a number of fundamental laws, it required the approval of two thirds of the existing Cortes plus the nation's endorsement in a referendum.

In presenting the bill to the nation, Suárez sought to establish himself as an impartial statesman acting on behalf of the monarch, whose chief aim was to guarantee a smooth transition from 'a system of legitimate delegation of authority to one with full and responsible participation'. The government, he observed, could have succumbed to the temptation of drawing up its own constitution but had preferred to invite the nation to express its views in the future democratic Cortes. Equally, it could have reached an agreement with the opposition alone, but since the right to speak on behalf of others could only be acquired through the ballot-box, this would have been undemocratic. Above all, Suárez was careful to underline that the reform 'originates in the existing fundamental legislation and will be undertaken in accordance with procedures foreseen therein'. It would have been difficult to summarise Fernández-Miranda's entire reformist philosophy in fewer words.[21]

Suárez would later acknowledge that the bill contained explicit references to the king in four of its five articles so as to allow its subsequent endorsement in a referendum to be presented as an indirect democratic legitimation of the monarchy. The latter was present in other, more explicit ways as well. The bill envisaged the survival of the Council of the Realm, ten of whose members were to be selected by the Cortes, while its president was to be appointed directly by the king. Juan Carlos appears to have felt a genuine need for an advisory body of this nature, and may also have been reluctant to reward the intellectual father of the bill by depriving him of a job. Finally, the king was empowered to submit any matter, constitutional or otherwise, directly to the nation by means of a referendum whose results would be binding on the government.

The Law for Political Reform was given a mixed reception by the opposition. *Coordinación Democrática* acknowledged that the government had made 'the maximum effort of which it is objectively capable' and admitted that until elections were held 'neither the government nor the opposition enjoy full democratic legitimacy', but it rejected the referendum and elections envisaged by the bill because they had not been negotiated with the opposition and fell short of a genuine constituent process. The PSOE was similarly unimpressed and took the government to task for trying to place some institutions, notably the monarchy, 'beyond the reach of the representatives of the people'. The wording of their communiqué, however, appeared to imply they might be willing to leave the institutional question to the future democratic Cortes. The Communists, for their part, publicly reminded Juan Carlos that General Berenguer's attempts to save the monarchy in 1930 had merely served to accelerate the advent of the Second Republic.[22]

The new strategy advanced by the king and his government seriously undermined the opposition's efforts to present a united front. Attempts to bring all opposition groups together in a single organisation, which culminated in the creation of the *Plataforma de Organismos Democráticos* in late October 1976, were once again hampered by disagreement over the king's role in the democratising process and its overall viability. Anxious to prevent expressions of undue hostility towards the monarchy, Múgica suggested that the demand for a plebiscite on the institutional issue be dropped in favour of a statement to the effect that 'popular sovereignty will freely determine the new constitution of the state', the formula finally adopted by the new organisation.[23]

Suárez's appointment had partly been determined by the king's faith in his ability to overcome the opposition of the more conservative Francoists, particulary in the armed forces. In late August the former was informed that General Santiago, in his capacity as deputy premier, was planning a meeting of all senior generals to discuss the political situation. After consulting the king, who was anxious not to transform 'the victors of the civil war into the vanquished of democracy', Suárez decided to call his own meeting in order to prevent them from taking a collective stand against him. On 8 September, in the course of a three-hour session, he met some thirty senior officers and sought to convince them of the need to accept certain inevitable reforms while reassuring them that these would never endanger the monarchy, Spain's national unity, or the armed forces. In reply to a question from one of the generals, Suárez stated that the legal-isation of the Communist Party was not possible with its current statutes. What he failed to explain was that he was already considering a possible negotiation with the PCE, which would include a change of statutes amongst its objectives. In the short term, however, the meeting was an unqualified success and Juan Carlos was elated to see that his confidence in Suárez had not been misplaced.[24]

According to General Gutiérrez Mellado, who attended the meeting, General Santiago barely spoke on this occasion and Osorio did not detect any uneasiness in him when the cabinet approved the Law for Political Reform two days later. On 21 September, however, Santiago confronted Suárez violently over the course the government was taking, leaving him no option but to dismiss him. Juan Carlos, who had thought it important to carry men like Santiago with him, was somewhat irritated by this decision, which Suárez justified on the grounds that the minister had been leaking confidential cabinet information to his fellow officers.[25]

The decision to replace Santiago with General Gutiérrez Mellado, who had actively cultivated Juan Carlos in recent years, was not well received by the more conservative senior generals. At Admiral Pita da Veiga's instigation, the three military ministers visited La Zarzuela to complain that Gutiérrez Mellado lacked seniority and was generally unsuitable for the job. Pita, appointed by Carrero in 1973, had felt passed over when Santiago was promoted to the deputy premiership in late 1975, and only by appealing to his patriotism and loyalty did the king avert a more serious incident on this occasion.

Several days after Santiago's dismissal, his friend General Carlos Iniesta Cano came to his defence in an open letter published by an extreme right-wing newspaper, prompting Suárez to relegate both of them to the reserve list. The king, who was anxious not to antagonise the likes of Santiago un-necessarily, was rapidly alerted to the fact that the government's action might not be lawful by Fernández Campo, currently serving in the Min-istry of Information, who narrowly failed to prevent Suárez from making his decision public. Weeks later a military court invalidated the govern-ment's sanction, much to Suárez's embarrassment.[26]

During these months the king continued to regard his tours of the Span-ish provinces as the best means of communicating with his subjects. In an interview with the BBC in mid-July, Juan Carlos had recalled that 'my father always used to tell me that the king of Spain must travel like a nomad throughout the country' and had justified these tours on the grounds that 'we can see [people's] faces and listen to what they say, which enables us to get an idea of what the country wants, of what the people want us to do as king and queen of Spain'. Later that month the monarchs embarked on their first official tour of Galicia, where, true to his aim of achieving public recognition for Spain's non-Castilian languages, the king spoke Galician during his visit to Santiago de Compostela.[27]

Some observers feared these tours merely strengthened certain populist tendencies already present in Spanish politics while causing confusion as to the king's powers and responsibilities. In the absence of democratic institutions, the mayors of the villages and cities visited by the monarch were falling into the habit of presenting him with a detailed catalogue of demands and grievances, as though their solution depended on him personally. In November, when the monarchs toured the Valencian region, the local provincial governor was instrumental in reversing this trend, while at the same time enabling his guests to meet a more representative cross-section of society than had hitherto been the case. The royal visit to Extremadura in February 1977, however, was marred by the unpopularity of the mayor of Cáceres, and the king's own speech was greeted with cries of 'facts yes, words no!' This was yet another unwanted consequence of Juan Carlos's anomalous position as constitutional monarch-to-be.

In the autumn of 1976 the future of the monarchy was inextricably linked to the fate of the Suárez reform in the Francoist Cortes. The Reform Bill was first sent to the National Council in late September, where a number of amendments were proposed aimed at limiting its impact. The Council's decisions were not binding, however, and the government sent the bill to the Cortes virtually unchanged. Although the king did not seek to influence the *procuradores* himself, Fernández-Miranda and the government made his wishes explicit to the more recalcitrant amongst them. Among those approached directly by the president of the Cortes was Gonzalo Fernández de la Mora, an influential opponent of the bill, who was simply told that 'the king has decided it and we are going towards a party system'.[28]

In the course of the three-day debate held in the Cortes in mid-November, the government presented the Reform Bill as an expression of the king's wishes and hammered home the idea that to disobey the king was tantamount to disobeying Franco's will. The most effective progovernment speaker was Primo de Rivera, a good friend of the king, who argued that it was possible for those who had served Franco to transfer their loyalty and obedience to Juan Carlos, as the former had wished. More importantly, he underlined that only the monarchy could guarantee the transition from 'a personal regime to one based on participation'.[29]

Not everyone was swayed by the government's spokesmen, however. One notorious diehard, José Fernández de la Vega, reminded the king of his oath to defend the regime's fundamental laws and principles, first taken in 1969 and renewed in 1975, and asked himself: 'How will this constituent process end, if it does away with Francoism, thereby depriving the monarchy of its firmest base?' His question was left unanswered by the government, which could not openly admit that it was seeking to create a new, democratic legitimacy for the post-Francoist monarchy.

The Reform Bill's future was soon seen to depend on the attitude of some 180 *procuradores* belonging to Alianza Popular (AP), a loose federation of conservative groups launched by Fraga in an attempt to restrain the Suárez government. Over the summer the king had done his best to convince Fraga to imitate his former associate, Cabanillas, in adopting a more centrist strategy, but to no avail. Juan Carlos had been greatly surprised by the formation of AP, which he privately described as 'an explosive mix', not least because it was led by former rivals such as Fraga and López Rodó. In October he made it clear to Fernández de la Mora, one of AP's 'magnificent seven', as its leaders were soon dubbed by the media, that he regretted their decision to form a party of their own instead of backing Suárez. AP was opposed to the election of the future Congress of Deputies by a system based on proportional representation, and, after a heated debate, agreed to back the bill in return for the introduction of a series of corrective devices. This paved the way for the bill's approval on 18 November by 425 votes in favour, 59 against and 13 abstentions.[30]

The Francoist Cortes' decision to vote itself out of existence was in many ways a foregone conclusion. Some *procuradores* believed their popularity and reputation alone would enable them to return to the Cortes as elected representatives, while others assumed they would have no difficulty in negotiating a place on the party lists of a government grateful for their support. Whatever their plans for the future, it was clear to all that the king wished the Suárez reform to succeed and that the bill's defeat would endanger the monarchy itself. By this stage, even the more reactionary *procuradores* could see that this was not in their best interest.

The opposition remained hostile to the government's efforts to transform the political system from within. In late November the *Plataforma de Organismos Democráticos* and its allies lay down seven conditions for their acceptance of the forthcoming referendum on the Law for Political Reform, which included the immediate legalisation of all political parties and labour organisations; the recognition, protection and guarantee of all political and syndical rights; the dissolution of the *Movimiento* and the political neutrality of the administration; a general amnesty; fair access to state-controlled media; the negotiation of all electoral and related legislation and the institutionalisation of regional political rights. Significantly, this list of demands did not include a plebiscite on the monarchy.

The opposition hoped to bring the government to the negotiating table before the referendum but this could not be done while Suárez's ban on the Communists remained in place. As Areilza informed Juan Carlos on 30 November after a supposedly secret meeting with Carrillo, Tierno, González and Ruiz Giménez, the opposition had effectively reconciled itself to a government victory in the referendum, but hoped this would pave the way for genuine negotiations prior to the first elections. This task was entrusted to a nine-man negotiating committee – the *Comisión de los Nueve* – which began its work after Christmas.[31]

The king was particulary concerned by the PSOE's continued reluctance to accept the monarchy. The Socialists had intended to hold their party conference in early November, but the government withheld its authorisation so as not to antagonise the Cortes on the eve of the vote on the Reform Bill. The PSOE had reacted angrily, warning that 'either the monarchy commits itself firmly to the establishment of democracy in Spain or the people will bring democracy without the monarchy'. The PSOE's highly successful conference, finally held in early December, produced some unexpectedly radical rhetoric, together with the by now traditional pronouncements in favour of a republican form of government. A young activist who appeared in the conference hall waving a large republican flag was given an ecstatic reception, forcing Múgica to drown out pro-republican slogans by playing the 'International' at full blast. The conference nevertheless enabled Juan Carlos to receive Willy Brandt, whose presence at La Zarzuela was seen as evidence of the Socialist International's recognition of the king's democratising endeavours.[32]

Increasingly uneasy at the PSOE's growing protagonism, on 10 December Carrillo gave a clandestine press conference in Madrid. The Communist leader admitted that 'everyone knows we disapprove of the way the king came to the throne', but went on to add that 'the king is there; it is a fact'. When the time came to draw up a new constitution the PCE would still vote in favour of a republic but would accept a democratically sanctioned constitutional monarchy. Carrillo was even willing to take part in a broad coalition government appointed by the king in order to guarantee fair elections, and once again offered to meet Juan Carlos in person to explain the PCE's position.[33]

The king could not intervene directly in the referendum campaign at home but could bring his influence to bear from abroad. In late October Juan Carlos and Sofía visited France, the first European country to receive them as king and queen of Spain. Efforts to present Juan Carlos as a Europeanist, democratising monarch in the French media were somewhat undermined by yet another wave of unrest in the Basque provinces coinciding with his arrival. As a result a visit to the École Polytechnique was cancelled in view of the threat of a student boycott. During his tour of Paris town hall, a Socialist councillor presented Juan Carlos with a document endorsing the Spanish opposition's programme and that of the PSOE in particular. Asked about its contents at a subsequent press conference, the king observed that 'everyone is entitled to an opinion'. Pressed further, in his characteristically informal manner he urged journalists to 'think of other European monarchs and you will see they are not easy to talk to'.[34]

Giscard's eagerness to impress his royal guests was reflected in details such as the presence of soldiers from the three services in the military parade that greeted Juan Carlos and Sofía on their arrival. Carrillo, who followed the visit closely, noted in his diary: 'Giscard is a fox ... the Frenchman must know that the king likes these things. During the parade Giscard kept looking at Juan Carlos as though observing the effect this military display was having on him, with a somewhat parternalistic, ironic air. He clearly wants to win the king over'. In the Communist leader's view, state-controlled media coverage of the visit amounted to blatant pro-referendum propaganda. Spanish television was indeed directed by one of the king's more zealous supporters, Rafael Anson, who was highly regarded at La Zarzuela. At home the visit was portrayed as evidence of Giscard's continued support for Juan Carlos's democratising efforts, and as an important step towards full recognition of the young monarchy by Europe's democracies.[35]

The king would have liked to see his standing – and that of his government – improve in Britain as well. In November 1976 Mountbatten, who watched Juan Carlos's progress with avuncular pride, suggested that he visit Britain privately with a view to meeting prominent Labour leaders in person. In the spring of that year James Callaghan, shortly to become prime minister, had told Areilza that socialists of his generation had always refused to visit Spain while Franco was alive. Michael Foot, a militant anti-Francoist of the old school, had at least agreed to attend the PSOE's conference in December. The king's visit, Mountbatten believed, 'would get our curious Labour government to see you in the right light, for up to now they don't seem to have understood the tremendous work you are doing in liberalising the constitution'. Unfortunately Juan Carlos was unable to take up his offer.[36]

The king's presence was very much in evidence in the run-up to the referendum. In early December a tour of the Valencian region, which could easily have been postponed, provided further opportunities for ample media coverage, which the opposition regarded as part of the government's somewhat overwhelming campaign in favour of a yes vote. In his televised broadcast to the nation on the eve of polling-day, Suárez presented his government's achievements to date as the natural consequence of the king's proclamation speech. 'The king', he declared, 'wishes to govern with society's assistance'. On 15 December Juan Carlos and Sofía were amongst the 77.4 per cent of the electorate who turned out to vote in defiance of the opposition's pro-abstention campaign. Of these, 94.2 per cent voted in favour of the Reform Law, while only 2.6 per cent voted against.[37]

These highly positive referendum results significantly modified the position of the king and the monarchy in Spanish political life. Hitherto Juan Carlos had owed his crown to Franco and to the very laws and institutions he was seeking to replace; with the referendum he began to acquire the democratic legitimacy he hoped would one day sustain him. This gave him greater self-confidence, already evident in his second Christmas Eve address, in which he claimed that 'the monarchy, the institutional form best suited to Spain, is capable of ensuring the unity of all Spaniards, freedom and the exercise of human rights in order and peace'.[38]

The king's optimism was by no means unjustified. According to a major independent poll conducted in January 1977, those in favour of a monarchy (61 per cent) vastly outnumbered those advocating a republic (20 per cent). At this stage 72 per cent of those polled regarded Juan Carlos's performance as good or very good, 23 per cent as indifferent and only 3 per cent as poor or very poor. As was perhaps to be expected, the king's standing was higher amongst those who described themselves as Liberals and Christian Democrats than amongst those who identified with socialism and communism. However, in spite of the PSOE's public stance, the ideological cleavage beyond which support for a republic began to predominate was that which divided potential Socialist voters from potential Communist ones. In spite of recent developments, at the other end of the political spectrum most of those who claimed to favour the continuity of the Franco regime appeared to have taken heed of the Caudillo's dying wishes, transferring their loyalties to the young monarch.[39]

Inevitably the outcome of the referendum also affected the king's relations with those closest to him. For almost six months Juan Carlos, Fernández-Miranda and Suárez had met for dinner at La Zarzuela virtually every Sunday to review the previous week's events and plan ahead; in the wake of the referendum these meetings were to become increasingly infrequent. This development was partly attributable to the fact that, once the Law for Political Reform had been put through the Francoist institutions, Fernández-Miranda no longer had such a prominent role to play. At the same time Suárez rapidly acquired a new sense of his own importance. During the second half of 1976, '*el Rubio y el Cebrereño*' – 'the blond and the one from Cebreros' (the village in Avila province where Suárez was born), as the premier liked to describe himself and the king in private – had been inseparable. The referendum marked his coming of age as a politician, and he became increasingly anxious to prove he had a mind of his own. Significantly, over Christmas he moved his office, staff and even personal residence away from central Madrid to La Moncloa, an eighteenth century palace on the outskirts of the city that was not unlike La Zarzuela and had previously been used by visiting dignitaries. It was not long before Otero Novas observed that Suárez no longer consulted his every move with the king and showed less interest than before in his telephone calls.[40]

In the wake of the referendum, the key issue facing the king was the future of the Communist Party. On 22 December Carrillo and other PCE leaders were arrested as they were leaving a clandestine party meeting in Madrid, forcing the government to come to terms with the problem. Juan Carlos subsequently received a telegram from their relatives demanding their release and Carrillo was freed on bail before the end of the year, prompting rumours of the imminent legalisation of the PCE.

January 1977 was to prove one of the most trying months of Juan Carlos's entire reign. On 23 January a student demonstrator was shot dead by a neofascist gunman. The following day the extreme left-wing organisation GRAPO, which had kidnapped a prominent member of the Council of the Realm, Oriol, shortly before the referendum, also seized General Emilio Villaescusa, president of the Supreme Council of Military Justice. Later that morning a police smoke cannister killed a young girl demonstrating in protest at the earlier death. That evening neofascist gunmen burst into an office in the Atocha district of Madrid and killed five people, four of them Communist labour lawyers. On 28 January GRAPO murdered four policemen. Several days later, after intense negotiations with the government, the PCE was allowed to hold a mass funeral for the victims of the Atocha outrage, its first tolerated demonstration. The spectacle provided by the five coffins engulfed in a silent sea of clenched fists and red carnations outside Madrid's Palace of Justice caused a deep impression on Juan Carlos, who is said to have witnessed the scene from a helicopter hovering overhead. In mid-February the king's faith in Suárez, which had been put to the test by these events, was fully restored when Oriol and Villaescusa were rescued by the police.

It was in February 1977 that Suárez first approached Juan Carlos with the suggestion that the PCE be legalised in time for the first elections. The government was due to amend the Law of Association to enable political parties to register with the Ministry of the Interior and the PCE was bound to submit its application along with other groups. The king's first reaction to Suárez's proposal was to remind him that 'I have something to say in this business too, Adolfo. The Army won't give us any problems so far as the Socialist Party is concerned, but it might well give us problems, and major ones, when it learns that we intend to legalise the Communist Party. So I am asking you not to do anything without consulting me first'. Suárez, however, succeeded in convincing Juan Carlos that the PCE's legalisation could be used to apply pressure on the PSOE, which still refused to recognise the monarchy. If the Communists could be made to acknowledge the monarchy – and by extension the entire reform process, including the future elections – in return for their legalisation, the PSOE would be deprived of much of its bargaining power and would eventually have to follow suit.[41]

With the king's permission, and in spite of Fernández-Miranda's grave misgivings, Suárez proceeded to meet Carrillo in secret on 27 February 1977. In the course of their six-hour interview the prime minister made frequent mention of the monarch's commitment to a full democratisation and to his belief that everyone, including the Communists, should ultimately benefit from the reform process. In return Carrillo assured him that in spite of its republican preferences the PCE would accept a king capable of establishing a fully democratic constitutional monarchy under which Communists could freely compete for office. 'If the king acts as a hinge between dictatorship and democracy he will have created a situation which, in practice, will be irreversible', Carrillo observed. What was more, he was willing to acknowledge that a plebiscite on the monarchy was no longer feasible. Although Suárez insisted that the legalisation did not depend exclusively on him or the king, Carrillo left the meeting with the conviction that his party would be taking part in the first elections. By way of proving his good will, Suárez authorised the Eurocommunist summit meeting hosted by Carrillo in Madrid several days later.[42]

The decision to legalise the Communist Party was thus taken at Suárez's initiative, with the king's consent and support. On 4 April the former informed his 'inner cabinet' that the time had come to recognise the PCE. With the exception of Osorio, everyone concurred. The latter was adamant that such a decision be based on a favourable ruling from a high-ranking judicial body, so that senior Army officers would not feel cheated by a government that had promised to abide by the law. 'Beware', Osorio warned, in a remark that made Suárez grimace, 'let us not gamble away the crown'. By way of reply, after a quick visit to La Zarzuela, the following day the latter assured him that the king himself saw no alternative but to proceed with the legalisation.[43]

Once the decision had been taken, it was implemented with military precision. Suárez soon obtained a favourable ruling from the attorney general, on which Martín Villa could base his decision to register the PCE. Everything was timed so as to announce the legalisation over the Easter weekend, when it was least expected. So as not to arouse suspicion, Suárez urged his ministers to leave on holiday as planned and encouraged Juan Carlos and Sofía not to cancel a private visit to France. Although this was left unsaid, it had crossed his mind that if the Army staged a coup it would be best if the king and other ministers were not trapped in the capital.[44]

Over the preceeding months Juan Carlos had canvassed military opinion in his weekly Monday audiences reserved for senior officers, while Suárez approached the three military ministers himself. Franco Iribarnegaray had assured the premier that the Air Force would not pose a problem, while Alvarez Arenas had expressed concern about the Army. Pita da Veiga went even further, warning him of a violent reaction in the Navy and admitted that he himself would have difficulty in accepting such a measure. On the whole, however, both the king and Suárez had reason to believe that, however disgruntled, the armed forces would remain loyal.[45]

The legalisation of the PCE was announced late on Saturday 9 April 1977, at a time when most Spaniards were enjoying their Easter holidays. On Monday Pita submitted his resignation, and Alvarez Arenas would have followed suit if Juan Carlos had not dissuaded him by appealing to his patriotism and personal loyalty. The king suggested that Pita be replaced by Admiral José Ramón González, who had been attached to his household, but the latter insisted on consulting his fellow officers first, in view of which Suárez offered the post to the only admiral who would take it, the reservist Pascual Pery Junquera. Several civilian ministers also considered resigning, but Osorio dissuaded them with the argument that this would undermine the king as well as the government.[46]

On 12 April the five-hour meeting of the Army's Supreme Council, attended, amongst others, by the captain-generals of the eleven military regions, was a turbulent affair. In spite of the harsh words spoken against Suárez and Gutiérrez Mellado, Generals José Vega Rodriguez and Antonio Ibáñez Freire between them induced their fellow generals to endorse a statement that repudiated the decision but accepted the *fait accompli*. Before this could be made public, however, a far harsher statement, drawn up by Army intelligence, was circulated without proper authorisation. This prompted Alvarez Arenas to issue an explanatory note that reaffirmed the Army's loyalty to the king and paid tribute to the government's dedication to the nation's well-being, its loyalty to the crown and even its affection for the armed forces. The council also sent a confidential letter to the king, warning him that his standing amongst Army officers had suffered a severe blow. Some generals accused Suárez of having deceived them at their meeting in September 1976, and Juan Carlos recalls that 'I had to speak to many of them to explain that nothing would happen, that Carrillo would remain calm, that there would be no red flags or demonstrations in the streets. For me, those were very difficult moments'.[47]

The king did not need to look beyond La Zarzuela to discover the impact of the PCE's legalisation on conservative senior officers. On 17 April Suárez and the secretary-general of the royal household, General Armada, had a blazing row in the king's presence concerning the mood of the Army. Two days earlier Armada had confronted Calvo Sotelo as he was leaving La Zarzuela, exclaiming: 'Nothing could be worse than to underestimate the gravity of the situation! I am shocked by your lack of information. One can do anything with a bayonet except sit on it. The government alone will be responsible for what might happen!' Contrary to what this outburst might suggest, in Osorio's view Armada's visits to a number of lieutenant-generals at the king's request contributed to restore calm. Years later Juan Carlos himself would admit that 'my contacts inside the armed forces informed me not only of the unrest caused by the PCE's legalisation but also of suspicious movements which succeeded in alarming me'.[48]

Carrillo, who was almost as surprised by his party's legalisation as the generals had been, called a meeting of the PCE's central committee for 14–15 April. On the second day of the meeting the secretary-general, acting in collusion with Suárez, unexpectedly warned his comrades of an imminent though unspecified threat to their newly acquired status, in view of which he proposed that the party formally acknowledge the monarchy and the symbols of the Spanish state. Carrillo went on to praise the crown's role in the democratising process and hinted that the PCE might endorse the monarchy in the future constituent Cortes. 'Today the option is not between monarchy or republic', he declared, 'today the option is between dictatorship and democracy'. Attempts to hold a proper debate on these momentous decisions were rapidly quashed and his proposals were adopted with little opposition. At the ensuing press conference Carrillo admitted that the restoration of the monarchy had initially caused the PCE 'serious misgivings', but recent developments suggested that Spain 'was indeed moving towards democracy under the monarchy'. In the secretary-general's view, if this trend continued the democratic forces represented in the future Cortes might well find a constitutional monarchy acceptable after all. Thereafter the PCE's long-standing opposition to Juan Carlos was rapidly transformed into growing support for the monarch who had made their legalisation possible after almost forty years of clandestine existence.[49]

The referendum and the subsequent reforms undertaken by the Suárez government also strengthened Juan Carlos's reputation and standing abroad, enabling him to play an increasingly confident role on the international stage. In February 1977 the king officially visited the Vatican, where he was greeted by Pope Paul VI. The purpose of this visit was formally to inaugurate an era of improved relations between the monarchy and the Holy See which would ultimately pave the way for the full separation of Church and state within Spain itself. The king and queen were also received by President Leone and Prime Minister Andreotti, though they did not officially visit Italy until 1978.

The democratising process instigated by the king was already having a significant impact on Spain's bilateral relations with some nations. Mexico, which had consistently refused to recognise Franco's regime and had allowed successive Spanish Republican governments-in-exile to operate from its capital, finally agreed to recognise the young monarchy in March 1977. This process was greatly facilitated by Juan Carlos's warm, down-to-earth manner, which immediately captivated President José López Portillo.[50]

In April 1977 Juan Carlos and Sofía made their first official visit to Germany, Spain's other major European partner and ally together with France. The king was very grateful to President Scheel for having attended his investiture and the latter went out of his way to endorse the young monarch's democratising efforts. More importantly, Chancellor Schmidt, who had closely watched developments in Spain for some time, spoke out in favour of Spanish membership of the EC, once the first democratic elections had been held.[51]

In the wake of the referendum Suárez agreed to meet the opposition's *Comisión de los Nueve* with a view to negotiating the terms of their participation in the forthcoming elections. In March the government recognised the right to strike, introduced a new electoral law that largely met the opposition's demands, and later granted a fresh political amnesty in an attempt to pacify the Basque country. A month later Suárez finally dismantled the *Movimiento* and legalised the hitherto clandestine trade unions. These measures paved the way for the first democratic elections, scheduled for 15 June 1977.

The legalisation of the major political parties finally enabled Juan Carlos to meet their leaders openly for the first time. On 2 May he received Tierno Galván, who left La Zarzuela fully convinced of the king's determination to remove the barriers that still stood in the way of democracy and even declared himself willing to preside a government under the monarchy. Three days later Juan Carlos saw Antón Cañellas, the opposition leader who had represented Catalonia on the *Comisión de los Nueve*, who discussed his region's demands.[52]

On 20 May it was González's turn to visit La Zarzuela for the first time, in the company of Javier Solana. The king, who generally used the informal '*tu*' form of address with his subjects, initially observed the more distant '*usted*', but soon reverted to the former as the tension eased. Before the meeting, PSOE leaders had debated whether they should raise the institutional issue with the monarch, finally deciding against it. Much to González's surpise, it was the king who lost no time in enquiring why the Socialists were republicans, to which the young leader replied that the monarchy had been consistently hostile to his party in the past. In order to illustrate the PSOE's current thinking González, who was very close to the Swedish prime minister, Olof Palme, told Juan Carlos of a famous exhange between King Gustav V and the Social Democrat Hjalmar Branting, held in the early 1920s. The Social Democrats had included the abolition of the monarchy in their electoral programme, in view of which Gustav proposed a gentleman's agreement whereby Branting would respect the *status quo* for a year as long as the king did not interfere with his government. A year passed, and Branting never raised the matter again. According to González, one of Gustav's arguments had been that his monarchy was cheaper than a republic because he did not have to stand for election every four years, an observation that greatly amused Juan Carlos. This first encounter paved the way for an increasingly warm relationship, which both men have partly attributed to the generation factor.[53]

The steps taken by the Suárez government since July 1976 gradually dispelled any doubts Don Juan and his aides may have harboured as to the future of the new monarchy, depriving Estoril of reasons to delay the count's renunciation any longer. In August Juan Carlos told a leading historian that his father no longer had any doubts about the consolidation of the institution, and therefore hoped to solve the matter in the autumn, but this was not to be. Don Juan spent Christmas in Madrid with his family, and revisited his son in late March and again in late April. When Fraga saw him in Estoril later that month he went away with the impression that the count 'had fully come to terms with the situation'.[54]

Suárez never attached any importance to Don Juan's renunciation, since he was only interested in the legitimacy the monarchy might acquire as a result of its role in the democratising process; as he told Osorio shortly after his appointment, he was only a monarchist in the sense that he was fully committed to Juan Carlos's cause. Furthermore the premier was under the impression that the king did not attach much importance to his father's renunciation either, an opinion that is corroborated by the fact that his son Felipe was formally proclaimed prince of Asturias in January 1977, several months before Don Juan's decision was implemented.[55]

If Don Juan's formal renunciation did not take place earlier it was largely because his son's closest advisers, notably Fernández-Miranda and Armada, were reluctant to accept his conditions. The Count of Barcelona had initially requested a televised ceremony to be held at the Royal Palace but this suggestion met the determined opposition of Juan Carlos's inner circle, a member of which went so far as to suggest that his renunciation should take the form of a letter to his son, 'like someone bidding farewell to a relative', as the indignant Don Juan would later put it. Fernández-Miranda agreed to a more modest ceremony at La Zarzuela, but clashed with Don Juan over the contents of his speech, and finally withdrew from the proceedings altogether. According to the Count of Barcelona the professor 'was horrified', for 'he regarded my renunciation as something which shattered the existing legal order . . . it was like telling them that what they were doing was not legal'.[56]

Fernández-Miranda's objections were not entirely unjustified. From the professor's point of view Franco had not restored the Bourbon dynasty that had reigned in Spain until 1931, but had created a new monarchy and dynasty of his own, whose first incumbent was Juan Carlos. On becoming king on 22 November 1975 Juan Carlos had also become head of the new dynasty; strictly speaking there was no legal or dynastic link between the king and Don Juan, who merely happened to be his father. It was therefore absurd for the state to acknowledge the latter's renunciation, since this would mean questioning Juan Carlos's previous right to the throne, and by extension the legality of everything carried out in his name since his investiture. The government's entire strategy had been based on the principle of respect for the existing legal order and its own mechanisms of reform. In Fernández-Miranda's view, if those in power failed to observe this maxim, they would release others from their obligation to do likewise, thereby endangering the entire transition process.

Don Juan's renunciation finally took the form of a low-key ceremony held at La Zarzuela on 14 May 1977. In his speech Don Juan restated his views on the monarchy, which he believed should be fully compatible with a democratic system of government, capable of adapting to rapidly changing social circumstances, tolerant of non-Catholic religions, and able to contribute to Spain's return to the international fold. Don Juan thus not only conferred on Juan Carlos the dynastic legitimacy he had lacked hitherto but provided him with a blueprint for the constitutional monarchy of the future. After the ceremony Don Juan privately handed over the plaque traditionally kept by the princes of Asturias – which he had asked Juan Carlos to surrender in 1969 – to his grandson Felipe.

Only weeks after Don Juan's renunciation Fernández-Miranda unexpectedly announced his own resignation. In late March the president of the Cortes had stated that he would remain in office for as long as he continued to enjoy the king's confidence and reminded journalists that he had been appointed for a six-year term. Although the professor had already declared that he did not intend to stand for election, according to the terms of the Reform Law the king could appoint him senator and later name him president of the new Cortes. A number of prominent political figures, amongst them González, subsequently took him to task for seeking to remain in office beyond the first elections. Whether or not these voices influenced his decision, on 23 May Fernández-Miranda submitted his resignation, which was not formally accepted until a week later.[57]

On 31 May the professor held a press conference in which he justified his decision as a logical consequence of the process initiated by the Reform Law. Although he admitted that when the latter was debated it was widely assumed that he intended to 'cross from one river bank to the other' by remaining president, he denied that this had ever been his intention, and claimed to realise that the future president would have to arbitrate between two democratically elected chambers, a task for which he thought himself unsuited. As soon as the press had begun to compare him to Mazzarino and the Count-Duke Olivares, he had realised his continued presence could only harm the monarchy. Fernández-Miranda hoped he would continue to enjoy the trust Juan Carlos had placed in him since 1960, and concluded by asserting: 'I have never used the king, I have only served him'.[58]

One of the few journalists to enjoy regular access to Fernández-Miranda later claimed that the king was initially unhappy with his decision to resign. According to Suárez, Juan Carlos was at a loss to explain the professor's motives, though he did partly attribute the decision to the fact that he had not been allowed to take part in talks with opposition leaders, a view he fully shared. At the time it was widely believed that the professor was unwilling to involve himself in talks of this nature, when in fact he had come very close to setting up a secret interview with Carrillo shortly before his resignation. More generally, Suárez admits that Fernández-Miranda found it increasingly difficult to accept his protegé's newly acquired autonomy and authority, and grew increasingly apprehensive about the outcome of the democratising process. Be this as it may, on the eve of his resignation he was barely on speaking terms with Suárez.[59]

In private Fernández-Miranda had often compared the reform operation to a theatre production, of which the king was the impresario, he was the author and Suárez the leading actor. To his dismay, by the spring of 1977 the author had discovered that the actor was beginning to write his own lines.[60]

Whatever Fernández Miranda's motives, his resignation caused the king considerable discomfort, for it drew public attention to the importance of his own role on the eve of the first democratic elections. If all had been well between them, the former could simply have announced that he did not wish to be considered for the post of president of the new democratic Cortes, leaving Juan Carlos free to appoint his successor. The king was genuinely grateful to his mentor for his services to the monarchy, however, and granted him not only a dukedom but also the highly coveted Order of the Golden Fleece.[61]

Suárez did not publicly announce his decision to stand in the first democratic elections until 3 May 1977. Even his closest advisers were surprised by his apparent reluctance to form his own political party or declare his support for any of the numerous parties and alliances that were hastily making themselves ready for the elections. At the time, even those closest to Suárez were unaware of the fact that in late 1976 he had approached Juan Carlos and Fernández-Miranda with a plan to form a government-sponsored party capable of winning the first elections. His aim had been to bring together independent professionals who had not taken part in the regime's official political life but who were nevertheless well known and respected in their towns and provinces. Much to his dismay, both the king and the president of the Cortes found his plan ill-advised, in view of which he requested that their opposition be noted in writing, so that he would not be accused of lack of foresight later on.[62]

Juan Carlos was well aware that the reform process inspired by the monarchy could only succeed with the support of the more conservative sectors of society as well as that of the left. Fraga and his allies were extremely critical of the manner in which Suárez had legalised the PCE and some feared they would not comply with the rules of the democratic game. Juan Carlos reacted by publicising his audiences with AP leaders, in order to let it be known that he welcomed their participation. Fraga was no doubt correct in suspecting that Juan Carlos did not wish to see AP win the first elections, but the king was genuinely grateful to him for having succeeded in interesting much of the neo-Francoist right in the democratic process. On the eve of the election, and in view of AP's increasingly backward-looking image, Juan Carlos even convinced López Bravo, a highly respected former minister, to join the party in an effort to improve its prospects.[63]

Osorio is of the opinion that in the crucial months leading up to the first elections, some of those with access to the king opposed the creation of a government-sponsored party because they assumed Suárez would not remain in office long. According to this interpretation, Juan Carlos saw in Suárez someone who was ideally suited to the task of dismantling the regime from within and coming to terms with the opposition, but not the leader of a political party capable of heading a government accountable to a democratically elected Cortes. The very fact that Suárez thanked Osorio profusely in February 1977 for having spoken to the king about the need to form a centre party under his leadership suggests that La Zarzuela harboured grave doubts about his future. Be this as it may, in the spring of 1977 Juan Carlos finally acknowledged that the time had come to allow Suárez to lead a party capable of winning the first elections.[64]

While Suárez busied himself with the democratising process, some of his ministers and their allies outside the government struggled to put together an attractive electoral vehicle for him to lead. Between mid-January and mid-February 1977 a number of Liberal, Social Democratic and Christian Democratic groups came together to form a new coalition, Centro Democrático. In March Suárez succeeded in removing Areilza from the leadership of the Popular Party, one of the more consolidated groups in the coalition, and in late April Calvo Sotelo left the cabinet in order to prepare his master's entry into the fray.

On announcing his decision to stand as a candidate in the Unión de Centro Democrático (UCD) lists on 3 May, Suárez went out of his way to emphasise that he was doing so 'without any support from the king, who is above options and contests'. This failed to convince his critics, some of whom felt he should not be allowed to benefit electorally from the political capital he had accumulated since July 1976 under the monarch's guidance. Worse still, given that for the past eighteen months Suárez's actions had been presented as an expression of the royal will, some feared his participation in the democratic process might compromise Juan Carlos unduly. These misgivings, however, were not widely shared by Spanish public opinion. Ironically, the only candidate accused of seeking to make use of his former association with the monarch for electoral purposes was none other than Arias Navarro, who failed to win a seat in the Senate for AP.[65]

On the eve of the elections much of the king's time was spent drawing up the list of forty-one royal nominees who were to sit in the new Senate. Although a number of left-wing and nationalist figures approached by Juan Carlos turned him down, the final, carefully balanced list included the Catalanist Maurici Serrahima and the republican Justino de Azcárate. When the king telephoned the latter to offer him a seat in the Senate, this former deputy objected that he was merely an old republican who had lived most of his life in exile, to which Juan Carlos replied: 'that is precisely why I would like you to accept'. Amongst those nominated were six of Suárez's ministers, who were barred from standing in the first elections by the new electoral law, and several of those who had contributed to the success of the Reform Law, including Fernández-Miranda. The king also included representatives of the three armed services, together with jurists, industrialists, academics and writers such as the novelist Camilo José Cela. Several of Juan Carlos's former tutors and two personal friends, Jaime Carvajal and Prado y Colón de Carvajal, were also amongst the nominees.

Amongst those initially considered by the king for the Senate was the secretary-general of the royal household, Armada, who had repeatedly expressed the wish to leave La Zarzuela in order to pursue his military career. Armada's departure was probably motivated by his fundamental disapproval of the course political life was taking under Suárez and may have been directly instigated by the premier himself. In the wake of the elections Armada was replaced by Fernández Campo, who had acquired valuable political experience in several civilian ministries since Franco's death. The Marquis of Mondéjar, who was awarded the Golden Fleece by Juan Carlos in recognition of his services, stayed on as nominal head of the royal household.[66]

On 15 June 1977 Spain finally held its first democratic elections since 1936. Juan Carlos was particulary pleased by the extremely high turnout – 81.2 per cent – which was seen as evidence of the democratic credibility of the electoral process. This was further corroborated by the dissolution of the Republican government-in-exile, still based in Mexico, later that month. With 34.4 per cent of the vote and 166 out of 350 seats, the government-backed coalition, UCD, narrowly failed to obtain an absolute majority in the Congress, much to Suárez's disappointment. The PSOE, with 29.3 per cent of the vote and 118 seats, emerged as the major opposition party, followed at some distance by the Communists with 9.4 per cent of the vote and 20 seats, and AP with 8.3 per cent of the vote and only 16 seats. The Christian Democrats who had refused to join Suárez's coalition failed to win a single seat in the lower chamber.[67]

Juan Carlos met many of Spain's democratically elected representatives for the first time at a large reception held at the Royal Palace on 24 June to celebrate his saint's day. Someone called Carrillo a 'murderer' behind his back as he advanced to shake hands with the royal couple and several senior officers refused to greet him. Much to his relief, Otero Novas noted that González and the other PSOE leaders behaved impeccably in the monarch's presence. One leading journalist described this event as 'the *fiesta* of national reconciliation', as it was the first time that Spain's democratically elected leaders met under the same roof.[68]

Shortly after the elections Juan Carlos wrote a long letter to the Shah of Iran, whom he had seen on several occasions since his first visit to Tehran in 1969, in which he provided a personal analysis of the Spanish political situation. The king began by explaining that 'forty years of an entirely personal regime have done much that is good for the country, but at the same time left Spain sadly lacking in political structures, so much so as to pose an enormous risk to the strengthening of the monarchy. Following the first six months of the Arias government, which I was likewise obliged to inherit, in July 1976 I appointed a younger, less compromised man, whom I knew well and who enjoyed my full confidence: Adolfo Suárez. From that moment onwards I vowed to tread in the path of democracy, endeavouring always to be one step ahead of events in order to forestall a situation like that in Portugal which might prove even more dire in this country of mine'.[69]

Juan Carlos then went on to discuss the legalisation of political parties and their efforts to equip themselves financially: 'the right, assisted by the Spanish banking system; Socialism by Willy Brandt, Venezuela and the other European Socialists; the Communists by the usual means'. While these groups prepared for the elections, Suárez, 'whom I had firmly entrusted with the responsibility of government, could only participate in the election campaign during its final eight days, bereft of the advantages and opportunities which I have explained above, and from which the other political parties were able to profit'. In spite of this, 'alone, and with an organisation still hardly formed, financed by short-term loans from certain private individuals, he managed to secure an outright and decisive victory'.

In the king's view the Socialists' unexpectedly good performance posed 'a serious threat to the country's security and to the stability of the monarchy, since I am reliably informed that their party is Marxist. A certain part of the electorate is unaware of this, voting for them in the belief that through Socialism Spain might receive aid from such major European countries as Germany, or alternatively from countries such as Venezuela, for the revival of the Spanish economy'.[70] In view of this, it was imperative that Suárez restructure and consolidate the UCD 'so as to create a political party for himself which will serve as the mainstay of the monarchy and of the stability of Spain. For this to be achieved premier Suárez clearly needs more than ever before whatever assistance is possible, be it from his fellow countrymen or from friendly countries abroad who look to the preservation of Western civilization and of established monarchies'. Juan Carlos went on to inform the shah that municipal elections were expected within the next six months, 'and it is there more than anywhere that we shall put our very future in the balance'. In view of this 'critical juncture', the king concluded by requesting a grant of $10 million as the shah's 'personal contribution to the strengthening of the Spanish monarchy'.[71]

Strictly speaking, Juan Carlos was not behaving unconstitutionally by intervening on Suárez's behalf in this manner, for he was still operating in the somewhat ambiguous context created by the Reform Law. The legislation on political parties adopted in June 1976, however, had outlawed the receipt of financial assistance from abroad. Had the contents of this letter been made public at the time, the king's prestige and authority would have been seriously undermined, both because it revealed the full extent of his willingness to interfere in the political process and because of the autocratic nature of the shah's regime.

It is difficult to judge the extent to which Juan Carlos was speaking his mind in this letter. It should of course be remembered that he was addressing an absolute monarch with little regard for the niceties of parliamentary democracy, and he may well have exaggerated the nature of the threat posed by the PSOE so as to justify his request for substantial financial support. His account of Suárez's predicament was certainly partial, for Juan Carlos knew full well that the former had enjoyed a number of advantages that were unavailable to his opponents, such as unlimited access to the state-controlled media and the support of provincial governors and other unelected officials. Similarly there is no evidence of a shortage of funding for UCD's campaign. On the other hand the PSOE had indeed declared itself Marxist at its party conference in December 1976 and, unlike the PCE, had thus far refused to acknowledge the monarchy. The PSOE's excellent performance in the first elections had surprised and alarmed influential conservatives such as Osorio, and Juan Carlos may well have shared their misgivings to some degree. Indeed the king's attempt to explain away the party's success by attributing it to the electorate's gullibility rings disconcertingly sincere.

Though warmly worded, the shah's reply – dated 4 July 1977 – displayed far greater caution, and it is not known whether Juan Carlos was succesful in his request.[72] The municipal elections alluded to in the letter, which the left had wished to call as soon as possible, were subsequently postponed by the government until April 1979, thereby depriving this appeal of much of its urgency and justification. The king no doubt greeted this decision with considerable relief. Though hardly bookish by nature, if there was one historical episode Juan Carlos knew well it was Alfonso XIII's decision to flee the country following the first fair municipal elections ever held in Spain on 12 April 1931.[73]

7 King of a Parliamentary Monarchy

The 1977 elections greatly improved Juan Carlos's standing and prestige both at home and abroad, as he was generally credited with the sucess of the Suárez reform. His role in Spanish political life, however, was to undergo major changes in the ensuing months. The king now found himself coexisiting with a democratically elected prime minister who had previously been accountable to no one but him, and who would in future have to take into consideration the wishes of his party, his electorate and the Cortes at large. Inevitably his trusted protegé was to become increasingly independent, if not distant, depriving the king of much of his former influence.

The king's speech at the opening of the Cortes on 22 July 1977 was far more than a mere formality. On entering the Cortes, Juan Carlos and Sofía saw most deputies rise to their feet to applaud them, with the ostentatious exception of those of the PSOE. At this stage the precise nature of the newly elected Cortes remained unclear and it was only when Juan Carlos explicitly announced his intention of becoming a constitutional monarch that the assembly's constituent role was formally acknowledged. As the king finished his speech, González and those in his immediate vicinity sprang to their feet to applaud and were promptly imitated by their fellow deputies. The Socialist leadership thereby underlined that their recognition of the monarch remained conditional on his ability to pave the way for a new democratic constitution.[1]

Juan Carlos and Suárez were initially uncertain as to how to proceed with the constitutional reform. Before the elections the government had considered drafting its own constitutional bill with a view to submitting it to a committee of experts, from whence it would be sent to the Cortes for a full debate. At one point, in order to ensure that the monarchy did not suffer the consequences of a possible government set-back, Suárez even studied the possibility of holding two referenda, one on the monarchy and another on the rest of the constitution, an option apparently favoured by Juan Carlos as well. In the wake of the elections, however, the government settled for a constituent process conducted entirely by the Cortes.[2]

The constituent process initiated in August 1977 with the appointment of a seven-man congressional drafting committee was to dominate Spanish political life for the next eighteen months. The king naturally followed developments in the Cortes very closely, for it was not only the nature of the future democratic system but also that of the monarchy itself that was at stake. Paradoxically, although a referendum on the monarchy would have entailed a far more blatant break with the past than the election of a *de facto* constituent assembly, it might well have served the government's long-term purposes better. By refusing to allow the monarchy to be put to a popular vote, the government made itself vulnerable to pressure from those parties, notably the PSOE, that had not yet recognised the institution. In spite of the presence of three UCD members on the seven-man committee, the PSOE was able to use this bargaining power to considerable effect.[3]

One of the most controversial issues the constituent Cortes would have to face, and which concerned the king greatly, was the future of Spain's regions. As we have seen, the Arias government had failed to make any significant progress in this area, while Suárez was of the opinion that little could be done until after the first elections. In late 1976 his government had been presented with a plan whereby Josep Tarradellas, the exiled president of the Catalan Generalitat (government) since 1954, would be restored to office in return for his recognition of the monarchy and Spanish national unity. This was an attractive proposition in that Tarradellas, widely acknowledged as the embodiment of Catalan aspirations, would be able to negotiate directly with Suárez on behalf of the entire Catalan opposition. Furthermore, unlike most nationalist leaders, the exiled president did not insist on the restoration of the 1932 Statute of Autonomy granted to Catalonia under the Second Republic, which the government refused to contemplate. Had it taken place before the elections, this pact could also have served to legitimise the monarchy in the eyes of many Catalans. In the wake of the referendum on the Law for Political Reform, however, Suárez lost interest in this proposal, preferring to negotiate with the moderate nationalists led by Jordi Pujol instead. Nevertheless in January 1977 Juan Carlos told the Catalan financier Manuel Ortínez, who had masterminded the Tarradellas operation, that he fully endorsed his efforts.[4]

The victory of the Catalan left and Pujol's relatively poor showing in the June 1977 elections forced Suárez to reconsider his strategy. Neither he nor the king could ignore the fact that the most voted party in the region, the Catalan branch of the PSOE, had not yet recognised the monarchy. Suárez therefore agreed to talks with its leaders, but little progress was achieved. On 21 June a delegation of Catalan Socialists led by Joan Reventós was received by the king, who sought to soften the impact of Suárez's refusal to comply with their demands. Reventós would later tell Tarradellas that the monarch had caused them 'a rather poor impression', and the Socialists abandoned all hope of reaching an understanding with Madrid.[5]

Shortly afterwards the recently elected representatives of the Catalan provinces joined to form an Assembly of Catalan Parliamentarians, following the example of their Basque counterparts. Juan Carlos was disappointed to learn that the Catalan senators appointed by him had been prevented from joining this assembly on the grounds that they had not been democratically elected, even though some boasted impeccable Catalanist credentials.[6]

Events in Catalonia led Juan Carlos and Suárez to conclude that the time had come to invite Tarradellas to Madrid. The latter travelled to the capital in a private jet provided by the Basque industrialist Luis Olarra, one of the senators recently appointed by the king. Tarradellas was adamant that the government should restore the Generalitat and at one point in their meeting Suárez lost his temper and exclaimed: 'Do not forget that I am the chief executive of a country of 36 million inhabitants and you were the president of a Generalitat which lost the civil war', to which the veteran politician replied: 'And you should not forget that a premier who is unable to solve the Catalan problem is placing the monarchy at risk'. Not surprisingly, both parties regarded the interview as an inauspicious start to their negotiations.[7]

Tarradellas's visit to La Zarzuela, initially planned for 28 June, was briefly postponed on account of the opposition of Francisco Coloma Gallegos, captain-general of Catalonia, who had not forgotten that the veteran politician had been responsible for the Republican war effort in Catalonia during the civil war. Having persuaded the general to reconsider, Juan Carlos finally received Tarradellas a day later. To the latter's delight, on his arrival he was greeted in his native language by the head of the royal household, Mondéjar, whose family hailed from Majorca, where a variety of Catalan is widely spoken. The Catalan leader thanked the king for seeing someone who intended to remain faithful to his republican convictions regardless, and went on to advocate an understanding between the monarchy and the restored Generalitat that would pave the way for Catalonia's acceptance of a future Spanish democracy. Juan Carlos surprised Tarradellas by questioning his claim to the presidency of the Generalitat, given the circumstances surrounding his election in 1954, a line of attack suggested to him by López Rodó. More generally, the king insisted that the restoration of the Generalitat could only be undertaken in agreement with the newly elected Cortes, and promised to encourage Suárez to find a viable legal formula. Throughout the interview Juan Carlos addressed the veteran Catalan leader as 'Don José' or 'señor Tarradellas', but later informed one of those present that he hoped to be able to acknowledge him as president of the Generalitat in the near future. Before leaving Madrid, Tarradellas told journalists that although most Catalans were republicans, he would accept a democratically sanctioned monarchy. He later wrote a letter thanking Juan Carlos for his hospitality, in which he concluded that 'Catalans, myself included, will always be grateful to the monarch who currently guides the destinies of the Spanish peoples'.[8]

The king's *de facto* recognition of Tarradellas as president of the Generalitat paved the way for more detailed negotiations with the government, which came to fruition in late August 1977. On 11 September over one million Catalans demonstrated in favour of the concession of autonomy, and on 23 October Tarradellas was finally able to return to Barcelona as president of the restored Generalitat. On the eve of his triumphal arrival in the Catalan capital, he revisited La Zarzuela to thank the monarch for making this historic agreement possible. At his swearing-in ceremony, Tarradellas promised to act 'with loyalty to the king', and paid tribute to Juan Carlos for having understood 'Catalonia's aspirations'. As both Suárez and he would observe on separate occasions, it was extremely fitting that Juan Carlos should restore the Generalitat, since it was the first Spanish Bourbon, Felipe V, who had abolished Catalan institutions in 1714.[9]

Although the provisional Generalitat could not be granted significant executive powers until Spain had approved a new constitution, its restoration represented a major contribution to the democratising process. A similar solution was badly needed in the Basque country, but the absence of a leader generally accepted as the embodiment of Basque national feeling made a repetition of the Tarradellas operation impossible. Unfortunately the Basque government-in-exile was a partisan institution, whose president, the PNV's Jesús María de Leizaola, could never have played a role similar to that of Tarradellas even if the Basque parties had allowed him to. Suárez eventually acceded to the creation of a Basque General Council comparable to the provisional Generalitat, which represented the Basque parties that had obtained seats in the recent elections. (A similar institution was later created in Galicia as well.) This failure to reach a pact between the Basque country and the monarchy early on in the democratising process was to have dire consequences for both.

The king watched over the opening of the constitution-drafting process with some apprehension. At this stage the acceptance of the monarchy by the parties of the left was by no means a foregone conclusion. The return of the monarchy had been undertaken at the behest of General Franco and was still regarded by many as part of an effort to perpetuate the authoritarian regime beyond the death of its founder. The king's fears were confirmed when, at a special meeting held at Sigüenza (Segovia) in early August 1977, the PSOE leadership adopted a constitutional draft that included the republican form of government amongst its clauses. It was also agreed that the party would defend a republican amendment until it was publicly defeated at some stage in the constitutional debates. By forcing a vote on the monarchy, the PSOE sought to emphasise that in future the institution would owe its existence to the will of the democratically elected constituent Cortes and not to that of General Franco.[10]

Given this state of affairs, on the eve of the first full meeting of the seven-man drafting committee, held on 22 August, Juan Carlos urged the president of the Congress constitutional committee, the UCD's Emilio Attard, to request party representatives to clarify their position on the institutional question. Attard subsequently drew up an eight-page report, destined for the king, in which he outlined their respective views.[11]

Speaking on behalf of the PSOE, Peces-Barba attributed his party's republicanism over the past fifty years to historical factors, notably Alfonso XIII's toleration of Primo de Rivera's coup in 1923, while reminding his colleagues that during the early years of its existence Socialists and Republicans had been adversaries rather than allies. As expected, the Socialist representative confirmed that his party would defend its republican amendment until it was defeated in the Cortes, but hastened to clarify that the PSOE would recognise the resulting constitution and would not hesitate to form a government under the monarchy in the future. In marked contrast the UCD representatives defended the monarchy as one of the essential pillars of the future constitution, while Solé Tura and Roca, acting on behalf of the Communists and peripheral nationalists respectively, announced that they would accept the institution from the outset. Fraga's attitude towards the monarchy was surprisingly lukewarm at this stage, probably so as to warn the UCD spokesmen that they should not take his support for granted. Determined to anchor the monarchy to the constitution as firmly as possible, on 25 August the UCD submitted a draft text stating that 'the political form of the Spanish state is that of a parliamentary monarchy', a formula that remained unchanged and was eventually incorporated into the constitution's preliminary title.[12]

At this stage Juan Carlos faced the daunting challenge of winning over the hearts and minds of the left while retaining the support of the right. Some former Francoists clearly believed that he was failing to achieve the latter. In late September López Rodo – who had won a seat in the Congress on AP's Barcelona list – warned him that resistance to change was leading some disgruntled conservatives to turn their back on the monarchy, to which the king retorted that their loyalty must have been suspect from the outset. Nevertheless Juan Carlos subsequently requested his support in convincing the AP leadership to initiate a press campaign in favour of the institution.[13]

The seven-man drafting committee debated the king's future powers in late September and early October 1977. Overall, the PSOE and the PCE sought to reduce the monarch's role to a purely symbolic level, while the UCD representatives struggled to provide the monarch with effective powers of arbitration and moderation. Comparatively speaking, the former wanted a monarchy such as that of Sweden or Japan, while the latter favoured the British, Belgian or Norwegian model. On the whole the UCD's views prevailed, largely thanks to the support provided by Roca, the Catalan representative. As indicated above, Fraga did not come to the UCD's assistance in this matter, forcing a number of AP deputies, notably López Rodó, to propose subsequent amendments aimed at increasing the monarch's powers, generally without success. Understandably, in the spring of 1978 Juan Carlos would privately complain that Fraga had not been very active in defence of the monarchy during the drafting stage of the constituent process.[14]

On the whole the king did his best to respect the work of the constituent Cortes and not prejudge the outcome of the institutional debate. As we saw above, his son Felipe had been proclaimed Prince of Asturias in early 1977, and the regional authorities had hoped to stage a solemn investiture in November. In the event this was transformed into a mere tribute by the people of Asturias so as not to offend the left's constitutional sensibilities, but Juan Carlos could not help referring to his son's future duties as king of Spain. Amongst those present was his former mentor Fernández-Miranda, who justified this reference on the grounds that 'everything depends on the answer one gives to the question: was the transition undertaken by means of a *reforma* or a *ruptura*? As far as I am concerned, the transition to democracy must be carried out within the law, by means of the law'.[15]

In late November 1977 a preliminary version of the constitutional draft produced by the seven-man committee was unexpectedly leaked to the press. At this stage the text clearly reflected the efforts of the left to limit the king's future powers, a goal facilitated by Fraga's passivity, a tendency that alarmed many monarchists and possibly the king himself. One of the most outspoken critics of the leaked text was the philospher Julián Marías, one of the senators appointed by the king, whom Suárez had to call to La Moncloa to reassure him as to Juan Carlos's future role.[16]

The most controversial issue concerning the king's future powers was his role in the appointment of the head of government. Fraga had initially succeeded in imposing a formula not unlike the Swedish, whereby the prime minister is elected by parliament from amongst the candidates proposed by the various parliamentary groups and is subsequently ratified by the monarch. In early December, however, Roca, acting in agreement with Herrero de Miñón, introduced an amendment enabling the monarch to propose a candidate to the Cortes. This formula was approved with the support of the UCD and the benevolent opposition of the left. Suárez, however, was unhappy with this change and by way of compensation he subsequently forced the UCD representatives to modify the article regulating the dissolution of the Cortes, greatly restricting the monarch's role. Juan Carlos would later tell a journalist that 'I think I am going to have fewer powers than the king of Sweden, but if that is what it takes for all political parties to recognise the monarchy, I am willing to accept it'.[17]

The king knew all along that the outcome of the institutional debate would ultimately depend on the PSOE. When the drafting committe completed its work in mid-December 1977, its members begged Peces-Barba to drop his party's republican substitution amendment. Personally, the PSOE representative would have been happy to oblige, but the party leadership refused to reconsider its position. This greatly alarmed the government, who demanded an explanation from González, currently on a tour of the Soviet Union. The Socialist secretary general stood firm but reassured the UCD leadership that his party would accept the resulting constitution even if its republican amendment was defeated.[18]

Throughout the constituent process Juan Carlos worked hard to improve his personal relations with the major leaders of the left, a task that was not without its difficulties. In mid-October 1977, in the course of a reception held in honour of the Mexican president, López Portillo, González approached Suárez and asked 'how is your *jefe*?', to which the latter replied 'well, my *jefe* and yours'. When the king appeared Suárez asked him 'is it not true that you are also Felipe's *jefe*?', to which Juan Carlos readily agreed. Embarrassed, González granted that he was happy to acknowledge the king's authority. Shortly afterwards, at another reception, the king came up to the PSOE leader from behind and asked him what colour his eyes were. Surprised, González looked up at him and answered: 'Grey'. 'In that case', Juan Carlos replied, only half in jest, 'you had better not go around saying, as you did recently, that the king is a young, tall, blue-eyed lad'. Shortly afterwards, in the course of their first encounter ever, González asked Don Juan whether the monarchy would accept a future Socialist victory at the polls, to which the count replied that the institution would not be fully consolidated until it proved itself compatible with a PSOE government. In January 1978 the king told a leading journalist that although his first meeting with González had been somewhat cold, the second, arranged by his friend Prado y Colón de Carvajál, had gone much better. This had led him to conclude that 'I think I can get on perfectly well with Felipe. We are almost the same age and have a great deal in common'.[19]

In spite of the age difference, the king appears to have made good progess with Carrillo from the outset. Their first full-length private meeting, lasting over two hours, took place on 5 December 1977. When the Communist leader was told that Juan Carlos generally used the informal '*tu*' form of address, he warned La Zarzuela that he would do likewise. The king was duly informed and decided to use the more formal '*usted*' and call him 'don Santiago' as well, a habit he has observed to this day, much to Carrillo's delight. During the meeting the latter assured the king that his party would not question the monarchy in the constitutional debates and would respect it as long as it proved compatible with democracy. The king in turn promised Carrillo that if the PCE ever won an election he would not hesitate to invite him to form a government.[20]

In the wake of this interview Juan Carlos privately described Carrillo as one of Spain's most skilful politicians, praising him for his ability to adapt to a situation such as he had never envisaged during the long years of opposition to the Franco regime. The king was particulary pleased to note that, unlike González, Carrillo rapidly acquired the habit of addressing him as 'your majesty'. He was also greatly relieved by the fact that neither the Communists nor Tierno Galván's PSP intended to question the monarchy in the forthcoming debates.[21]

While seeking the approval of the left, Juan Carlos also struggled to appease the right. The government had been careful to introduce a clause acknowledging the armed forces' role in guaranteeing 'the sovereignty and independence of Spain' as well as 'its territorial integrity and the constitutional order', and another enabling the king to 'exercise supreme command of the armed forces'. However the constitutional text leaked in November had also publicised the fact that the UCD had accepted the word *nacionalidades* (nationalities) to describe Spain's historic regions, a term many conservatives regarded as a denial of the existence of a Spanish nation. At the traditional *pascua militar* celebration[22] held in early January 1978, Defence Minister Gutiérrez Mellado admitted that the military were following the constitutional debates closely and described the prevailing mood as 'concerned but confident, tense but disciplined'. Echoing the views of many senior officers, the minister solemnly declared that 'there is only one Spain and we Spaniards are not going to allow it to be broken up'. In his own speech, the king urged his audience to accept and understand the necessary political changes they were witnessing, even if these were not always to their liking. Speaking as a fellow officer, Juan Carlos observed that if civilians had the right to expect their political neutrality, they in turn were entitled to demand respect for the rules regulating the internal life of the armed forces.[23]

This exhortation illustrates the king's ability to bridge the divide that still separated the civilian and military spheres. As king of Spain, he could transmit the views of civilian politicians who were fearful or suspicious of the armed forces and were anxious to uphold the principle of civil supremacy. At the same time, as commander-in-chief, he could air and share his fellow officers' fears and concerns and ensure that the civilian authorities were made aware of them. It goes without saying that this was a role that almost by definition, an elected president could never have performed. Most importantly, unlike his grandfather Alfonso XIII, Juan Carlos was performing the role of soldier-king in a manner that was fully compatible with the democratic aspirations of his people.

Although the monarch was careful not to become personally involved in the constitutional debates, he was kept well informed of developments by senior figures such as the new president of the Cortes, Antonio Hernández Gil, as well as by individual deputies and senators whom he knew personally. In private at least, he appears to have been quite explicit as to his personal preferences. In mid-April 1978, for example, he informed López Rodó, a member of the Congress constitutional committee, that he wished to retain the power to appoint at least twenty senators, and had already thought of several candidates, amongst them the poet Vicente Aleixandre, a recent Nobel prize winner, and Hernández Gil. (The Cortes, however, subsequently decided that it would have been anachronistic to retain directly appointed royal senators.) Juan Carlos also appears to have favoured the survival of an up-dated Council of the Realm, on which he could rely for non-partisan advice.[24]

Quite exceptionally, clauses relating to the monarchy were directly inspired by La Zarzuela. It was thus at Juan Carlos's insistence that a clause was introduced forbidding those with a right to the throne from marrying without royal consent. In the final stages of the constitutional debate, however, this was slightly modified so that the king would not be able to deprive anyone of their rights without the approval of the Cortes.[25]

Juan Carlos not only kept a watchful eye over the constituent process but intervened when necessary to ensure a satisfactory outcome. In early March, irritated at the development of a tacit understanding between Fraga and the UCD representatives that allowed the latter to impose their views, Peces-Barba unexpectedly walked out of the seven-man drafting committee. The king subsequently approached González in the course of a dinner held in honour of the governor-general of Canada to ensure the Socialists did not exclude themselves from the process. Although Peces-Barba never returned to the committee, he did endorse the fruit of its labours. More importantly, in May 1978 Suárez reconsidered his overall strategy, opting for a far-reaching understanding with the PSOE, largely at the expense of AP.

Juan Carlos was equally concerned that the resulting constitution should prove acceptable to the more conservative sectors of Spanish society. Aware of the difficulties Fraga faced within his own party, many of whose leaders were reluctant to accept the constitutional text currently taking shape, in early March he invited him to La Zarzuela to discuss his misgivings. According to the conservative leader, at this point the king's concern was matched by his determination not to interfere in the debates, not even with regard to the definition of his future powers.[26]

The king's fears concerning the future of the monarchy were no doubt partly allayed by the results of the numerous opinion polls carried out on the institutional question during these months. According to a major study conducted at the government's request, at this stage 38 per cent of those questioned regarded the monarchy as the ideal form of government in the abstract, while 20 per cent preferred a republic and 30 per cent expressed indifference. Similarly, 38 per cent regarded the monarchy as being conducive to political stability, while only 15 per cent associated this quality with a republic. As to the type of regime they wished to see established in Spain, 44 per cent of those polled wanted a monarchy and only 16 per cent opted for a republic, while 18 per cent remained indifferent. Most significantly, perhaps, 36 per cent of those questioned approved wholeheartedly of Juan Carlos's performance to date and a further 35 per cent gave him their partial endorsement, while only 14 per cent disapproved outright. The PSOE leadership was no doubt quick to note that 45 per cent of respondents believed the monarchy to be compatible with a future Socialist government, a view still rejected by 27 per cent of those polled.[27]

Peces-Barba was not alone in thinking that the PSOE had gone far enough in defence of its republican heritage. At a press conference held in April 1978, Tierno Galván, recently appointed honorary president of the PSOE as a result of his own party's dissolution, argued in favour of dropping the republican amendment in the presence of Luis Gómez Llorente, the party spokesman responsible for defending it in Congress. The latter responded by explaining that the future of the amendment would depend on the government's response to his party's objections to the remainder of the constitutional text. The Socialists thereby admitted that the whole point of their amendment was not so much the need to legitimise the monarchy by democratic means but rather the fact that it represented a crucial card in their negotiations with the government.

The institutional question was finally debated in the Congress constitutional committee in early May 1978. By way of explaining the PCE's position, Carrillo attributed his party's traditional opposition to the monarchy to King Alfonso XIII's cohabitation with the Primo de Rivera dictatorship in the 1920s, since when the party had always defended the republican form of government even though the Second Republic had not always been grateful for this support. The Communist leader was brave enough to admit that unlike better informed – or more opportunistic – parties, the PCE had initially 'nourished not only reservations but even an evident hostility towards the figure of the head of state, which seemed an inheritance from the previous dictatorship'. However, during the transition the PCE had come to understand that Juan Carlos 'had learned to echo our democratic aspirations, and had assimilated the idea of a democratic parliamentary monarchy'. Carrillo acknowledged that the king had played a crucial role in the democratising process, acting as 'a hinge between the state apparatus and the profound democratic aspirations of civil society'. Indeed had it not been for him, 'the state apparatus and civil society would have clashed, and civil society itself would have been divided, with dramatic consequences for the peoples of Spain'. The Communists had therefore agreed that 'as long as the monarchy respects the constitution and popular sovereignty, we will respect the monarchy', and Carrillo concluded by reaffirming his faith in 'a young man who has shown us he identifies with the Spain of today rather than that of yesteryear'. Several weeks later Juan Carlos personally thanked Carrillo for these words, which amply compensated the difficulties he had faced in April 1977 as a result of his decision to legalise the PCE.[28]

The PSOE, on the other hand, justified its republican amendment in the light of the constituent nature of the Cortes, which entitled the democratic political forces to examine the merits and demerits of every major institution, including the monarchy. While reaffirming his party's preference for a republic, Gómez Llorente accepted that a parliamentary monarchy 'which respects popular sovereignty and the reformist aspirations of the majority of the people at any given time' was compatible with the PSOE's programme. It was also claimed that the PSOE was duty-bound to advocate a republic out of respect for its heritage and out of loyalty to its electorate, sectors of which had voted Socialist in 1977 because republican parties were not legalised until after the first elections. Another speaker, the Catalan Socialist Eduardo Martín Toval, argued that given the Spanish right's historical tendency to usurp the monarchy for its own ends, in order to 'save the current king from falling into the hands of undemocratic forces' it was necessary to strip him of the powers the latter might covet. This argument led him to conclude that 'today only a monarchy which is, so to speak, republican, can be regarded as legitimate by democrats'.[29]

The PSOE was by no means alone in its criticism of the monarchy. Heribert Barrera, sole representative of Esquerra Republicana, a leftist Catalan nationalist group, regretted that the institution had never been put to a referendum, and rejected the 1976 referendum on the Law for Political Reform as an acceptable substitute. The Catalan deputy did not deny Juan Carlos's contribution to the transition to democracy, but argued that it was impossible to know whether it would have been more difficult without him, a view few of those present could share. Barrera went on to compare the decision to constitutionalise the monarchy out of gratitude to the king to medieval legends in which gallant knights were rewarded for saving damsels in distress by being allowed to marry them. More seriously, he challenged Carrillo's assumption that there was still a need for a royal 'hinge' to prevent a conflict between the remnants of the Francoist state apparatus and civil society, and argued that although the armed forces would undoubtedly have resisted a republican coup, they would also have accepted the result of a popular vote on the institutional question.[30]

Francisco Letamendía, spokesman for Euskadiko Ezkerra, the most radical of the Basque parties represented in the Congress, was similarly outspoken in his opposition to the king and the monarchy. Letamendía acknowledged that 'contrary to what was initially feared, the king is not the monarch of fascism', but objected that Juan Carlos 'is the monarch of the Reform, and the Reform cannot heal the Basque country's wounds'.[31]

Acceptance of the monarchy by the more mainstream moderate Basque nationalists of the PNV was conditional on the institution's ability to contribute to the achievement of a satisfactory relationship between the Basque country and the rest of Spain. Encouraged by Herrero de Miñón, the PNV had warmed to the idea of reestablishing the Basque provinces' historic links with the Spanish monarchy by means of a special pact with the crown, sanctioned by the constitution. In practice this formula would have been not unlike the agreement that had paved the way for the return of the Generalitat to Catalonia, but the left rejected it on the grounds that it was anachronistic in the context of a late twentieth-century parliamentary monarchy. Sadly, the UCD failed to find an acceptable alternative, in view of which the PNV felt unable to endorse the new constitution.

The UCD and AP were thus the only parties to speak out in defence of the monarchy as an institution, as opposed to the king's performance during the transition. Fraga defended the institution on theoretical grounds, reminding his audience that in other European countries the monarchy had greatly facilitated 'the transition from a traditional community to a democratic society'. Speaking on behalf of the UCD, Pérez Llorca defended the monarchy as a rational solution to the problems posed by the existence of a head of state in a democratic political system, and was the only speaker to address the difficulties facing presidential republics by way of comparison. In a similar vein, the centrist Oscar Alzaga argued that it was preferable to speak of 'crowned democracies' rather than 'crowned republics', since, contrary to the left's assumptions, 'democracy' and 'republic' were not necessarily synonymous. Most importantly, Alzaga referred to the monarchy's unifying strength, which could prove decisive in inducing different peoples to live peacefully under the same constitutional roof.[32]

Much to the king's relief, on 11 May the PSOE's republican amendment was defeated in the Congress constitutional committee by 13 votes in favour, 22 against and one abstention. Shortly afterwards the committee adopted the clause stating that 'the political form of the Spanish state is that of a parliamentary monarchy' by 23 votes in favour and 14 abstentions. Significantly, once their amendment had been defeated the PSOE deputies preferred to abstain rather than vote against the monarchy.

With the republican amendment out of the way, in the last week of May Juan Carlos was free to invite González, Fraga and Rafael Arias Salgado (the UCD chairman) to La Zarzuela to question them about the remaining stages of the constitutional debate. Several days earlier Silva Muñoz, acting on behalf of AP in Fraga's absence, had walked out of the constitutional committee in protest at the behind-the-scenes talks involving the UCD and the PSOE, which would soon lead to a far-ranging consensus on major issues. Alarmed by this decision, Juan Carlos urged Fraga to return to the committee, to which the latter agreed.[33]

On leaving La Zarzuela, González had declared that the king was untroubled by the imminent discussion of his future powers by the Congress constitutional committee. Much of this debate was dominated by individual and group amendments aimed at raising the monarch's constitutional profile. López Rodó, who appears to have believed he was acting on the king's behalf, defended the creation of an advisory Council of the Crown, which was far too reminiscent of the Francoist Council of the Realm to prove acceptable to the left. (Significantly, the UCD did not come to AP's support but was presumably prevented from doing so by its overall agreement with the PSOE, rather than by prior knowledge of the king's wishes.) López Rodó had envisaged a six-man council, to include the most senior general in the armed forces, thereby allowing the military to have regular, institutionalised access to the monarch, which was precisely what the left sought to prevent.[34]

López Rodó was also in favour of granting the king special powers to meet exceptional circumstances in which the major political institutions could not function normally. In order to prevent the monarch from over-reaching himself, these powers would only be exercised in agreement with the head of government and the president of the Cortes. By way of reply, Peces-Barba argued that if, for example, either the Cortes or La Zarzuela fell under the control of hostile forces, it would be impossible to satisfy these requirements, in view of which it was best not to attempt to legislate in anticipation of a virtual *coup d'état*. Many observers were to remember this exchange in the light of the events of the night of 23 February 1981.

The articles pertaining to the king's powers were finally approved by the Congress constitutional committee on 30 May 1978. Several days earlier, over dinner with a group of journalists, the king had expressed satisfaction at the manner in which the constitutional debates had been conducted and, with hindsight, even appeared to welcome the PSOE's republican amendment, without which the monarchy would never have been put to a vote. According to some of those present, Juan Carlos would have been happy to hold a referendum on the monarchy, so confident was he of winning it, but had been advised against it by the government.[35]

Having been through the committee stage, the articles that referred to the monarchy were put to a full meeting of the Congress in July 1978, at which point only the Catalan nationalist Barrera defended a republican amendment to the text. On this occasion he argued that it was contradictory to expect the king, whom he regarded as the supreme representative of military interests, to be able to defend the constitution from interference by the armed forces. In his view, this vain hope was proof enough that Spain was not yet a democracy, since 'if we were really living in a democracy there would not be so many monarchists', a remark that prompted loud protests from fellow deputies. In spite of Barrera, the clause constitutionalising the monarchy was duly passed with 196 votes in favour (including those of the PCE), 115 abstentions (mainly those of the PSOE) and only 9 votes against.[36]

Shortly afterwards a major poll was published, according to which 56 per cent of those questioned favoured a parliamentary monarchy while 24 per cent were against. At this stage some 75 per cent of AP and UCD voters endorsed the clause recently adopted by the Congress, which was also true of 58 per cent and 31 per cent of PSOE and PCE voters respectively. In other words, while the Socialist leadership was acting broadly in keeping with its voters' wishes, its Communist counterparts were clearly running a significant risk by endorsing the monarchy in this manner.[37]

As the king had feared, not all parties could bring themselves to vote in favour of the complete constitutional text finally submitted to the Congress on 21 July. This was duly adopted with 258 votes in favour (including those of the PSOE), two against (those of Silva Muñoz and Letamendía) and 14 abstentions (including the rest of AP and Esquerra Republicana). The PNV, which had failed to convince others of the viability of a 'pact with the crown', expressed its dissatisfaction by staying away. As if to test Barrera's arguments, that same day ETA murdered a general and a lieutenant-colonel, forcing the joint chiefs of staff to issue a statement solemnly reaffirming the Army's loyalty to king and government alike.

Even before the adoption of the new constitution Juan Carlos was increasingly expected to behave like the sovereign of a parliamentary monarchy. In August 1978, when the government announced a forthcoming royal visit to Argentina, the PSOE and other groups opposed it on the grounds that it would only serve to legitimise the ruling military junta. The UCD government justified the visit with the argument that it would enable the monarch to apply pressure on General Videla and his colleagues and duly defeated a Socialist motion in the Congress' standing committee by 20 votes to 16. Although the visit went ahead as planned, the incident served to alert the king and the government that they were entering a new phase in which their actions would be subjected to ever-greater scrutiny.[38]

In view of the left's largely successful efforts to limit the monarch's powers as much as possible, when the constitution came under the scrutiny of the Senate in September a number of royal appointees, acting of their own accord, sought to reverse this trend, though to little avail. Osorio, for example, was of the opinion that the king should have the power to submit to a referendum controversial laws that had not been promulgated within the allotted time. This option was rejected with impatience by the UCD spokesman, who reminded him that Alfonso XIII had lost his throne precisely for opposing his parliament.

As far as the monarchy itself was concerned, the most important amendment adopted was undoubtedly that proposed by the veteran monarchist Satrústegui, which described Juan Carlos as 'the legitimate heir of the historic dynasty'. The purpose of this was to underline the fact that the monarchy was an age-old institution that pre-dated the constitution. Additionally, Satrústegui was anxious to remove all trace of the restored monarchy's Francoist origins and to emphasise the fact that Juan Carlos had inherited his right to the throne from Don Juan in May 1977. Ironically, this impeccably monarchist amendment amounted to an outright rejection of Francoist legitimacy and was therefore in contradiction with the constitutional strategy originally conceived by Fernández-Miranda, which had made the transition possible in legal terms. Not surprisingly perhaps, the king's former mentor, an increasingly rare visitor to La Zarzuela, chose to abstain when the monarchy was eventually put to the vote in the Senate.

Before this could happen, in late September 1978 Fraga and other AP leaders launched a campaign aimed at convincing the king of the need to appoint a government of supposedly non-partisan notables as soon as the constitution was adopted, and entrust them with the task of calling both local and general elections. This was justified on the grounds that Suárez had undoubtedly benefited from his association with the monarch in the 1977 elections and that, given the king's new constitutional status, it was important for him to be seen to be neutral. Juan Carlos, however, greatly resented being dragged into the political arena in this manner and refused to become involved. Other options briefly contemplated by some political actors in anticipation of future elections were a UCD–PSOE coalition, which the king opposed, and a UCD–AP coalition, which he knew to be inviable.[39]

The constitution was put to a final vote in the Cortes on 31 October 1978. In the Congress it passed with 325 votes in favour, 6 against (those of five AP deputies and Letamendía) and 14 abstentions (including those of 3 AP deputies, seven PNV deputies and Barrera). In the upper chamber 226 senators voted in favour, 5 against and 8 abstained. The three military senators appointed by the king were amongst those who voted against, while Fernández-Miranda and Marías stayed away altogether.

The king's satisfaction at the outcome of the constitutional debates was unexpectedly undermined on the eve of his departure to Mexico, Peru and Argentina. On the night of 16 November he was informed of the existence of a plan to storm La Moncloa palace while the cabinet was in session and force Suárez to appoint a government of 'national salvation' in his absence. The leaders of the so-called 'Galaxia operation', named after the Madrid cafeteria where it was conceived, police Captain Ricardo Sáenz de Ynestrillas and Lieutenant-Colonel Antonio Tejero of the Civil Guard, had hoped to enlist the support of Army and police units outraged by a recent wave of ETA killings. Satisfied that the coup attempt had been aborted, on 17 November Juan Carlos left for Mexico as planned.[40]

The king attached a great deal of importance to his Mexican visit. After the civil war, Mexico had welcomed thousands of Spanish political refugees, including leading Republican figures, and had consistently refused to recognise the Franco regime thereafter. By visiting the country, Juan Carlos was paying tribute to the Republican diaspora, and expressing his determination to achieve a genuine national reconciliation. Juan Carlos and Sofía insisted on meeting María Dolores Rivas, widow of the former president of the Second Republic, Manuel Azaña, who paid tribute to the king's role in restoring democracy and effectively acknowledged the legitimacy of the new regime. In turn, Juan Carlos assured her that 'your husband and you yourself, *Señora*, are as much part of the history of Spain as I am'.[41]

Though symbolically less important, the royal visit to Argentina later that month was also charged with political significance. Oreja vividly recalls the royal party's arrival in Buenos Aires, and in particular the head of the military junta's attempts to embrace the king warmly, and the latter's determination to prevent him from doing so. Juan Carlos later spoke out in favour of democracy and human rights at several functions presided by the military junta, in spite of the latter's evident displeasure. On one occasion the king outmanouvered his hosts by ordering his speech to be widely distributed beforehand. Additionally, Juan Carlos insisted on being allowed to meet leading members of the Argentine opposition and interceded on behalf of numerous political prisoners. This was the first of many overseas visits in which the king was able to make a significant contribution to the promotion of democracy.[42]

Intentionally or otherwise, these visits, which took place in the run-up to the referendum on the constitution, undoubtedly improved the king's standing amongst left-leaning Spaniards. With the exception of the PNV and radical nationalists in both Catalonia and the Basque country, the entire parliamentary spectrum, including AP, campaigned for a yes vote. On 6 December 1978, 67.7 per cent of the population voted, of whom 87.7 per cent endorsed the constitution; as had been feared, however, the abstention rate was highest in the Basque provinces, where it reached 53 per cent. As in 1976, the king and his family lent the referendum their personal support by turning out to vote. Both at home and abroad, the adoption of a new democratic constitution was seen as a great personal triumph for Juan Carlos, who was enthusiastically congratulated by President Jimmy Carter, the ubiquitous Giscard d'Estaing, Italian President Sandro Pertini, who was to become a close friend, and Chancellor Schmidt, amongst many others. Shortly thereafter Juan Carlos was nominated for the Nobel Peace Prize on account of his contribution to Spain's successful transition to democracy.

In recognition of their efforts to draw up a constitution that was acceptable to the vast majority of Spaniards, Juan Carlos invited the executives of the major political parties to a special audience at La Zarzuela. In effect, the visit by the PSOE delegation on 12 December 1978, the first of its kind in Spanish history, marked the party's formal acceptance of the new monarchy.[43] The Socialists expressed the hope that the king would

take an oath of obedience to the new constitution, as the latter required of
future monarchs, but it was eventually decided he would merely sanction
it. The PSOE had opposed this formula on the grounds that it amounted
to a recognition of Juan Carlos's proclamation as king of Spain in 1975,
and hence of Francoist legality.[44]

On 27 December 1978 the king formally sanctioned the text in the
presence of the Cortes. Juan Carlos assured his audience that 'as it is
the constitution of all and for all, it is also the constitution of the king of
all Spaniards', and promised to 'abide by and serve it'. Significantly, he
referred in passing to his proclamation speech, no doubt so as to remind
those present that he had been king of Spain since 22 November 1975. On
this occasion only the PNV deputies failed to join in the enthusiastic
applause that greeted the king's arrival and departure.[45]

The adoption of the 1978 constitution marked the end of a process
initiated by Juan Carlos shortly after his proclamation as king of Spain,
whereby he gradually shed the powers ascribed to him by the Francoist
fundamental laws in order to become a Western-style constitutional monarch. In theory at least, by early 1979 his powers were not unlike those of
the Queen of England. In practice, however, his influence remained far
greater, due to both the importance of his role in recent political events
and the need to consolidate Spain's fledgling democracy.

8 Consolidating – and Defending – Democracy

During the next few years the king was to make a substantial contribution to the consolidation of the democratic system he had done so much to bring about. Above all, he would play a decisive role in inducing the armed forces to accept some of the more visible consequences of the change of regime, and in particular the process of decentralisation that was to lead to the creation of a semi-federal state. Unfortunately this process was accompanied by an escalation of terrorist violence largely aimed at provoking the armed forces into some form of military intervention, which eventually took place in February 1981.

Juan Carlos also played an important role in the strictly civilian political sphere. Contrary to what many had expected, the UCD, a party hastily assembled in early 1977 in an ad hoc fashion, was to remain in power until late 1982. This proved discouraging both to the left, which had made substantial sacrifices for the sake of a widely accepted constitution, and to the right, whose enthusiasm for the latter was initially lukewarm. Juan Carlos took it upon himself to integrate these forces within the newly erected democratic system, encouraging them to contribute to the overall process of consolidation. Additionally, he strove to make the increasingly important peripheral nationalist parties aware of their stake in the success of Spanish democracy as a whole.

ETA wasted no time in seeking to destabilise the new constitutional system. In early January 1979 the organisation killed an Army major in Vizcaya and the military governor of Madrid, General Constantino Ortín. At the latter's funeral, dozens of Army officers hurled abuse at Defence Minister Gutiérrez Mellado, who presided the ceremony, and later disobeyed orders by marching to the cemetery with Ortín's coffin on their shoulders. Alarmed by this act of collective insubordination, Juan Carlos used unusually harsh language in his *pascua militar* speech, openly expressing his disgust at these events. At the same time he referred to the recent decision to bring the three services under a new Ministry of Defence, and praised Gutiérrez Mellado's role in this major undertaking, while acknowledging the difficulties it would pose to all those concerned. Significantly, the monarch did not miss this opportunity to remind fellow officers that the new constitution made the government responsible for military administration and the defence of the state, and explicitly mentioned the role of the Cortes in supervising these major changes.[1]

Once the constitution was adopted, Suárez could either call fresh elections or seek his confirmation from the existing Cortes. The king appears to have favoured the former course of action, as it allowed the prime minister to obtain a fresh mandate. Suárez duly announced the dissolution of the (*de facto*) constituent Cortes on 29 December and called general elections for 1 March 1979. Contrary to what many had anticipated, the results were virtually identical to those of 1977, in view of which there was no doubt as to who would be invited to form the first constitutional government of the new parliamentary monarchy. In spite of this, before proposing Suárez's candidature the king saw the representatives of all parties represented in the Cortes, with the sole exception of Herri Batasuna, the Basque equivalent of Sinn Fein, which turned down his invitation. Amongst those who officially visited the king for the first time were the Catalan nationalist Pujol and the PNV leader Carlos Garaicoechea, as well as Euskadiko Ezkerra's Juan María Bandrés and the neofascist Blas Piñar. One of the monarchy's most outspoken critics during the constitutional debates, Barrera, also made his way to La Zarzuela, though not before having been driven to the theatre of the same name by mistake by a novice taxi driver. In all Juan Carlos saw a total of fourteen party representatives, a figure that aptly reflected the complexities of Spanish political life.

The king was soon made aware of the difficulties inherent in exercising his newly acquired powers of moderation and arbitration. The PSOE favoured postponing Suárez's investiture until after the first democratic local elections, scheduled for 3 April 1979, on the grounds that the UCD would otherwise benefit from the additional media attention. Juan Carlos could have satisfied this demand by waiting several days before submitting a name to the Cortes, but given that there was only one viable candidate, such a delay would have been unjustified, and Suárez was duly invested on 30 March, in spite of the proximity of the local elections.

One of the unforeseen consequences of the PSOE's defeat in the 1979 elections, and one that Juan Carlos no doubt welcomed, was González's move to reverse his party's decision to define itself as Marxist, adopted at the 1976 conference. Surprisingly, the PSOE conference held in May 1979 refused to comply with his wishes, in view of which he stood down as secretary-general, depriving the party of its most valuable asset. The king had long since concluded that the consolidation of democracy – and hence the monarchy – necessitated the presence of a moderate Socialist party, and was greatly alarmed by these developments. Four months later, however, González – or Felipe, as he was almost universally known – bounced back to power on his own terms.

Juan Carlos attached special significance to the formal opening of the first Cortes elected in keeping with the new constitution, held on 10 May 1979. In his speech he spoke of the need to strike a reasonable balance between the past and the future, and urged the political class to safeguard 'that which is permanent and indisputable in the legacy of our nation's history', while at the same time satisfying 'the need to renew, modernise and protect the rights and wishes which our people are requesting with tenacity'. This ability to combine elements of both continuity and change was to become a hallmark of Juan Carlos's official statements.[2]

While the king sought to consolidate the newly established democratic system, others did their best to disrupt it. In mid-April Juan Carlos was forced to bring his authority to bear on senior members of the armed forces, who reacted badly to the appointment of José Gabeiras as chief of the Army General Staff. The logical candidates by seniority were two generals notorious for their Francoist leanings, Jesús González del Yerro and Milans del Bosch.[3] By way of revenge, a military court in Milans' jurisdiction acquitted General Juan Atarés, who was accused of having shouted abuse at Gutiérrez Mellado at a meeting held in Cartagena in November 1978, attended by several hundred officers and men. Later that month, at a ceremony held at the General Staff, Juan Carlos once again underlined the importance of accepting decisions adopted with the support of the majority of the population. Shortly afterwards, on 25 May, the eve of the Armed Forces Day, ETA murdered Lieutenant-General Luis Gómez Hortiguela, together with two colonels and a driver. To cap it all, the following day the mysterious left-wing terrorist organisation GRAPO detonated a bomb in a popular Madrid cafeteria, 'California 47', killing eight people. During the military celebrations presided by Juan Carlos in Seville that day, hard-line right-wingers heckled the head of state with total impunity.

It was against this backdrop that the Suárez government began to negotiate the Catalan and Basque statutes of autonomy. In Catalonia, the restoration of the Generalitat and the absence of terrorist activity facilitated the negotiation between the provisional Catalan government and Madrid. Negotiations between the Suárez government and the Basque parties posed far greater difficulties, but an agreement was eventually reached in July 1979. Juan Carlos had hoped to ease the tension by travelling to the region himself, but was discouraged from doing so until after the statute had been approved.

As far as the more intransigent sectors of the armed forces were concerned, the statutes of autonomy negotiated by the Suárez government merely confirmed the fears raised a year earlier by the introduction of the term *nacionalidades* in the constitution and marked the beginning of the

end of Spanish national unity. To make matters worse, ETA proved relent-
less in its efforts to provoke a military backlash. Thus on 20 September
they murdered a colonel and a major in Bilbao, killing the military governor of Guipúzcoa three days later. These events led a number of senior
officers to plan yet another unsuccessful occupation of La Moncloa on
the eve of the referenda on the Catalan and Basque statutes of autonomy,
held on 25 October 1979.

Juan Carlos followed these developments very closely and did his best
to diffuse pent-up tension in military circles. In an attempt to rekindle his
personal loyalty, the king granted General Milans del Bosch a private
audience in November and later met a large group of officers from the
Army's crack Brunete armoured division stationed outside Madrid. Its
commander, General Luis Torres Rojas (who was later transferred from
the division on account of his role in the recent conspiracy), spoke for
them all when he expressed outrage and impotence at the stream of ETA
killings. Not for the first time, Juan Carlos insisted that they should face
the crisis in unity and discipline.

In view of the political climate, the king sought to reassure the more
conservative sectors of Spanish society in his traditional Christmas Eve
address. Aware of the fears raised by the recently approved statutes, Juan
Carlos solemnly declared that 'we are Spaniards – Spaniards from all the
regions of our *Patria* – and must feel the pride of being such'. He went
on to chide those who seemed obsessed with the country's recent past,
either out of nostalgia or hatred, and condemned the former's attempts to
resuscitate that which no longer existed and the latter's efforts to erase all
trace of it. Weeks later, in his January 1980 *pascua militar* speech, Juan
Carlos reiterated this defence of Spanish national unity as well as his call
for military discipline.[4]

Echoes of these words were to reverberate in mess rooms throughout
the country in the ensuing months. In early January 1980 the new head of
the Army, General Gabeiras, sought to reassure an increasingly uneasy
civilian population that 'nobody must think of us that we pose a threat to
liberty, because there is no reason for it'. The following month Spain's
first civilian defence minister since Franco's death, Agustín Rodríguez
Sahagún, visited the Brunete armoured division, and assured its officers
that nobody would tolerate the dismemberment of Spain, a nation 'forged
over the centuries by God and the will of our forebears'. In March an
Italian newspaper conveniently carried an interview with Juan Carlos, which
was widely reproduced in Spain, in which he attributed the success of the
transition process to the unity of the armed forces. In the interview the
king reminisced about his hurried visit to the troops stationed in the Sahara

in November 1975, only to conclude that 'from then on, the Army has always had confidence in me'.[5]

Military unrest was only one of many problems facing the Suárez government. In particular, the latter appeared to have lost control of the devolution process. The 1978 constitution envisaged 'fast' and 'slow' routes to regional autonomy, the first of which was originally intended for the 'historic' regions, namely Catalonia, the Basque country and Galicia. Andalusian institutions, however, unexpectedly opted for the 'fast' route, which necessitated the calling of a referendum in late February 1980. Anxious to deter other regions from following suit, the government urged voters to abstain, advice that went largely unheeded. To make matters worse, in March 1980 UCD came fourth and fifth in the first Catalan and Basque regional elections respectively. In an attempt to compensate for the government's increasingly strained relations with peripheral nationalists, in a rapid succession of audiences Juan Carlos met the presidents of the newly elected Catalan and Basque governments, Pujol and Garaicoechea, as well as representatives from Andalusia and Navarre. Not for the first time, it was the king's presence that prevented centre–periphery tensions from reaching breaking point.

During these months it was increasingly felt that Suárez had lost his sense of direction, and was allowing his government to drift. Anxious to hear the opposition's views, in April Juan Carlos invited González and Fraga to La Zarzuela. The Socialist leader subsequently declared that the king was anxious to exercise his powers of arbitration and moderation, which were clear in theory but needed careful definition in practice. González complained to the king of Suárez's tendency to behave like a head of state instead of a head of government, delegating the day-to-day running of the country on his deputy premier, Fernando Abril Martorell, a habit that was undermining confidence in the major democratic institutions. Fraga, whose political influence was far greater than his paltry nine seats in Congress suggested, adopted an even more alarmist tone, warning the king of an imminent crisis of the newly established democratic system, for which Suárez alone would be held responsible. In June Juan Carlos held a similar meeting with Carrillo, who advocated some form of coalition government as the only solution to the conundrum.[6]

In the late 1970s the Spanish economy, which had recovered somewhat in the wake of the all-party Moncloa Pacts of late 1977, had gone into recession as a result of the second world oil crisis. This resulted in high inflation and rapidly growing unemployment, which greatly undermined confidence in Suárez and his government. The PSOE sought to exploit this by presenting a motion of censure in late May 1980, which the government narrowly survived thanks to the abstention of Fraga's conservatives and Pujol's nationalists. Juan Carlos was apparently very pleased by the interest with which this parliamentary debate was followed by the average Spaniard, which he read as evidence of the consolidation of the country's major democratic institutions. Additionally, the king hoped that a challenge from the Socialists would force Suárez to seek a stable majority in the Cortes and pay closer attention to public opinion at large.[7]

Juan Carlos listened carefully to leading political figures who warned their countrymen of an imminent political crisis. In May 1980 the former president of the Generalitat, Tarradellas, publicly declared that unless there was a '*golpe de timón*' (change of tack), only an iron surgeon would be able to provide the necessary solutions. The following month his own father, Don Juan, broke a three-year silence to express his concern at what he saw as the excesses committed by peripheral nationalists. Needless to say his remarks reminded some observers of the philosopher José Ortega y Gasset's famous '*no es esto, no es esto*' (this [the Republic] is not it), prompted by the radicalisation of the Second Republic.[8]

These warnings failed to impress the ruling party, however. In early July a group of leading UCD figures met at a country house near Madrid to discuss Suárez's leadership, and narrowly agreed to renew their support. Later that month however, Abril Martorell, Suárez's most trusted cabinet minister since the 1977 elections, resigned from the government. It was at this point that rumours first began to circulate concerning the possible formation of a caretaker government presided by a senior military man, supposedly with the king's blessing.

Suárez briefly appeared to regain his self-confidence in September 1980, when he formed a government that included many of his critics within the UCD leadership. The change of government, however, merely deepened the internal rift that had already emerged in UCD on account of the future divorce law. Shortly afterwards the prime minister sought a vote of confidence from the Cortes, which he narrowly obtained with the support of Pujol's nationalists and the Andalusian Socialist Party, a rival of the PSOE. This was to be Suárez's last victory in the Cortes.

Throughout the autumn of 1980 La Zarzuela continued to gather evidence of mounting military unrest. Shortly before the summer recess the Cortes had begun to debate a bill whereby former members of the anti-Francoist UMD, dismantled by Milans del Bosch in 1975, would be allowed to return to the armed forces. An earlier bill had contemplated putting an end to the military status of the Civil Guard, hitherto led by Army officers. Juan Carlos was duly informed of the indignation with which these proposals were greeted in military circles, and received numerous reports from senior Army officers listing their complaints. On the whole the king 'listened to them carefully, and when their arguments struck me as departing too far from reality I tried to make them see reason. But I also made it clear that in no case could they count on me to cover up for the slightest action against a constitutional government like our own'.[9]

In view of the UCD's evident weakness, the PSOE leadership decided to test the waters of military opinion in anticipation of a general election they hoped to win. It was thus that two prominent Socialists, Reventós and Múgica, sat down to lunch with General Armada, the former secretary-general of the royal household and current military governor of Lérida, on 22 October 1980. Armada was extremely critical of the Suárez government, and is said to have discussed the formation of a broad-based emergency coalition government led by an independent figure, possibly a general. Prominent PSOE figures also canvassed leading Basque and Catalan nationalists, amongst them Pujol, in an attempt to learn whether they would find such a solution acceptable, though to little avail. Similarly, a number of prominent UCD dissidents raised this possibility with members of other parties, as did the Communist leader Ramón Tamames, who was immediately disowned by Carrillo. The idea that only a 'De Gaulle-style operation' could forestall a violent coup and the establishment of a military junta gradually gained ground in civilian circles.[10]

In view of the growing tension, Juan Carlos repeated his round of talks with major party leaders. Earlier, Fraga had written to him expressing his 'very grave concern at the rapid deterioration of the situation', as well as his belief that the king should intervene to prevent 'a crisis of institutional and historical transcendence'. In late November the conservative leader openly discussed the rumours of a military coup with the king and advocated a UCD–AP coalition government as the only antidote to chaos. In December Juan Carlos saw González, who was reluctant to come to Suárez's assistance, and Carrillo, who once again defended the need for an all-party government of 'national salvation'. At these meetings Juan Carlos made it abundantly clear that he was not contemplating extra-constitutional solutions. Indeed in his last major interview before the coup with the writer Jorge Semprún, the king reiterated his determination to uphold the constitution. Juan Carlos also admitted having resisted requests to use the Army in the Basque country, on the grounds that 'it is very easy to call out the troops, but much harder to return them to their barracks'.[11]

Many Spaniards only became aware of the seriousness of the situation on hearing the king's traditional Christmas Eve address. In marked contrast with previous occasions, which had been characterised by their informal, almost festive atmosphere, Juan Carlos appeared without his family, sitting at his desk in his office at La Zarzuela. In his brief exhortation, an unusually grave Juan Carlos urged those in government and in opposition, as well as the major institutions of the state, to put 'the defence of democracy or the well-being of Spain above transient personal, group or party interests' and encouraged them to 'protect and consolidate that which is essential lest we should wish to deprive ourselves of the basis or occasion to implement that which is accessory'.[12]

Without exception, since Franco's death the Spanish royal family had spent at least part of their Christmas holidays skiing at the Catalan resort of Baqueira Beret. It was there that the king and his prime minister held a crucial interview in late December 1980. Juan Carlos warned Suárez of the very real possibility of a military coup, and urged him to do everything in his power not to provide the conspirators with fresh motives for proceeding with their plans. Suárez had contemplated the possibility of calling early elections, but all the polls conducted at his request predicted a sweeping Socialist victory, which he feared would trigger precisely the type of military response they sought to avoid. Given his refusal to form a coalition government with any of the opposition parties, this left only one option, namely his replacement by another UCD leader.[13]

Given that Baqueira Beret was in the province of Lérida, nobody expressed surprise when Armada, its military governor, paid the monarchs a courtesy visit on 3 January, as he had done on many previous occasions. Earlier the general had sent the king a detailed report, via Fernández Campo, the secretary-general of the royal household, which analysed the political crisis and proposed possible solutions. A week later Armada saw Milans del Bosch in Valencia and told him of his conversation with the monarch. The captain-general – who had not seen Juan Carlos since January 1980 – would later claim to have been assured that the king favoured extraordinary measures to overcome the current crisis and that, in the event of a coup, he would agree to 'redirect' it. Milans also specified that, according to Armada, the king wanted a new civilian government, while the queen had expressed support for a military junta. Given the outcome of Constantine's disastrous experience with the Greek military, it is patently clear that one or both of the generals was lying.[14]

The *pascua militar* celebrations of January 1981 thus took place at a time of unprecedented military unrest. As on previous occasions, Juan Carlos strongly condemned the mindless acts of terrorism that so obsessed the armed forces and expressed his full sympathy and support. (In 1980 alone there had been 124 victims of terrorism in Spain, a figure never equalled before or since.) This time, however, he explicitly referred to the existence of limits beyond which the enemies of Spanish democracy would not be allowed to go. It was also the king's hope that 'if you remain united, fully committed to your profession, respectful of the constitutional norms on which our democratic state is based, and if you retain your trust and confidence in your superiors and your commander-in-chief, together we shall succeed in overcoming the difficulties inherent in any transition process'.[15]

Aware of Armada's growing influence, Juan Carlos sought his appointment as deputy Army chief of staff, presumably so as to have him under closer watch in Madrid. Neither Suárez nor Gutiérrez Mellado were in favour of this promotion, and on 22 January the king and the prime minister had a heated exchange of views on the matter, which did little to improve their already somewhat strained relations.[16]

By this stage Suárez had lost all hope of reestablishing his personal authority within the UCD and on 26 January he informed his inner cabinet of his decision to resign. That same day Ricardo de la Cierva, who had until recently been Suárez's minister of culture, found the king deeply concerned about the divisions within the ruling party, which he feared would lead to a major political crisis long before the elections scheduled for 1983. Although he appeared to have lost much of his former faith in Suárez, he nevertheless continued to support him, and seemed to have no inkling of what awaited him. The prime minister did not inform the king of his plans until the following day, in the course of a five-hour interview at La Zarzuela, their longest ever. Relations between them had soured to the extent that Suárez informed Fernández Campo before seeing Juan Carlos so that the latter would be unable to take credit for his resignation. This was also the reason why he had let some of his ministers in on the secret before going to La Zarzuela. In Suárez's own words, it was his duty to 'protect the king even from the king himself'.[17]

The king had already announced his first official visit to the Basque country in early February, as well as a meeting with Ronald Reagan, which would have made him the first European head of state to meet the new American president, and did not conceal his irritation at having to revise his plans. According to Suárez, Juan Carlos begged him to reconsider and encouraged him to appeal to his voters over the heads of his party leadership if necessary, but to no avail. Other sources claim that the king did not plead very hard and lost no time in consulting Fernández Campo as to how they should proceed with the appointment of a successor, a reaction Suárez found deeply offensive. It was during this meeting that Juan Carlos promised him a dukedom, an offer he subsequently judged excessive and which only Suárez's persistence prevented him from withdrawing.[18]

On 29 January, after consulting his text with the royal household, Suárez addressed the nation on television. The latter explained that he was resigning 'without anyone having asked me to do so', and in spite of 'the request [presumably, that of Juan Carlos] and the pressures for me to remain at my post'. Somewhat enigmatically, he went on to explain that the continuity of the task he had set himself was best assured by others, only to conclude that 'I do not wish the democratic system we have all desired to be yet another parenthesis in the history of Spain'. Since then, Suárez has consistently denied having bowed to military pressure, attributing his resignation to his difficulties with his own party. At the time, many observers believed that the monarch had not gone out of his way to retain him, a suspicion fuelled by Suárez's own solemn reaffirmation of loyalty to the crown in his farewell speech. While admitting that 'I was accused of letting Adolfo down', Juan Carlos has argued that 'such accusations disregarded the part which it is proper for the king to play in a parliamentary regime. I had no powers to impose a political solution of my own liking'.[19]

In spite of the uncertainty caused by Suárez's resignation, the king chose not to cancel or postpone his long-awaited visit to the Basque country. On 4 February Juan Carlos and Sofía landed at Vitoria, where they were greeted without enthusiasm, rapidly moving on to a somewhat warmer reception in Bilbao. The following day, in what was seen as the high-point of the visit, the king was due to address a gathering of members of the Basque parliament and provincial councils assembled at the Casa de Juntas in Guernica, the town traditionally associated with Basque freedoms. As soon as he began to read his speech, Juan Carlos was interrupted by several dozen members of Herri Batasuna who clenched their fists at him while singing the *Eusko gudariak*, or Basque soldier's hymn. The king, who had anticipated trouble, remained calm, and even put a cupped hand to his ear, as if to encourage them to sing louder. Once the hecklers were removed, and before continuing with his speech, Juan Carlos solemnly reaffirmed his faith in democracy and the Basque people, even in the face of 'those who practice intolerance, scorn our efforts to live in peace, and have no respect for institutions or the basic rules regulating freedom of expression'.[20]

The royal visit to the Basque country was accompanied by a proliferation of hostile graffitti, notably in the most nationalist of the three provinces, Guipúzcoa. In its wake, Herri Batasuna claimed that the king's protection had required even more policemen than used to be necessary when Franco visited the region, and with a similar impact on the local community. The extreme right, for their part, read the Guernica incident as an outrage to Spain, and an insult to the commander-in-chief of the armed forces. However, at a subsequent meeting with the Basque socialist leader José María Benegas, Juan Carlos seemed pleased with this first attempt to win over Basque minds and hearts *in situ*.

In the wake of Suárez's resignation the king was increasingly seen as the guarantor of the democratic system, and the monarchy acquired an unusually high profile. In late January Tarradellas took part in the presentation of a new book about Juan Carlos, using this opportunity to underline the importance of his role in the democratising process. Several weeks later, state-owned television showed a highly complimentary BBC documentary on the king of Spain. In the course of this interview, Juan Carlos ruled out the possibility of a military coup and reiterated his determination to uphold the constitution. Shortly afterwards both *Newsweek* and *L'Express* dedicated their cover stories to the king. According to one senior journalist, all of this was part of a carefully orchestrated campaign aimed at filling the power vacuum left by Suárez's departure.[21]

The premier's resignation provided Juan Carlos with a unique opportunity to exercise his powers of arbitration. The situation was novel in that a new head of government had to be appointed without there having been a general election. To complicate matters, the UCD's second party conference, due to have been held in late January in Majorca, was postponed for a fortnight on account of an air traffic controllers' strike. In view of this, after consulting the leaders of the major parties, Juan Carlos decided to wait for the UCD to elect a new candidate before proposing him to the Cortes. When Fraga saw him on 30 January he obtained the impression that the king 'was not in a hurry, taking nothing for granted', and that on this occasion his consultations were more than a mere formality.[22]

The absence of a prime minister and the UCD's inability to provide a sense of direction fuelled fresh speculation in anticipation of a royal decision to form a caretaker government presided by a senior general. On 31 January a prominent journalist, Emilio Romero, openly stated what many had been whispering in private, by declaring Armada the ideal candidate. Several days later it was announced that the general was to be made deputy Army chief of staff, in spite of Suárez's opposition. Shortly after the latter's resignation, Defence Minister Rodríguez Sahagún had finally agreed to his appointment at the insistence of General Gabeiras, who thereby hoped to ingratiate himself with the king.[23]

The king and Armada met on a number of occasions on the eve of the attempted coup. Juan Carlos telephoned the general to congratulate him on his imminent appointment on 3 February and invited him to Baqueira three days later. Armada subsequently claimed they were unable to discuss political matters because shortly after his arrival the queen was informed that her mother had been taken seriously ill in Madrid. Following Queen Frederica's death, in the course of the Greek orthodox funeral held in her honour on 11 February, Juan Carlos told Armada that he needed to see him urgently. Two days later they had a long talk at La Zarzuela, after which the king asked him to see Gutiérrez Mellado. According to the latter, Armada showed little interest in strictly military matters, but seemed obsessed with 'other issues which affect our *Patria*, and in particular his majesty the king'. The general informed him that the latter's prestige within the Army was at its lowest level since his proclamation and was highly critical of both the recent BBC documentary and the visit to the Basque country. According to Gutiérrez Mellado, he gave such a display of monarchist feeling that 'I came to believe that, in order to save the crown as he saw it, he might even accept solutions contrary to the best interests of his majesty'.[24]

The death of Queen Frederica in Madrid on 6 February 1981 provided Juan Carlos and Sofía with fresh food for thought. Partly as a result of the pressure applied by the Spanish royal family, the Greek authorities allowed the exiled King Constantine to enter his country for the first time since 1967 in order to attend his mother's funeral. The contrast between the almost clandestine arrival of the deposed monarch and that of Juan Carlos, who was greeted with full military honours, could not have been more eloquent. What was more, the funeral, held at the former royal residence of Tatoi where Sofía had lived as a child, was on the verge of being taken over by far-right demonstrators. As a number of observers were quick to point out, the essential difference between the two monarchs was that Juan Carlos had been a staunch defender of popular sovereignty and had consistently refused to bow to military pressure, however intense.

The UCD party conference duly elected Calvo Sotelo as its new leader, enabling Juan Carlos to propose him to the Cortes on 10 February. In his speech the future prime minister announced that the transition was over and looked forward to a new era, in which constitutional mechanisms would be able to function 'free of any foundational emotion', an obvious reference to the king's special relationship with Suárez. On 20 February Calvo Sotelo failed to obtain the 176 votes he required for his investiture as head of government, in view of which a second meeting of the Congress became necessary.

In the early evening of 23 February 1981, Juan Carlos was getting ready to play squash with his friend Ignacio Caro when an aide informed him that Lieutenant-Colonel Tejero had burst into the Congress with several hundred Civil Guards in the midst of the voting for Calvo Sotelo's investiture. Some twenty minutes later news reached La Zarzuela that Milans del Bosch had decreed a state of emergency in the Valencia military region and that tanks were patrolling the streets of the Mediterranean city. The captain-general also issued a manifesto, modelled on Franco's *pronunciamiento* of 18 July 1936, banning political parties and trade unions. Additionally, a number of units from the Brunete armoured division stationed near Madrid had begun to occupy key locations in the capital, including the headquarters of the state-owned television and leading radio stations.

By the time Caro arrived at La Zarzuela for his squash match, the king was busy giving precise orders that were obeyed without hesitation. His first priority was to inform the military hierarchy that, contrary to the impression intentionally created by Milans and others, the coup did not enjoy his support. Juan Carlos was greatly assisted in this task by the key members of his staff, all of whom were Army officers. It was thus Mondéjar, a cavalry general, who convinced a fellow cavalry officer to leave television headquarters and return to his barracks, while Lieutenant-General Joaquín Valenzuela, head of the king's military household, was crucial in guaranteeing the loyalty of the parachute regiment stationed outside Madrid. Fernández Campo, for his part, acted as a buffer between the king and the rebels.

Amongst the first to be informed of the king's determination to uphold the constitution was the president of the four-man junta of chiefs-of-staff (or JUJEM, in Spanish military jargon), Lieutenant-General Ignacio Alfaro Arregui, who proceeded to relay the message throughout the armed forces. Alfaro had intended to issue a statement promising to restore order, but the king disallowed it out of fear of creating the impression that the military were fully in command. Given that the out-going government was being held hostage in the Congress, it was essential to have an alternative civilian structure capable of acting on its behalf. Juan Carlos therefore encouraged the creation of a parallel government, formed by the secretaries and undersecretaries of state of the key ministries, and chaired by Francisco Laína, of the Ministry of the Interior. 'One of my chief concerns during those dramatic hours', the king would later recall, 'was to be scrupulously careful in preserving democratic legality'. In practice, however, Laína did not move a finger without consulting him.[25]

Ironically it was the officers of the Brunete division who accidentally provided the king with the vital clue as to the true nature of the plot. In the absence of their commander, General José Juste, several senior officers had prepared their vehicles for an advance on Madrid. When Juste returned, this was justified on the grounds that Milans and Armada, allegedly with the king's approval, were taking steps in anticipation of momentous events at the Cortes. In order to overcome his reticence, his subordinates made the fatal mistake of encouraging him to telephone Fernández Campo, who promptly confirmed that Armada 'is not here, nor do we expect him'. It was only then that Juste called the captain-general of the Madrid region, Guillermo Quintana Lacacci, who ordered him to recall the units which were already heading towards the capital. Juste's enquiry aroused the suspicions of Fernández Campo, who rushed to inform Juan Carlos, only to find him speaking to Armada on another telephone. The latter had offered to go to La Zarzuela to assist the king but was immediately forbidden to do so. (Armada would later claim his offer had been prompted by the memory of an earlier crisis, that of Carrero Blanco's assassination, which he had spent at Juan Carlos's side). It was thus that the king and his entourage first became aware of Armada's involvement in the uprising. Presumably, once inside La Zarzuela, he would have volunteered to contact the captain-generals on Juan Carlos's behalf. Had he been allowed to do so, it would have been extremely difficult to convince others that the king was not in on the plot as well.[26]

In spite of Tejero's reputation as a hot-head, Juan Carlos tried to reason with him through Fernández Campo, but it soon became apparent that he would only obey Milans del Bosch. Shortly before eight that evening, the king called the captain-general of Valencia, who claimed he had brought out his troops to save the monarchy, in spite of which he refused to obey his orders. Instead, this supposedly monarchist general *par excellence* sought the support of the colonel commanding the region's major air base, a former fellow cadet of the king's, who turned him down and informed La Zarzuela instead.[27]

In the course of the evening, Juan Carlos sought to confirm the loyalty of the other ten captain-generals, most of whom were unequivocally against the coup from the outset. Several, however, were reluctant to speak to the king and were to remain in frequent communication with Milans throughout the night. The captain-general of the Canaries, González del Yerro, a reactionary who nevertheless opposed Milans' leadership, is said to have told Juan Carlos: 'I will obey your majesty's orders . . . but what a pity!'[28]

In the government's absence, it was left to La Zarzuela to inform and reassure civil authorities throughout Spain, as well as party activists, trade unionists, and foreign diplomats and their governments. Amongst the heads of state who called with words of encouragement were Presidents Giscard d'Estaing and Pertini, as well as King Baudouin of Belgium, King Hassan of Morocco, King Hussein of Jordan and Queen Elizabeth. (Much to Juan Carlos's disappointment, there was no word from Washington.) The king also spoke to the presidents of the Catalan and Basque governments, Pujol and Garaicoechea, to reassure them that the situation was under control. Pujol immediately informed journalists of this conversation – 'relax, Jordi, relax', Juan Carlos had told him – thereby revealing that La Zarzuela had not been overrun as well. It goes without saying that had the king been unable to communicate freely with the outside world, the outcome of the coup could have been very different indeed. The fact that those involved never even contemplated the possibility of controlling his movements is in itself highly revealing of their confidence in Armada's ability to win him over to their cause.[29]

By early evening an impasse had been reached in that, although Tejero still controlled the Congress, none of the other captain-generals had joined Milans. Shortly after nine Juan Carlos ordered Gabeiras, who had been with the other members of the JUJEM since shortly after Tejero's entry, to return to Army headquarters to keep an eye on Armada. On his arrival the latter informed him that, in view of the magnitude of the crisis, the only viable solution was an all-party emergency government presided by himself. At Gabeiras' insistence Armada repeated his suggestion to the king, who forbade him to put any such proposal to the Congress. Armada insisted and once again requested permission to go to La Zarzuela, in view of which Juan Carlos passed the call over to Fernández Campo. The latter was particularly struck by Armada's confidence in his ability to convince the deputies to vote his investiture, in spite of their being held at gun-point.

Since Tejero refused to take orders other than from Milans and Armada, the king eventually allowed the latter to go to the Congress, but only on the understanding that he would not invoke his name. Armada hoped to submit the creation of an all-party government to the deputies and offered Tejero and his men a plane in which to leave the country. Outraged by this proposal, the lieutenant-colonel ordered him to leave the building. The only solution acceptable to the fiery Civil Guard was a military junta led by Milans del Bosch.

From the outset Juan Carlos had been aware of the importance of reassuring public opinion as to his own intentions, but was initially prevented from doing so by the presence of rebel troops at television headquarters. These were not withdrawn until well after nine, and it was almost eleven before a television crew finally reached La Zarzuela. The king's message was recorded shortly after midnight and finally went on the air at precisely 1.23 am. This delay was subsequently attributed to the king's reluctance to publicly oppose the coup until there was sufficient evidence of its failure, but can be convincingly explained in terms of the practical difficulties involved.[30]

Looking tired but authoritative in his captain-general's uniform, Juan

Carlos was brief and concise as never before. After announcing that he had ordered all civil and military authorities to defend the democratic *status quo*, he solemnly proclaimed that 'the crown, symbol of the permanence and unity of the *Patria*, cannot in any way tolerate the attempts of any persons, by their actions or their attitude, to interrupt by force the democratic process determined by the constitution and approved by the Spanish people by means of a referendum'. This message, watched by millions of anxious viewers who had refused to go to bed without hearing from Juan Carlos, was to have a decisive impact. Above all, it revealed that those involved in the coup who had claimed to act on behalf of the king – and even in his defence – had been using his name in vain. Additionally, it encouraged many key institutions that had hitherto remained silent, such as the leading employers' federation, to issue statements in support of democracy.[31]

One of the few Spaniards not to greet the royal message with relief was Armada, who complained that it would split the armed forces and turn many officers against the crown. In spite of the king's categorical opposition to unconstitutional solutions of whatever nature, Armada still had the *sang froid* to propose himself to Laína as head of a military junta, on the grounds that it was the only formula that might induce Tejero to lay down his arms.

In the early hours of 24 February the king and Milans held a second telephone conversation, in which the former reiterated his commitment to the democratic *status quo*, and once again ordered him to withdraw his tanks and obtain Tejero's surrender. This was followed by a telex reaffirming his determination to stand by the constitution, and a warning that 'after this message I cannot turn back', by which he meant that unless Milans obeyed immediately, he would hold him responsible for the consequences of the coup. (During the subsequent trial, this text was quoted as evidence of the monarch's initial hesitation.) Juan Carlos also stated that 'no *coup d'état* of any kind whatsoever can shelter behind the person of the king; it is against the king', and concluded: 'I swear to you that I will neither abdicate nor leave Spain'. Defeated, Milans agreed to cancel his manifesto, and gradually withdrew his tanks from the streets of Valencia, though not before making one final attempt to convince La Zarzuela of the merits of the 'Armada solution'.[32]

Abandoned by Milans, in the morning of 24 February Tejero finally agreed to negotiate his surrender, and requested that Armada act as mediator in order to humiliate him. Shortly before noon, after several hours of talks, the lieutenant-colonel finally released his hostages. Unaware of events outside the Congress, as soon as he was freed, Suárez drove to La Zarzuela, where he began to apologise for not having trusted Armada in the past, only to be told that he had been right all along. At a meeting of the defence junta that same afternoon, Juan Carlos is said to have choked with rage when presented with fuller evidence of Armada's involvement. When Suárez ordered General Gabeiras to arrest Armada at once, the Army chief of staff turned to the king, prompting the acting premier to shout: 'Don't look at the king, look at me!'[33]

That same evening the leaders of Spain's major parties, most of whom had spent the night in a heavily guarded room in the Congress, converged on La Zarzuela for what the king himself has described as 'a very emotional' gathering. When Carrillo arrived, 'he came over to me, took my hands between his own and said, "your majesty, thank you for saving our lives!"' According to Fraga, González was more restrained, while Suárez and the recently appointed UCD president, Rodríguez Sahagún, spoilt the occasion by liberally distributing blame on the officers involved.[34]

Juan Carlos read out a prepared statement in which he agreed that the rebels should be brought to justice, but without alienating those who had remained loyal. His main concern, he would later explain, was 'that there must be no grudge held against the armed forces as a whole'. He went on to warn them that 'the king neither can nor should face incidents of such gravity again on his own responsibility', in view of which they should do their utmost to prevent the political situation from deteriorating to the extent it had on the eve of the coup.[35]

The monarch's words had an immediate impact on Fraga and the Catalan nationalists, who voted in favour of Calvo Sotelo's investiture as prime minister forty-eight hours later. When the president of the Congress, Lavilla, opened the session with a reference to the king's crucial role in thwarting the coup, the deputies rose to their feet and gave Juan Carlos, who was not present, their most enthusiastic standing ovation to date. Hitherto, many on the left had regarded Spain's parliamentary monarchy as a lesser evil, an unexpected and largely unwanted byproduct of the transition to democracy. The king's behaviour on that fateful night may not have prompted many institutional conversions but it undoubtedly resulted in a spectacular increase in the number of devoted *Juancarlistas*.[36]

Although there are still many unanswered questions concerning the precise nature and scope of the aborted coup, it is widely believed that there were several conspiracies in progress by late 1980, which converged somewhat haphazardly on the night of 23 February. The first of these, sometimes described as the 'spontaneous' or 'primitive' option, was led by Tejero, and was fully in keeping with the spirit of the 'Galaxia operation' discovered in 1978. Its goal was simply to capture the Congress and hold the government hostage, in the hope that major Army units would join at a later stage, thereby facilitating the creation of a military junta. The second option, loosely modelled on the coup carried out in Turkey in September 1980, was apparently backed by a number of senior generals, and also aimed at overthrowing the constitution and installing a military junta. This plan was largely based on the notion that the occupation of Madrid by the Brunete armoured division would trigger a nation-wide military uprising, and enjoyed the vociferous support of the extreme right-wing press, as well as that of prominent civilian Francoists. Milans del Bosch was initially involved in this plot, but later broke away on account of its hostility to the monarchy. The general favoured a Primo de Rivera-style *pronunciamiento*, leading to the establishment of an authoritarian monarchy such as that of the 1920s. In his determination to prevent any of these plots succeeding as originally envisaged, Armada – who greatly admired De Gaulle – developed the notion of a 'soft' coup, which would initially respect the constitution and prove acceptable to the major parties as well as the military. This scheme, which necessarily required royal approval, envisaged the formation of a largely civilian government led by Armada, which would set out to combat terrorism and reform the constitution. Milans was eventually persuaded that this plan enjoyed the king's tacit support and modified his own project accordingly. This was done in partial agreement with Tejero, who was never fully informed as to Armada's true objectives.

In the wake of the coup, there was much discussion in Spain concerning the extent of the king's prior knowledge of these various plots, as well as the degree of royal support for the so-called 'Armada solution'. Doubts concerning Juan Carlos's role were first raised in public in the course of the ensuing military trial as part of a clever – though ultimately unsuccessful – legal strategy, and have never fully dissipated since. It is not impossible that in his private conversations with Armada the king, alarmed by the difficulties facing the Suárez government, unintentionally led him to believe that he would not be averse to a pseudo-constitutional solution to a major institutional crisis. After all, Juan Carlos has never been noted for his discretion and Armada had once been a trusted member of his inner circle. However, the latter's ambition and capacity for wishful thinking were such that he hardly needed prompting by the king to justify his own intentions. In this respect, Juan Carlos's most serious mistake was to think he could appease Armada with a promotion which not only took him to Madrid but placed him at the heart of the Army's key decision-making centre. Unfortunately, unlike Milans and Tejero, Armada has consistently denied his involvement in any form of conspiracy whatsoever, and we may therefore never learn the true nature of his role in these events.

Paradoxically, the monarch's special relationship with the armed forces proved decisive in both aborting the coup and in making it possible in the first place. It was largely by invoking the king's name that Tejero was able to recruit a substantial number of Civil Guards and gain entry to the Congress, and it was the belief that Armada would be issuing orders from La Zarzuela that mobilised senior officers in Valencia and the Brunete armoured division. Indeed it is more than a little ironic that the two most senior generals involved were also the Army's staunchest monarchists. Had Juan Carlos been unable to clarify his position to the captain-generals, it is more than likely that several would have imitated Milans, with unforseeable consequences. Not surprisingly the king has never concealed his irritation with those who regard the coup as a mere 'operetta conspiracy'.

Juan Carlos himself has acknowledged that 'the military obeyed me not just because I was one of them, but also, indeed primarily, because I was commander-in-chief of the armed forces'. By and large, most of those who obeyed him did so out of loyalty to the king, and not in defence of the constitution. Indeed one of the most alarming aspects of the coup was that it revealed that the armed forces continued to see themselves exclusively in terms of their relationship with their commander-in-chief, regardless of the role defined for them by the constitution.[37]

The '23-F' – as the coup attempt came to be known in Spain – was thus similar to the 1967 coup in Greece in that the rebels invoked the king's name, but different in that Juan Carlos, unlike his brother-in-law, refused to bow to military pressure. In the light of the Greek experience, the alternatives were perhaps more clearly defined for the Spanish monarch. If he sided with the generals, he would become a mere puppet in their hands, and his reign would not outlive the resulting military dictatorship. By confronting them he would earn the everlasting gratitude and support of his fellow countrymen if he succeeded, and their undying admiration and respect if he did not.

The king's main concern in the wake of the coup was that the newly appointed Calvo Sotelo government should restore popular confidence in the nation's democratic institutions and provide a new sense of stability to Spanish political life. Juan Carlos had been pleased by the UCD's selection of Calvo Sotelo, a life-long monarchist whose seemingly humourless façade hid a humane, witty personality. Nevertheless his relationship with the new premier was to be very different from that he had enjoyed with Suárez, both because it was a fully constitutional one, and because Calvo Sotelo was too much in awe of the institution ever to regard himself as the king's friend.[38]

The king's immediate task in the wake of the coup was to build bridges between the armed forces and the rest of society, in an attempt to restore mutual trust. In March 1981 he invited the Supreme Councils of the three services, totalling over forty generals, to a formal session in the Royal Palace, where he urged them to obey the country's laws, which could be modified 'by the established legal procedures, but never by force or disobedience'. Juan Carlos admitted having understood and shared their concern and anger in the past, but insisted that military dissatisfaction be expressed through the appropriate channels, thereby preventing 'the existence of a military influence which indirectly conditions the nation's political life'. Earlier, at a meeting at La Zarzuela, the Army Supreme Council had publicly reaffirmed its loyalty to the king, democracy and the constitution. In late May the king and queen presided the Armed Forces Day celebrations held at Barcelona, which proved a great success with the public. Juan Carlos and Sofía had not returned to Catalonia on an official visit since 1976, and were greeted with considerable popular enthusiasm.[39]

Given his crucial role in preventing the rebels from achieving their goals on the night of 23 February, it was inevitable that future attempts to emulate them would seek to neutralise the king. In June 1981 the arrest of several 'ultras' with associates in the armed forces enabled the police to stymie a plot that aimed to storm La Zarzuela and force Juan Carlos to abdicate. Hostility towards the monarch also surfaced in a number of minor incidents, which revealed the impact of recent events. One of Milans del Bosch's sons, also an Army officer, who had been accused of publicly insulting the king at a riding club, was punished with a mere month's arrest. More importantly, in late 1981 one hundred officers serving in the Brunete division publicly expressed their support for those involved in the coup, in a document that barely concealed their contempt for their commander-in-chief. Partly in response to this, and largely at the king's suggestion, the government appointed a new JUJEM in early 1982.

Politicians initially appeared to take heed of Juan Carlos's February 1981 plea. In the wake of the coup González had wanted a coalition government, something Calvo Sotelo opposed, but was nevertheless happy to support major government initiatives aimed at shoring up democracy. Thus in March 1981 the Cortes passed a law in defence of the constitution, granting the government new powers in its struggle against military rebels and terrorists alike. This did not prevent yet another ETA bomb attack in May, in which the head of the king's military household, General Valenzuela, almost lost his life. Most importantly, in August the government and the PSOE negotiated a major bill aimed at controlling the devolution process. Although much of this law was later judged unconstitutional, at the time it served to appease those who feared the imminent dissolution of the Spanish state.

One issue on which the Calvo Sotelo government did not seek a broad consensus was Spanish membership of NATO. In theory the UCD had always been committed to this foreign policy goal, but Suárez was never fully convinced. Indeed some observers believe this was one of the few ideological issues over which Juan Carlos and his premier had seriously disagreed in the past. In Calvo Sotelo's mind, however, there was no doubt that membership would facilitate Spain's entry into the EC and had the added advantage of providing the armed forces with a badly needed challenge. Fully aware of the imminence of a PSOE victory, Calvo Sotelo rushed NATO membership through the Cortes in May 1982 in the hope that his successor would accept the *fait accompli*.[40]

Given the political context, it is highly unlikely that Calvo Sotelo would have defended NATO membership with such tenacity without the king's support. As a statesman, Juan Carlos had always regarded NATO membership as a way of anchoring Spain firmly in the Western world and a means of overcoming decades of ostracism. As a soldier, he was painfully aware of the limitations of the Spanish armed forces and saw in NATO membership a means of furthering their long-overdue modernisation and professionalisation. What was more, Spain's presence in the Atlantic alliance would substantially reduce its dependence on the US, which had always troubled the king. Juan Carlos thus left Reagan in no doubt as to his support for NATO membership when he finally visited Washington in October 1981. Following this interview the KGB circulated a letter supposedly written by Reagan, in which he urged Juan Carlos to 'act . . . with despatch to remove the forces obstructing Spain's entry into NATO'. The purpose of this forgery was to suggest that the king was a puppet of the US administration, but it was so crude – it referred to a mysterious group of '*Opus Dei* pacifists', for example – that it failed to have any impact whatsoever. In May 1982, after visiting Juan Carlos, Chancellor Schmidt confided to Spanish journalists that in the king's view NATO membership would also contribute to the consolidation of democracy.[41]

In anticipation of the forthcoming military trial, throughout 1981 the 'ultra' press and its allies did their best to cast doubt on the king's commitment to democracy and his behaviour on the night of 23 February. This was accompanied by a proliferation of libellous pamphlets and leaflets signed by a so-called *Union Militar Española*. Deeply irritated, in his *pascua militar* speech of January 1982 Juan Carlos denounced this 'insidious and deceitful propaganda' in the strongest terms, while urging the armed forces to adapt to changing circumstances. In February, at a centenary celebration of the foundation of Zaragoza Military Academy, where he had studied, the king went even further, openly defending his choice of the democratic path for Spain. The Calvo Sotelo government and the major opposition parties duly rallied around the monarch, amidst reminders that he would have been forced into exile had the coup succeeded. Contrary to what the 'ultras' had expected, the campaign against the king merely served to strengthen his popularity, while undermining that of the armed forces.[42]

Juan Carlos followed the '23-F' trial, which finally came to a close in June 1982, with mounting apprehension. In spite of his much-flaunted loyalty to the crown, Armada allowed his silence to be interpreted as evidence of the king's connivance, whilst Milans openly admitted his intentions. This possibly explains why the king always regarded the former's behaviour as treasonable, and the latter's as misguided and obtuse but ultimately well-meaning. Ironically, the military court passed a thirty-year sentence on Milans, while Armada was given a mere six years.[43]

In spite of the king's repeated warnings the UCD was unrepentant and by March 1981 the party was once again riven by internal disputes. In July, 70 dissenting deputies led by Herrero de Miñón formed a so-called 'moderate platform', in response to which leading Social Democrats left the UCD to form their own party. In October the UCD suffered a major defeat in the Galician elections at the hands of Fraga's AP, prompting party leader Rodríguez Sahagún to submit his resignation. Shortly afterwards Suárez himself left the party's executive committee. Calvo Sotelo came under mounting pressure to call early elections but refused to do so until the '23-F' trial was over. The premier sought to appease his critics by forming a new government, in spite of which Herrero de Miñón deserted to AP in February 1982. In May the UCD suffered another humiliating defeat in the Andalusian elections. A month later Calvo Sotelo himself resigned as UCD president, and announced he would not seek reelection. To cap it all Suárez left the UCD to form his own party, the Centro Democrático y Social (CDS). Juan Carlos intervened at this point to urge party leaders to find a viable solution to the political stalemate. In view of the situation, in August Calvo Sotelo finally dissolved the Cortes and called elections for October, a decision the king greeted with relief.

Though closer to the UCD ideologically, Juan Carlos looked forward to a PSOE victory, which would provide Spain with firm political leadership after almost three years of instability that had put the crown itself at risk. Interestingly, González himself had come to this conclusion by September 1982. Indeed as early as 1980 Juan Carlos had told a journalist: 'They say the king wants the Socialists to govern, but I always want whatever the people want. If I do not respect the will of the people, where will we end up?' Most importantly, he had yet to prove that the monarchy was compatible with the party that had largely inherited the democratic, secular values that many still associated with Spain's republican tradition, and which had advocated a republican form of government as recently as 1978.[44]

On the eve of the elections the police uncovered a military plot to storm La Zarzuela and depose the king on grounds of perjury. Juan Carlos responded with a fiery speech in Cádiz on 12 October, in which he spoke out in defence of Spain's constitutional liberties. Several days later the royal guard was put on the alert when the police detected a column of military vehicles apparently heading for La Zarzuela in the middle of the night. This proved to be a false alarm, but the incident is highly indicative of the tense preelection atmosphere.

Juan Carlos invited major party leaders – including Roca and Javier Arzallus, representing Catalan and Basque nationalism respectively – to a joint meeting at La Zarzuela on the eve of the elections and urged them to remain united in the face of the twin threats of military conspiracy and terrorism. By this stage there was little doubt as to the scale of the PSOE's imminent victory and Juan Carlos was anxious to ensure its acceptance by all sectors of society. The king also expressed concern over a possible power vacuum after the elections, which was interpreted as a request to Calvo Sotelo to hand over the reigns of government as quickly and smoothly as possible. After the meeting, which González described as 'important and moving', the PSOE leader criticised those who strove to present his party as an enemy of the monarchy in order to undermine its electoral appeal.[45]

As anticipated, the elections of 28 October 1982 produced an unprecedented landslide, with the PSOE winning 48 per cent of the vote and 202 seats while Fraga's Coalición Popular obtained 26 per cent of the vote and 106 seats. The great looser was the UCD, with only 6 per cent of the vote and a mere 12 seats, a number matched by the Catalan nationalists. Suárez's CDS failed to profit from the UCD's collapse, winning only two seats in the Congress of Deputies. The PCE's poor showing, with a mere 4 per cent of the vote, effectively put an end to Carrillo's political career.

On this occasion Juan Carlos consulted a total of nine party leaders before submitting González's name to the new president of the Congress, Peces-Barba. The latter's speech at the opening of the new parliament on 25 November 1982 contained a highly significant defence of the monarchy, which was justified not only out of gratitude to the king for his role in the transition and the coup, but on its own merit. Peces-Barba identified the institution with 'stability, equilibrium and potential for progress', and praised it for its ability to guarantee the deep-rooted identity of a community while remaining fully compatible with change. Most strikingly, he urged Spaniards to move beyond *Juancarlismo*: 'I believe', he concluded, 'that the positive values of a parliamentary monarchy are general and more permanent, and transcend the person who currently embodies the institution'.[46]

In his reply, Juan Carlos praised the armed forces for their endurance in the face of cowardly terrorist attacks to which they could not respond in kind, while reminding them that political violence would not be solved by authoritarian means. The king was particularly critical of those who manipulated military outrage to foster disobedience, comparing them to the terrorists themselves. He also reaffirmed his determination to prevent the will of a minority from prevailing over the democratically expressed wishes of the majority, and announced that Spain was turning over a new leaf and would soon enjoy a fully consolidated democracy.

Not surprisingly, perhaps, when Peces-Barba visited La Zarzuela on 3 December 1982 to obtain his signature ratifying González's appointment, Juan Carlos was visibly pleased. As the president of the lower house stood up to leave, the monarch embraced him warmly and observed: 'If my grandfather had been able to have this sort of relationship with Pablo Iglesias (the founder of the PSOE), we could have avoided the civil war'. To this Peces-Barba replied: 'Perhaps, Sir, it was necessary to live through that in order to reach the point where we are now'.[47]

9 Juan Carlos at Home and Abroad

The PSOE victory of October 1982 opened a new phase in Juan Carlos's political life. The party in office enjoyed an absolute majority in the Cortes for the first time, which reflected its unprecedented popular support. In many ways democracy could be said to have been consolidated, even though the changes sanctioned by the constitution of 1978 had not yet been fully assimilated by all sectors of the population.

The king was forced to live with the consequences of the February 1981 coup for several years to come. In April 1983 the Supreme Court increased the prison sentences decreed by the military court a year earlier in 22 out of 33 cases. Most significantly, Armada's prison sentence was raised from six to thirty years, in recognition of his leading role in the conspiracy. Whether or not it was these stiffer sentences that deterred possible emulators, this was the last serious coup attempt carried out by the military.[1]

The fact that the armed forces no longer posed a threat to Spanish democracy did not diminish the king's concern for their well-being. Juan Carlos continued to use the *pascua militar* to communicate with fellow officers, who experienced dramatic changes in the 1980s as a result of both internal reforms and Spanish membership of NATO. Additionally, the king made a point of presiding the annual Armed Forces Day celebrations, which helped to improve civil–military relations. These events attracted considerable media attention and proved remarkably popular; in May 1986, for example, some 100 000 people turned out to watch the military parade held at Santa Cruz de Tenerife.

The king's first concern in the wake of the 1982 elections was to demonstrate that the monarchy was fully compatible with a Socialist government, a task in which he enjoyed the full collaboration of González, with whom he soon formed an excellent working partnership. Juan Carlos's relationship with Suárez, particulary during the early period, had been far more intimate, but the former had learnt that this could prove counter-productive. Like many European monarchs before him, the king would come to appreciate the respect and formality that have often characterised the attitude of left-wing prime ministers towards the institution.

The relationship between the king and his government was somewhat closer in Spain than in other European monarchies. Cabinet ministers, including the premier, took up office after a swearing-in ceremony held at

La Zarzuela in the monarch's presence much as they had done under Franco. In February 1983 Juan Carlos and González began to meet once a week, generally on Tuesday mornings, except in August, when the prime minister – or the deputy prime minister if he was unavailable – travelled to Majorca to brief him. Additionally, the king occasionally presided over cabinet meetings, in theory at the head of government's request. Juan Carlos, who had very rarely attended cabinet meetings under the UCD, started this tradition in August 1983, and presided over a total of seven meetings in the ensuing decade, generally at La Zarzuela and occasionally at the Royal Palace. During the constitutional debates it was pointed out that the king might become too closely associated with government decisions as a result, but this fear would prove unfounded. These meetings generally served to inform Juan Carlos of major non-partisan issues, such as the state of membership negotiations with the EC, or to analyse the consequences of international crises, such as the Gulf War. At the third such meeting, held in January 1985, the king himself justified this custom as 'a symbol of a collaboration which signifies neither fusion nor intrusion'. Nevertheless in September 1991 Juan Carlos's presence at a cabinet meeting was widely read as a desperate attempt by González to bolster his government's authority at a time of acute economic and political difficulties.[2]

The PSOE government's determination to avoid constitutional conflicts with the monarch was put to the test very shortly after their sweeping 1982 victory. The king's January 1983 *pascua militar* speech – which Juan Carlos was unable to deliver in person due to a recent skiing accident – boldly stated that the monarchy 'does not depend, indeed cannot depend, on an election, a referendum, or a vote', because its usefulness derived precisely from the fact that it owed its existence to 'the plebiscite of history, the universal suffrage of past centruries'. Some critics deemed this passage incompatible with the principle of popular sovereignty, but the government rushed to the king's aid by urging that it be read in the context of the overall defence of the constitution contained in the same speech. This was not entirely convincing, however, and it was subsequently claimed that Juan Carlos had not been able to check the text carefully prior to its release.[3]

Several months later, in the course of a royal visit to Brazil, it was discovered that a speech prepared for the king by the Foreign Ministry had been lifted from a recent article by González in *Le Monde*. In theory this did not pose a political problem, since the views of a constitutional monarch are supposedly those of his government, but as Foreign Minister Morán subsequently admitted, it was desirable that the former's opinions should seem 'more general and politically neutral'. Juan Carlos went out of his way to reassure the government that he had not taken offence, and a senior diplomat subsequently resigned over his *faux pas*. In official circles this incident was read as evidence of La Zarzuela's shortage of qualified personnel capable of detecting oversights of this nature.[4]

The government was nevertheless occasionally accused of manipulating the crown for its own ends. In January 1985, for example, the Communist mayor of Córdoba, Julio Anguita, accused the Socialist authorities of exploiting Juan Carlos's visit to the city, while preventing him from inaugurating the new town hall. In the ensuing row, the royal household postponed the visit to avoid further controversy. What is perhaps most significant about the incident is that Anguita, the PCE's candidate to the presidency of the Andalusian regional government, saw the king's presence as a contribution to his own political legitimation. (When Anguita eventually became secretary general of the PCE in 1988, however, the PCE abandoned Carrillo's strategy and reintroduced the republican form of government amongst its long-term goals.)

Occasionally, opposition parties also raised objections to the premier's proximity to the monarch. In July 1991, for example, both the centre-right and the Communists accused González of accompanying the king on a visit to Mexico and Morocco in order to derive political capital for himself. This appears to have irritated Juan Carlos considerably, given the unusually strong language used by the royal household in refuting this claim. According to La Zarzuela, the king's role as head of state was not constitutionally comparable to that of his hosts, and he therefore required the prime minister's presence.

In some instances, however, the king did appear to resent the PSOE government's efforts to associate itself too closely with the monarchy. This was particulary true of the ceremony at which Prince Felipe swore the constitution in the presence of the assembled Cortes on coming of age in January 1986. This occasion was largely stage-managed by the Socialist authorities, with the result that the heir shared the limelight not only with the president of the Cortes, which was perhaps understandable, but also with the head of government, which was uncalled for. Most surprisingly, neither the king nor his son were invited to address the Cortes on this occasion. Although Peces-Barba described the monarchy as the most appropriate institution for Spain and paid tribute to Don Juan's contribution to its restoration, a reference that visibly pleased Juan Carlos, he also went out of his way to emphasise that the ceremony was taking place under a Socialist government that enjoyed an absolute majority in the Cortes. Similarly, in his own speech González assured the prince that he could count on 'the loyalty and sympathy of the government', an endorsement that was perhaps somewhat out of place. Although the commitment to the monarchy expressed by the Socialists augured well for its future, some observers could not help feeling that it was as if the institution's survival depended on the government's largesse. The king himself is said to have felt that the solemnity of the occasion and its dynastic – as opposed to strictly constitutional – dimension had been somewhat marred by governmental interference.[5]

On occasion it was the king who was criticised for lending undue support to González and his party. In September 1991 for example, he congratulated the government for its foreign policy and its 'efforts to face up to the difficulties which threaten us', at a time when González was widely thought to be running out of steam. Similarly, in April 1992 Juan Carlos told a Portuguese interviewer that the decade of Socialist rule had been 'a necessary experience', an opinion many Spaniards may have shared, but which nevertheless constituted a rare departure from his usual impartiality. In general the king clearly welcomed the existence of stable Socialist governments capable of implementing their political programmes, even though some of their policies may not have been to his liking.[6] Indeed there is evidence that, very occasionally, the king's opinion may have had a decisive influence on González. Although the latter was generally far less willing to share his thoughts with Juan Carlos than Suárez, in September 1988 he unexpectedly informed him that he was toying with the idea of not standing as the PSOE's candidate in the forthcoming elections. Shocked by this suggestion, the king actively discouraged him from even contemplating it, on the grounds that Spain was not yet ready for the change of government that would undoubtedly result from his withdrawal. The prime minister duly reconsidered his position, and went on to win his third general election in 1989.[7]

In the early 1990s the steady decline in the PSOE's fortunes placed fresh strains on the king's relationship with the executive. In June 1991, during a visit to Andalusia, a traditional PSOE stronghold, Juan Carlos argued that 'the administration sometimes lags behind society instead of leading from in front', and referred to the need to eradicate idleness and corruption. These remarks, which some construed as criticism of the Socialist authorities, prompted a debate as to the function of royal speeches generally and there were even calls for this aspect of the king's activity to be regulated by law. Six months earlier, however, Juan Carlos had been criticised for failing to mention Spain's increasingly frequent corruption scandals in his Christmas Eve address.[8]

The era of political stability inaugurated by the 1982 elections finally came to an end in 1993, when economic recession and a succession of political scandals combined to deprive the PSOE of its majority in the Congress of Deputies, forcing González to rely increasingly on the support of the Catalan nationalists. Additionally, under the leadership of José María Aznar the Partido Popular became increasingly attractive to the electorate, performing better than the PSOE in the 1994 elections to the European Parliament. The political scandals which had done so much to erode the PSOE's credibility resulted in considerable friction between the executive and the judiciary, and threatened to undermine public confidence in the major institutions. In view of the stalemate some commentators demanded that Juan Carlos act in keeping with his constitutional duty to 'arbitrate and moderate the regular working of the institutions' (article 56), apparently oblivious of the fact that he lacked the authority to dismiss the prime minister or call early elections. In practice, there was little Juan Carlos could do other than urge party leaders, judges and prominent journalists to act responsibly.[9]

The most significant challenge still facing the young democracy when the Socialists came to power in 1982 was the transformation of a formerly highly centralised unitary state into a semi-federal one by means of the development of the *Estado de las Autonomías*. This process affected the king directly, both in his capacity as commander-in-chief of the armed forces and because of his constitutional status as symbol of the 'unity and permanence' of the Spanish state. His main task in this area was to compensate for the centrifugal tensions institutionalised by the *Estado de las Autonomías* and the resulting party system, particularly with regard to the 'historic nationalities'.

It is important to note that due to Franco's tendency to appropriate all Spanish national symbols for his regime, after his death many of his former opponents continued to associate them with authoritarianism and repression. Indeed their aversion was such that in the mid-1970s most Communists and Socialists could not bear to utter the word 'Spain', and referred to 'the Spanish state' instead. During the civil war Franco had banned the Republican flag and anthem, and had restored the monarchist symbols removed in 1931. This meant that, with the exception of the Bourbon coat of arms, which replaced Franco's modified Habsburg eagle in 1982, the external symbols of the parliamentary monarchy were identical to those of the preceding regime, a fact that hindered its full acceptance by both the left and peripheral nationalists. This explains the importance attached by Juan Carlos to events such as the commemoration of the two hundredth anniversary of the Spanish flag in May 1985, which sought to dissociate it from the Franco regime by emphasising its eighteenth-century origins.

Ever since his proclamation, and in particular since 1978, one of the

king's major goals was to reconcile his countrymen to the notion of a
united yet plural, multi-cultural Spain. In the past this view of Spanish
society had been rejected both by hard-line Spanish nationalists and their
peripheral counterparts, but it gained considerable ground in the 1980s, to
the extent of winning the acceptance of the vast majority of the population, albeit with some reservations. As in Belgium, and to some extent in
Britain, the monarchy thus proved essential in holding the country together.
In Spain, a country that would never elect a Catalan head of government
regardless of his ideology, this was largely possible because, unlike most
politicians, the king was not associated with any particular region or locality.

One theme to which the king returned time and again in his speeches
was that of cultural diversity and linguistic tolerance. According to the
1978 constitution, Castilian is the official language of the state, but the
other Spanish languages (that is, Catalan, Basque and Galician) are also
official in their respective autonomous communities. In keeping with this
philosophy, in October 1992, at a ceremony held at the monastery of
San Millán de la Cogolla in La Rioja, traditionally associated with the
study of both Castilian and Basque, Juan Carlos vigorously defended the
coexistence of Spain's languages as a cornerstone of the new democratic
monarchy.

Following his father's example, Juan Carlos went out of his way to
familiarise himself with Spain's other official languages, encouraging
his son to do likewise. Nobody could expect him to speak them fluently,
however, particularly in the case of Basque, an extremely difficult language to learn only spoken by a quarter of the Basque population. Indeed
for the king to address the inhabitants of the 'historic nationalities' exclusively in these languages would be to undermine an important linguistic
principle embodied in the constitution, namely that all Spaniards have the
duty to know and the right to use the Spanish language.

Juan Carlos was always acutely aware that for historical, demographic
and economic reasons, Spain's viability as a democratic state depended
largely on its ability to accommodate Catalonia. For much of the 1980s
Catalan political life was characterised by the tension between a Socialist
central government and a Generalitat controlled by Convergencia i Unió,
the moderate nationalist coalition led by Pujol. The king's main goal during
these years was to consolidate the monarchy's standing in Catalonia while
doing his best to avoid getting trapped in the cross-fire between the Madrid
and Barcelona governments.

In May 1985 Juan Carlos visited Catalonia officially for the first time
since the restoration of the Generalitat. The king had felt comfortable with
Tarradellas, who presided the Generalitat until 1980, but found it much

harder to get on with his successor Pujol, for both political and temperamental reasons.[10] In return for his acceptance by those in power, Tarradellas, like Carrillo before him, had gone out of his way to demonstrate his loyalty to the king, the monarchy and Spanish national unity. Pujol, however, found it politically expedient to display far greater reticence and ambiguity in his attitude towards these institutions. Although he soon developed the habit of paying the royal family courtesy visits whenever they went skiing in the Catalan Pyrenees, relations were initially cool.

The 1985 visit proved to be a turning point in the crown's relationship with the Generalitat. Juan Carlos explicitly acknowledged the existence of a Catalan national identity and paid tribute to the Catalan language by speaking it on several occasions. (Most observers were quick to comment on the marked improvement in his pronunciation since his first official visit in 1976.) Characteristically, Pujol insisted that he preside a meeting of the Catalan *Consell* (executive), thereby establishing an implicit parallel with the rare occasions when Juan Carlos attended the Madrid government's cabinet meetings. Much to Pujol's discomfort, however, the king took this opportunity to express concern at the rate at which Catalan was being introduced in schools at the expense of Spanish, a process that even native Catalan speakers such as the opera singer Montserrat Caballé had criticised in his presence.[11]

In April 1987 Pujol visited the king to inform him at length about the difficulties encountered by the Generalitat in developing the Catalan Statute of Autonomy, adopted in 1979. This interview was criticised by those who feared the king would become involved in the central government's on-going quarrel with the Generalitat, but Pujol justified it on the grounds that, as head of state, Juan Carlos was entitled to both sides of the story.

Determined to establish a direct link with La Zarzuela independently of La Moncloa, Pujol subsequently invited Juan Carlos to preside the commemoration of Catalonia's millennial in April 1988. The central government – which was not invited to the events – feared that Pujol would manipulate the king's presence in order to ingratiate himself with the non-nationalist electorate, but Juan Carlos was determined to attend. Although his presence triggered the usual protests from radical nationalists, it undoubtedly helped to strengthen the Generalitat's links with the crown, and by extension the monarchy's standing in Catalonia.[12]

This hard-won mutual confidence was unexpectedly jeopardised in September 1989, during the opening ceremony of the Athletics World Cup, held at the recently restored Montjuich stadium originally inaugurated by Alfonso XIII in 1929, the central venue for the forthcoming Olympic Games. Much to the king's annoyance, the royal family's presence was greeted with a hostile demonstration staged by hundreds of youths belonging not only to radical nationalist organisations but also to the youth section of Pujol's own party. Ironically, Pujol himself had urged party members to impress Juan Carlos with a display of Catalan nationalist feeling, but was later forced to issue a formal statement condemning these incidents and reaffirming his loyalty to the king.

Catalonia once again dominated Juan Carlos's attention in December 1989 when, at the suggestion of the radical Esquerra Republicana party, the Catalan parliament passed a resolution stating that its acceptance of the 1978 constitution did not imply that it would not seek to exercise its right to national self-determination in the future. By way of reply, the king's traditional Christmas Eve address reminded nationalists that the constitution proclaimed 'the indissoluble unity of the Spanish nation'. Pujol subsequently sent the king a personal letter reassuring him of his loyalty to the crown and the constitution, in which he explained that a nationalist party such as his could not fail to endorse the principle of national self-determination, even if it had no intention of exercising it.

The prince of Asturias's first official visit to Catalonia in April 1990 provided the Catalan government with a fresh opportunity to demonstrate its commitment to the constitution and the monarchy. One of the aims of this visit was to underline the Spanish monarchy's medieval roots, and hence the notion of an intimate relationship between successive Spanish monarchs and their Catalan subjects. It was in this spirit that Felipe, whose status as crown prince made him Prince of Gerona, Count of Cervera and *Señor* of Balaguer, duly visited the towns to which these titles referred. In his speech to the Catalan parliament, the heir went as far as the constitution would allow in recognising Catalan national identity, in spite of which five radical deputies walked out in protest. So pleased was Pujol by the prince's performance that he subsequently urged the PSOE government to take heed of the heir's words.

It was thus not without apprehension that Juan Carlos looked forward to the 1992 Barcelona Olympics, a venture he had wholeheartedly endorsed in 1986. In March 1992 Esquerra Republicana raised the political temperature by promising to expel the monarchy from a future independent Catalonia. After a meeting with Juan Carlos in April, Pujol declared that their relationship was one of 'mutual loyalty'. Shortly afterwards, however, he advised the king not to travel to Ampurias to receive the Olympic flame as it reached Spain. Pujol no doubt knew that the organisers of a 'Freedom for Catalonia' campaign – his eldest son amongst them – would use this occasion to make their presence felt. The Catalan president subsequently requested that the royal family be respected during the opening ceremony, which proved a great success. When Prince Felipe, a member of the Olympic yachting team in his own right, made his appearance carrying the Spanish flag, spectators responded with wild enthusiasm, a reaction the local activists had not anticipated. During the ensuing weeks the continued presence of the royal family at key events and an unexpectedly good performance by the national team combined to produce an explosion of Spanish nationalist sentiment as had not been witnessed in recent years. As the king had hoped, in spite of the friction between Pujol and the Socialist mayor of Barcelona, Pascual Maragall, the image projected by the Olympics within Spain was one of peaceful coexistence. Juan Carlos, who had sailed for his country in the 1972 Olympics, thoroughly enjoyed the games, as he rushed from one event to the next, determined to be the first to embrace successful Spanish athletes.[13]

Although membership of both a Spanish and a Catalan national community was increasingly seen as compatible by the inhabitants of Catalonia, the monarchy continued to be rejected by a radical minority. Thus Juan Carlos's visit to Barcelona in September 1993 once again resulted in minor acts of protest. Two months later, at the Catalan monastery of Sant Jeroni de la Murtra, where Columbus once informed Ferdinand and Isabella of his discoveries, the king reiterated his faith in a plural yet united Spain. In March 1994, however, for the first time since its creation, the Catalan parliament heard a vitriolic attack on the monarchy from one of its more radical deputies, who accused the king of active belligerence against Catalonia.

Juan Carlos was similarly anxious to consolidate the monarchy's standing in the Basque country, the autonomous community that had proved most reluctant to accept the outcome of the transition process inspired by the crown. Juan Carlos never got on well with Garaicoechea, the Basque *lehendakari* (president) from 1980 to 1984, on account of his ambivalent attitude towards Spanish national unity and its symbols. In May 1983, for example, Garaicoechea initially refused to attend the Armed Forces Day celebrations to be held at Burgos, where the VI Military Region, which included the Basque country, had its headquarters. Juan Carlos sent the *lehendakari* a personal message warning him that his absence would constitute an insult to the state, the crown and himself, in the light of which Garaicoechea reconsidered his decision.[14] The king's relations with the Basque authorities improved considerably after the replacement of Garaicoechea by José María Ardanza, and the formation of PNV–PSOE coalition governments after 1987. In marked contrast with his predecessor, shortly after his appointment the new *lehendakari* travelled to Madrid to pay his respects to the king.

In view of the incidents that had accompanied the first royal tour of the Basque country in February 1981, during which Spaniards first became familiar with the extremist cry of *erregeak kampora* (royals go home), the Madrid authorities were extremely reluctant to allow Juan Carlos to repeat the éxperience. When Juan Carlos briefly visited Bilbao in October 1986 to commemorate the one hundredth anniversary of Deusto University, councillors belonging to HB, the city's third largest party, stayed away in protest. In February 1988, during the king's first tour of Navarre, an autonomous community that some nationalists continued to regard as an integral part of the Basque country, he was greeted with hostility by radical groups staging violent protests, resulting in numerous arrests. On this occasion even the supposedly moderate PNV criticised the monarch for endorsing Navarrese autonomy, which was in fact supported by a majority of the region's population by this stage.

Remarkably it was not until July 1991 – a full decade after his first visit – that Juan Carlos was able to return to the Basque country in an official capacity. Over the years the PNV–PSOE coalition government had gradually succeeded in creating a reasonably stable political environment and ETA, though still active, had lost much of its former support. Though somewhat marred by violent incidents in Bilbao instigated by HB – whose leaders compared the king's arrival to the recent invasion of Slovenia by Yugoslav tanks – the royal visit was widely seen as a success.[15]

Two years later Juan Carlos returned to Bilbao to support Basque industrialists who had refused to abandon their native land in spite of more than two decades of ETA violence. More generally, the king praised Basque society for its civic courage in standing up to the terrorists, and reaffirmed his faith in a democratic solution to this problem. A poll taken in the wake of this visit revealed that Juan Carlos's popularity in the Basque country had increased significantly in recent years, reaching levels comparable to those of other areas.[16]

The king's concern over centre–periphery tensions remained unabated, however. In the wake of the June 1993 elections, narrowly won by the PSOE, HB representative Jon Idigoras was received at La Zarzuela for the first time, and even wore a tie for the occasion, something he had not done since his wedding day some twenty years earlier! Several months later the HB leaders accused of insulting the king during his visit to Guernica in 1981 were finally acquitted after a legal battle that had meandered its way through several courts for over a decade. In late 1993, however, the PNV unexpectedly blamed the Army for standing in the way of Basque self-determination. By way of reply, in his January 1994 *pascua militar* speech the king argued that 'the diversity which enriches us should unite and not separate', and called on Spaniards to overcome the 'disunity' that had proved so costly in the past, thereby provoking further criticism from the PNV.[17]

Juan Carlos's determination to be regarded as 'king of all Spaniards' – a goal he shared with both Don Juan and Alfonso XIII – manifested itself in other spheres as well. If the king was proud of his contribution to the transition to democracy it was above all because it had brought about a genuine national reconciliation, allowing Spaniards of different persuasions to coexist in peace. This explains his decision to mark the tenth anniversary of his proclamation, on 22 November 1985, with the inauguration of a votive flame in Madrid's Plaza de la Lealtad, under the inscription 'honour to all those who gave their lives for Spain'. For the first time ever, this ceremony brought together representatives of those who had fought on both the Republican and Nationalist sides in the civil war.

The king's other major contribution to Spanish political life since the consolidation of democracy was in the field of foreign policy. Juan Carlos was exceptionally active in this area on account of the need to make up for almost forty years of relative international isolation, imposed on Spain as a result of the non-democratic nature of the Franco regime. Monarchs have traditionally been regarded as good ambassadors on account of their ability to identify with and represent their countries. This was particularly true of Juan Carlos, who was greeted abroad as the leading protagonist of a highly successful democratising process that was enabling Spain to play an increasingly prominent international role.[18]

As we have seen, during the pre-constitutional phase of his reign Juan Carlos played an exceptionally active role in the foreign policy sphere. During these years it was not unheard of for the king to intervene directly in the appointment of an ambassador, as happened in the case of Juan José Rovira, who was sent to Washington after contributing decisively to the 1976 treaty. More generally, the king appears to have restrained Suárez from replacing ambassadors whom he suspected of being lukewarm about the democratising process with his own political appointees.[19]

As in other parliamentary monarchies, after 1978 Spain's foreign policy was formulated and conducted by the government of the day. Nevertheless the king's standing abroad, his special relationships with numerous heads of state and his not inconsiderable knowledge of the international scene were assets that successive premiers naturally sought to exploit. In turn Juan Carlos encouraged successive governments to pay special attention to certain issues and areas that were of particular concern to him. The king soon established the habit of receiving all Spanish ambassadors whenever they took up a new posting, an interview that in many cases was far more than a mere formality.[20]

Since his proclamation in 1975, Juan Carlos had invariably expressed himself as an enthusiastic Europeanist and a leading advocate of Spanish membership of the EC, a goal shared by all major parties and public opinion at large. As in other foreign policy areas, the king's public discourse was characterised by the notion of a reencounter or reconciliation, in this case between Spain and the European democracies. Inevitably the question of EC membership dominated the king's dealings with leading European statesmen in the late 1970s and early 1980s, and he is generally thought to have made a significant contribution to the Spanish cause. This was formally acknowledged in May 1982 when he was awarded the prestigious Charlemagne prize for his contribution to the establishment of democracy in Spain and the cause of European unity. It was thus fully appropriate that the signature of the EC accession treaty by Spain in June 1985 should have taken place in the king's presence, in the course of a solemn ceremony held at the Royal Palace. The British foreign secretary, who had just attended a similar event in Lisbon, would later observe that 'the earlier spontaneity of the Portuguese Republic contrasted with the restrained grandeur of the Spanish ceremonial, engagingly offset, as it was, by the relaxed style of the Spanish monarch and his consort'. In May 1986, once membership had become effective, Juan Carlos reaffirmed Spain's commitment to the EC in a speech to the European Parliament.[21]

Juan Carlos was forced to play a far more discreet role in relation to NATO, membership of which was opposed by the parties of the left and a substantial proportion of the population. The king undoubtedly endorsed González's decision to keep Spain in NATO and to postpone the referendum originally promised in 1982 until 1986, by which stage the government was in a position to justify its U-turn to its electorate. However in the wake of his January 1985 *pascua militar* speech, in which he stated that 'Spain's neutrality or isolation would prove suicidal', critics accused Juan Carlos of taking sides in favour of NATO. Indeed the Catalan leftist Barrera, who had been so active during the constitutional debates, concluded from this incident that 'there will only be a genuine democracy in the Spanish state the day we have a republic'. Several months later the king privately expressed his preference for Spain's full integration in NATO's military structure, as opposed to the half-way-house negotiated by the PSOE government. True to the precedent established in 1976 and 1978, in March 1986 the royal family voted in the NATO referendum, by which Spaniards narrowly endorsed the government's terms.[22]

During the first decade of his reign the king's major foreign policy goal, which reflected that of successive governments, was to achieve Spain's full acceptance by the major European powers. The first two European states visited by the king were France and Germany, without whose support

Spain's application for EC membership in July 1977 could never have succeeded.

Giscard d'Estaing, who had cultivated the monarch assiduously since his proclamation, officially visited Madrid in June 1978, the first French president to do so since 1906.[23] Giscard, whose illusions of grandeur led him to see himself as a latter-day Bourbon monarch, often succumbed to the temptation of patronising his Spanish '*petit frère*', and tended to treat Suárez with open contempt, preferring to deal directly with the king. Unfortunately his ambassador in Madrid, Jean-François Deniau, was also given to lapsing into eighteenth-century habits and often behaved as though he were the Élysée's special envoy to La Zarzuela. In spite of this supposedly cosy relationship with Juan Carlos, after appearing to support Spain's entry to the EC, Giscard abruptly changed his tune on the eve of the French presidential elections, much to Madrid's irritation.[24]

The king's relations with Giscard's successor, Mitterrand, were initially cooler but ultimately more productive. Like many other European Socialists, Mitterrand had refused to visit Spain while Franco was in power, and initially accepted the exiled opposition's verdict of the young king. Indeed an entry in his diary for October 1975 described Juan Carlos as 'a third-hand monarch', whom he pitied on account of 'the tidal wave which will soon overwhelm him'. When Areilza visited him in early 1976, however, he admitted having underestimated the king and was more optimisitic about the monarchy's chances. Anxious to make up for his earlier scepticism, on coming to power in 1981 Mitterrand personally telephoned Juan Carlos in an attempt to improve relations.[25]

In the course of the president's first, somewhat tense visit to Spain in June 1982, Juan Carlos firmly requested his assistance in the never-ending EC negotiations and in the struggle against ETA, which continued to operate freely from the French Basque country. Although it was widely felt that Mitterrand had come to Madrid empty handed, he took back with him a far clearer idea of Spain's demands. Indeed it was partly thanks to the king that he began to understand that the urgency with which Spain demanded EC membership was an expression of essentially domestic factors relating to the consolidation of democracy.

In November 1983, in the course of a visit to Paris to attend a UNESCO gathering, Juan Carlos saw Mitterrand in private, once again broaching the ETA issue. This was followed by a private visit by González, who obtained the clear impression that the French government was about to change its tune. The Spanish ambassador in Paris, the Catalan Socialist Reventós, subsequently concluded that it was the first of these visits that had proved crucial in overcoming the deadlock. By the time Mitterrand visited Madrid again in 1984, the most serious obstacles to Spanish membership of the EC had been removed. This paved the way for Juan Carlos's return visit in July 1985, widely hailed as a definitive turning point in Franco–Spanish relations. In 1993, at Mitterrand's suggestion, the king became the first foreign head of state to address the French legislative assembly since 1919.[26]

Juan Carlos also cultivated key political figures in Germany, the country that ultimately facilitated Spain's accession to the EC. The king and queen first visited the country in April 1977, where they obtained the enthusiastic backing of Chancellor Schmidt, who always took pride in his contribution to Spain's transition. The latter visited Madrid officially in 1980, and was followed by President Karl Carstens a year later. Schmidt, who received Juan Carlos again in 1982, would later publicly reflect on Spain's great good fortune at having had at its disposal such an 'energetic democrat'.[27]

Juan Carlos and Sofía proved decisive in improving Spain's bilateral relations with most European powers, notably other parliamentary monarchies. This was perhaps truest of Britain, a country with which Spain could have enjoyed far better relations had it not been for the Gibraltar imbroglio. The king was initially anxious not to create the impression that his family ties with the British royal family would jeopardise the Spanish claim and was careful to publicise his support for this by-now traditional foreign-policy goal in his proclamation speech. This did not prevent Juan Carlos and Sofía from visiting their British relatives in a strictly private capacity on numerous occasions, and they deeply regretted not being able to attend Prince Charles' and Lady Diana's wedding in 1981, on account of their choice of Gibraltar as the starting-point of their honeymoon.[28]

Anglo–Spanish relations were nevertheless good enough for the king to believe he could mediate in the Malvinas/Falklands conflict. In May 1982, in a letter to the UN secretary-general, Javier Pérez de Cuellar, Juan Carlos expressed the anguish he felt 'as a Spaniard, as a soldier and as king' and urged him to negotiate a ceasefire, which would give him time to explore new avenues with London and Buenos Aires. Had he succeeded, Juan Carlos would no doubt have obtained the Nobel Peace Prize for which he was first nominated in 1978, and which has eluded him ever since.[29]

It was the British government's agreement to include the question of sovereignty in future talks on Gibraltar in 1984 that paved the way for Juan Carlos and Sofía's decisive state visit in April 1986, in the course of which the king became the only European monarch ever to have addressed the assembled Houses of Parliament. In spite of referring to Gibraltar as 'a colonial relic' in his speech, the king was greeted with unprecedented enthusiasm, to the extent that the speaker concluded his salutation with a resounding 'Viva el Rey! Viva España!'[30] At Oxford University, where he received an honorary degree, following the precedent established by Alfonso XIII in 1926, Juan Carlos was greatly amused to hear a description of his role in aborting the 1981 coup read out in Latin by the public orator.

It was in the wake of this tour that the Prince of Wales and his family stayed with the Spanish royal family in Majorca over the summer, a visit they would repeat on three consecutive years. Given the media attention they attracted, these holidays did more for the improvement of Anglo–Spanish relations than years of diplomacy could ever have achieved. Queen Elizabeth II finally carried out her own long-awaited state visit to Spain in October 1988, and a year later Juan Carlos returned to Windsor to receive the Order of the Garter.

As with Britain, the royal family played a crucial role in bringing about Spain's reconciliation with the Netherlands. The atrocities committed by Spanish troops in the Low Countries under Habsburg rule in the sixteenth and seventeenth centuries had occupied a prominent place in the Dutch national consciousness, and the Franco dictatorship had merely served to confirm centuries-old stereotypes. Indeed, together with the Scandinavians, the Dutch had been amongst Franco's most determined antagonists, systematically opposing Spanish membership of NATO and the EC during the dictator's lifetime. Juan Carlos and Sofía broke the ice with an official visit to the Netherlands in 1980, which Queen Beatrix returned in 1985. Spain's relations with Belgium also benefited from the royal family's close ties with Baudouin and Fabiola, who visited the country officially in September 1978.

Although Spain's commercial and political links with Scandinavia were weaker than with the Benelux, Juan Carlos and Sofía also contributed to bring Spain closer to the populations of these countries, a task facilitated by their warm personal relations with their respective monarchs. Norway had been consistently hostile to the Franco regime and initially regarded Juan Carlos with some reticence. The king's role in thwarting the 1981 coup – to which King Olav V paid public tribute during his visit in April 1982 – was thus decisive in facilitating Oslo's recognition of Spanish progress towards democracy. The same could be said of Sweden, whose monarch first visited Spain in March 1983, and of Denmark, whose queen travelled to Madrid later that year.

Juan Carlos's easy-going personality and linguistic skills enabled him to establish unusually intimate relationships with a number of foreign statesmen. Prominent amongst these was the Italian president, Pertini, an octogenarian whose affection for him was such that he once described Juan Carlos as the son he would like to have had. Pertini visited Spain officially in 1980 and received the king and queen in Rome a year later. In 1982, when he returned to watch Italy play the World Cup final, his excitement was such that he spent much of the match hugging Juan Carlos. Characteristically, when the king revisted his native Rome in 1984, Pertini insisted on taking him to his favourite *trattoria* in the Trastevere quarter.

The presence of a royal family in Spain proved more damaging than useful in the country's bilateral relations with only one state, namely Greece. President Karamanlis, who never forgave Queen Frederica for having forced him into exile in 1963, visited Madrid officially in 1984, providing Sofía with an excuse to wear the Greek royal family's most splendid decorations. In view of continued Greek official hostility towards its royal family, Athens remains the only EC and NATO capital the Spanish king and queen have yet to visit officially.

Juan Carlos also paid considerable attention to Spain's relations with the United States, which had largely dominated Franco's foreign policy. As we saw in an earlier chapter, it was his determination to obtain official recognition for the fledgling Spanish democracy that took him to Washington in June 1976, in his first state visit abroad. Juan Carlos subsequently established a good relationship with Carter, who visited Spain in 1980. The king and queen returned to the US in late 1981 at the invitation of the Reagan administration, thereby helping to improve relations that had been somewhat soured by Washington's apparent indifference to the outcome of the aborted coup. The king was also in contact with Reagan during the Malvinas/Falklands conflict, and in May 1982 he sent the president a letter urging him to make 'one last effort' to achieve a 'negotiated, fair and honourable' solution.

In May 1984 a new bilateral agreement replaced the treaty negotiated by Kissinger and Areilza in 1976, paving the way for Reagan's visit in May 1985. Two years later Juan Carlos and Sofía embarked on their third US tour, which included visits to California, Texas and New Mexico, where the king defended the coexistence of the English and Spanish languages. Juan Carlos would later admit that the tour had been an eye-opener, revealing just how little was known about the new democratic Spain in the US. At the time Madrid was negotiating a reduction in US military presence on Spanish soil, and the visit was somewhat marred by what were seen as Washington's efforts to undermine the government's position by circulating rumours of alleged discrepancies between Juan Carlos and González over this issue. Earlier, in his January 1987 *pascua militar* speech, the king had urged Spanish negotiators to exercise 'tact and prudence' in their dealings with the US.[31]

Juan Carlos would also develop a good working relationship with

Reagan's successor, George Bush, on account of the negotiations leading to the 1991 Middle East peace summit held in Madrid. Indeed Bush would later declare that the king had acted as a catalyst in his own relationship with Mikhail Gorbachev, and he visited Madrid privately on several occasions after leaving office.

One of the most pleasant surprises that awaited Juan Carlos as king was the warmth with which he was greeted by the inhabitants of Spain's former American colonies. During his first visit to the Latin American mainland in October 1976 the king stopped at Bogotá, where small children trotted alongside his motorcade shouting 'Our king is back! Our king is back!' A year later a Costa Rican academic moved him deeply when he greeted him with the words: 'Sir, we are a small country, inhabited by simple, peace-loving people. We have been waiting for you for four hundred years. Thank you for coming'. Since 1976 Juan Carlos has visited every Latin American country, with the sole exception of Cuba.[32]

In the late 1970s and early 1980s Spain's highly successful transition to democracy and the prospect of EC membership rendered it a far more attractive partner in the eyes of Latin Americans than it had ever been in the past. This was particularly true of countries that had recently experienced, or were in the process of undertaking, their own transitions to democracy, where the king was seen as a symbol of the Spanish 'miracle'.

Juan Carlos first became fully aware of his importance as promoter of democracy in the course of his fifth Latin American tour in May 1983, which included visits to Brazil and Uruguay, countries with military regimes slowly moving towards civilian rule. In Uruguay the head of the military junta, General Gregorio Alvarez, had recently opened talks with representatives of the democratic opposition, a process that was experiencing numerous setbacks. On his arrival the king was hailed as the champion of Spanish democracy by the enthusiastic crowds that thronged the streets of Montevideo, and his public appearances were spontaneously transformed into massive pro-democracy rallies, much to the junta's embarrassment. As he had already done in Argentina in 1978, Juan Carlos insisted on meeting the leaders of the major democratic parties, including several who were currently banned from political activity. When one of them established a parallel between the situation in Uruguay and that in Spain after Franco's death, Juan Carlos was quick to point out a fundamental difference, namely that in the latter case it was Franco himself who had appointed him successor, thereby guaranteeing the obedience of the military. The king also advised them as to how to deal with their own armed forces and emphasised the importance of allowing them an 'honourable' withdrawal from politics.[33]

The Spanish government subsequently commissioned a poll to gauge the impact of the royal tour on Uruguayan public opinion. This revealed that an extremely high proportion of the population of Montevideo had followed it with interest, to the extent that 65 per cent of those polled had seen the royal couple with their own eyes. Furthermore the king's meeting with opposition leaders was seen as the most important aspect of the visit, and his references to democracy were the most widely remembered. Indeed 39 per cent of those questioned believed Juan Carlos had contributed significantly to Uruguay's transition to democracy. This was certainly the opinion of Uruguay's first democratically elected president, Julio Sanguinetti, who travelled to Spain in 1985 to thank him for his support.[34]

The king played a similar role with regard to the Argentine transition. Juan Carlos enjoyed considerable prestige and popularity on account of his role in the Spanish process and, by associating with him, the protagonists of the restored Argentine democracy legitimised themselves in the eyes of their own population. The representative of the new Argentina, President Raúl Alfonsín, visited Madrid in 1984 and received Juan Carlos in Buenos Aires a year later. In 1990 the king was finally able to visit Chile, where he publicly admitted not having wanted to go sooner on account of General Pinochet. President Patricio Aylwin's presence in Madrid a year later, like that of Alfonsín and Sanguinetti before him, was read as proof of these countries' definitive acceptance by the European democracies. In his dealings with Latin America the king thus played a role not unlike that performed earlier by senior European statesmen with regard to Spain.

It was thus largely Juan Carlos's ability to exploit the prestige and authority acquired during the Spanish transition that enabled him to fulfil the constitutional mandate by which 'the king ... assumes the highest representation of the Spanish state in international relations, especially with those nations belonging to the same historic community' (article 56.1). In theory this community included Fidel Castro's Cuba, which partially succeeded in mitigating the effects of the US embargo thanks to the Spanish connection. Juan Carlos was the only European head of state who regularly saw the Cuban autocrat, in spite of an incident provoked by Castro in 1990 when he publicly questioned the democratic nature of parliamentary monarchies such as that of Spain. It is unlikely, however, that the king will be able to do much for Cuban democracy. As he himself has admitted, when they met in 1991 Castro was 'very amiable', but 'we both knew we couldn't talk about anything really serious'.[35]

Not surprisingly, given the love–hate feelings that often characterise relations between former imperial powers and their erstwhile colonies, the king's presence in Latin America sometimes proved controversial. In particular the crown's vigorous promotion of the celebrations marking the fifth centenary of the discovery of America – first announced by Juan Carlos in his 1984 Christmas Eve address – was resented by some sectors of Latin American society, even though much was done to involve the indigenous populations. In 1990, for example, the leftist Mexican leader Huautemoc Cárdenas turned down a royal invitation to attend these events on the grounds that he could not condone a genocide. Ironically, during that same visit to Mexico the Indians of Oaxaca requested the king's support in their struggle to obtain official recognition of their property rights from the government. Several months later, during a visit to Chile, the Mapuche Indians insisted on meeting the king on their own territory, much to the irritation of the Santiago authorities.[36]

Virtually since his proclamation, Juan Carlos had spearheaded Spanish efforts to promote the concept of an 'Iberoamerican Community of Nations' as a way of forging closer links between the Hispanic peoples (including Portuguese speakers). These efforts, galvanised by the events of 1992, have so far resulted in four summit meetings of Iberoamerican heads of state, held in Mexico (1991), Spain (1992), Brazil (1993) and Colombia (1994). According to Juan Carlos, at the first of these meetings 'whenever one of them rose to speak he first addressed our host, Carlos Salinas de Gortari: "*Señor Presidente* . . ." Then, immediately afterwards, he would turn to me: "Your Majesty . . ." It gave me gooseflesh every time. They all showed me a respect and affection that no one had obliged them to show'.[37] This modesty underlines a fundamental difference between the Iberoamerican Community and the British Commonwealth, namely that the Spanish monarch's standing is identical to that of his fellow heads of state.

Together with Latin America, Spain's other traditional sphere of influence had been North Africa and the Arab world. Over the years Juan Carlos patiently nurtured his relationship with King Hassan of Morocco, a country of vital interest to Spain for strategic, economic and political reasons. Juan Carlos's friendship with Hassan dated back to the early 1970s, when the latter stayed at La Zarzuela for several days during a private visit arranged by Don Juan. Thereafter the two monarchs often spoke on the telephone to discuss international developments of mutual interest as well as bilateral relations. As we saw in an earlier chapter, this personal relationship did not prevent the Moroccan king from putting Spain and its future monarch in an extremely difficult position in late 1975, but their friendship survived the crisis.[38]

Hassan, who ruled not unlike a mid-nineteenth century European monarch, was reluctant to allow his government too great a say in dealings with foreign powers and treated Spanish ministers as mere personal emissaries of his 'brother'. As a result, any major negotiation between

Spain and Morocco necessarily required the king's intervention, as the PSOE government publicly acknowledged when it thanked Juan Carlos for his role in bringing about a crucial fishing agreement in 1983.

Dealing with semi-absolute monarchs, however, could have its drawbacks. Whenever the Spanish press was critical of Morocco and its king, Hassan would call Juan Carlos and demand that he put a stop to it. Despite his efforts to convince him that in a democracy a king does not control the press, Juan Carlos could not help feeling that 'although he is a very intelligent and very experienced man, Hassan just cannot understand me. Sometimes I wonder if he even believes me'.[39]

Juan Carlos first officially visited Morocco in 1979 and returned to celebrate the twenty-fifth anniversary of Hassan's coronation in 1986. The latter did not visit Spain officially until 1990, a visit that paved the way for a crucial bilateral treaty signed by Juan Carlos in Morocco the following year. Important though it was, the king's special relationship with Hassan did not prevent the latter from pursuing Morocco's claim to the Spanish enclaves of Ceuta and Melilla, and Juan Carlos was careful to stay away from these territories so as not to antagonise his 'brother' unnecessarily.

Under Franco, Spain had actively cultivated its ties with the Arab states in an attempt to mitigate the regime's postwar isolation. This proximity enabled Juan Carlos to develop unusually close relationships with a number of Arab monarchs, some of which dated back to his early travels as Prince of Spain. Juan Carlos and Sofía came to regard King Hussein of Jordan as a close family friend, to the extent of travelling to Amman to celebrate his fortieth birthday, while the latter visited the king in Madrid after one of his skiing accidents. The fact that both monarchs were enthusiastic amateur radio operators no doubt contributed to keeping their friendship alive in spite of the distance. Juan Carlos was also on close terms with King Fahd of Saudi Arabia, who visited Spain in 1984, even though 'the Saudis don't like speaking languages other than their own, so one is rarely alone with them'.[40]

The king's relations with the monarchs of the leading oil-producing countries proved particularly useful to Spain, a country chronically dependent on imported crude. Already in 1974–75, during the first oil crisis, Juan Carlos had interceded with Crown Prince Fahd of Saudi Arabia on behalf of the Franco government in order to guarantee additional oil shipments. Several years later, during the second oil crisis, it was again at his request that Fahd offered Spain 100 000 daily barrels of crude at a special price. In spite of this, by January 1980 Spanish oil reserves reached an all-time low, in view of which the government turned to the king once again. On this occasion Fahd added a further 50 000 barrels a day to what oil experts came to describe as 'the king's quota'. Juan Carlos subsequently obtained additional crude from the rulers of Qatar, the United Arab Emirates and Kuwait, all of whom he visited in 1980–81.[41]

The king's personal relations with these monarchs was put to the test in 1986, when Spain and Israel finally established diplomatic relations. The State of Israel had always refused to have dealings with Franco on account of his war-time association with the Axis powers and resented his close relations with its Arab neighbours. In return for their support in the United Nations and elsewhere, Franco had actively supported the Arab cause, including demands for a Palestinian state.

Juan Carlos had always wanted to establish relations with Israel, and had encouraged Areilza and Oreja to take steps in this direction in the late 1970s. However, he was also anxious that this should be done without undermining Spain's standing in the Arab world. The king first raised this issue with Fahd and Hussein in late 1982, during their private visits to Madrid. A year later, following a visit to Tunisia, the local press claimed he had given assurances that there would be no *rapprochement* with Israel. By 1984 the Israeli press was beginning to describe Juan Carlos as an impediment to his government's diplomatic overtures, a view shared by some in Washington. In view of this, in late 1985 Juan Carlos sent González two so-called 'institutional notes' – or written statements of his position – urging the government to establish relations as soon as possible.

As had been feared, this decision was not well received by the Arabs. However, as the king himself has admitted, 'as a personal friend of many Arab leaders I was able to intervene behind the scenes. I told my Arab brothers: look, this is not a question of betraying a friendship, still less of ignoring our fraternal bonds. You can ask a lot of me, but you can't insist that a democratic state like Spain should not have diplomatic and commercial relations with other democratic states, including Israel'. In the end they accepted his point of view, albeit reluctantly. As Juan Carlos himself has observed, 'they might not have reacted in the same way to explanations from a republican president'.[42]

Spain's new ties with Israel enabled Juan Carlos to mediate in the Middle East conflict with some success. In January 1989 the king saw Yasser Arafat in Madrid, and openly endorsed the PLO's talks with Washington. A month later he saw Israel's President Chaim Herzog and urged him to come forward with fresh proposals in the light of the PLO's increasingly moderate stance. In recognition of these efforts, the king's Arab friends proposed Madrid as the venue for the decisive Middle East peace conference of October 1991, which was held at the Royal Palace at his suggestion.

Juan Carlos and Sofía were finally able to visit Israel in October 1993, a month after the signature of the Israel–PLO agreement in Washington. In his speech to the Knesset, Juan Carlos – the first European monarch to address the Israeli parliament – defended the right to Palestinian self-determination and endorsed the 'land for peace' formula. Although this was badly received by some deputies, Prime Minister Yitzhak Rabin urged the king to continue to act as a bridge between Israel and the Arab world in the future. The visit contributed to the mutual reconciliation sealed in 1986, even if the royal party was unhappy with Israeli comparisons of the expulsion of the Jews from Spain in 1492 with the Holocaust.

Given the king's personal ties with a number of Arab leaders, some observers expected him to play a leading role in the crisis resulting from Iraq's invasion of Kuwait in August 1990 and were critical of the fact that he did not interrupt his holidays in Majorca on this account. King Hussein travelled to Palma during his emergency tour of Europe to inform Juan Carlos in person of events in the Gulf, but the latter's critics claimed he had been too busy studying the plans for a new yacht to brief himself properly beforehand. This criticism was totally unfounded, however, and there was in any case little Juan Carlos could do other than inform the government of his conversations with the Emir of Kuwait and Hassan II as well as Hussein. Quite exceptionally, some Spanish publications sub-sequently expressed criticism of the fact that the king was sailing in Majorca while Spanish recruits were being forced to man the frigates with which Madrid contributed to the naval blockade of Iraq.[43] By way of reply, in his annual Christmas Eve address Juan Carlos demanded that the media perform their duties with moderation and respect for the truth, a remark that irritated some commentators.

The king's reputation as promoter of democracy also enabled Spain to strengthen its hitherto tenuous links with Central and Eastern Europe. In the 1980s Spain's transition became an exportable commodity, which nobody could sell better than Juan Carlos himself. In 1987 the king visited Hungary and Czechoslovakia, where he spoke out in favour of democracy and human rights, and went on to Poland in 1989. Like so many other Western statesmen, the king got on famously with Gorbachev, who went to Spain in 1990 and would later become a regular visitor. His successor, Boris Yeltsin, travelled to Madrid in 1994, and publicly compared his role in Russia to that of the king in Spain, an analogy that may not have pleased the latter. President Vaclav Havel was in Madrid in 1990, and visited Juan Carlos privately in Palma the following summer, where he may have discovered some of the clues as to his host's success. To his amaze-ment the king took him to a bar, where he was greeted by everyone as if he were an old acquaintance and later paid for their drinks himself in spite of the owner's remonstrations. 'Doing anything like this is absolutely out of the question in Prague!', the Czech president would exclaim.[44]

Juan Carlos always knew that it was one thing to promote democracy, and quite another to 'export' the monarchy. During his tour of Bulgaria in May 1993 he was received with wild enthusiasm by numerous pro-monarchy demonstrators, but was careful to keep his distance. Juan Carlos thought it unwise to foster the belief that the return of the monarchy could solve a country's problems overnight, something he had often discussed with his friend King Simeon II of Bulgaria, who lived in exile in Madrid and was married to a Spaniard. This scepticism was partly born of his awareness that the situation in Spain in 1975 and that of the former Soviet bloc countries in the late 1980s had little in common. As Juan Carlos himself would explain, 'I inherited a country which had known forty years of peace, a period during which a powerful and prosperous middle class came into being: a social class which was practically non-existent at the end of the civil war, but one which very soon became the backbone of my country'. In the far less auspicious environment of the former Soviet bloc countries, a monarch unable to provide answers to unprecedented socio-economic problems could only expect to be 'thrown out as enthusiastically as he had been welcomed back'.[45]

Finally, the king also played a key role in Spain's relations with the Vatican. Although the 1978 constitution sanctioned the separation of Church and state, Catholicism remained the religion of a majority of Spaniards and it was therefore important that the head of state should enjoy good relations with Rome. At home the king's close association with successive popes undoubtedly improved his standing in the eyes of the more conservative sectors of society.

As we saw in an earlier chapter, Juan Carlos's visit to the Vatican in early 1977 had helped to put Spain's relations with Rome on an entirely new footing after Franco's death. The king had hoped that John Paul I would become the first pope to visit Spain, and was greatly saddened by his sudden death in 1980. It was thus the irrepressible John Paul II who toured Spain in 1982, shortly after the decisive October elections won by the Socialists. Juan Carlos and Sofía became regular visitors to the Vatican and developed a good rapport with Wojtyla, who returned to Spain in 1984, 1989 and 1993.

In spite of the separation of Church and state, Juan Carlos respected many of the crown's traditional ties with the Catholic Church. The king and queen frequently attended major Catholic events, such as the traditional offering to Spain's patron saint held at Santiago de Compostela,

Seville's famous Easter celebrations, or the Corpus Christi procession in Toledo. With characteristic good humour, in his July 1982 offering to Santiago, Juan Carlos included himself amongst the sinners on whose behalf he sought the saint's intercession and claimed his burden was such he could barely enter the cathedral through its vast door.

Ever since he was a child, Juan Carlos has always regarded himself as a devout, unquestioning Catholic, while Sofía's spirituality is perhaps more akin to that of Prince Charles, though she has naturally brought up her children in the faith. La Zarzuela houses its own private chapel, where the royal family regularly attend mass when they are in residence, and the king has his own father confessor, a member of the Dominican order.[46]

In spite of his close personal association with the Catholic Church, Juan Carlos has carefully avoided any form of religious controversy. The king – who cannot refuse to sanction a law passed by the Cortes, according to the constitution – duly put his signature to legislation relating to divorce (1981) and abortion (1985). In the latter case the bishop of Cuenca warned that the royal sanction would pose Juan Carlos a serious moral dilemma, but his concern was not widely shared.[47] The king has often voiced conservative views on issues such as family values in his Christmas Eve addresses, but to date this has never proved controversial.

In his determination to become 'king of all Spaniards', Juan Carlos became increasingly sensitive to the demands of other religious communities present in Spain. As part of the crown's struggle to reconcile Spain with its own history, he publicly associated himself with Islam and Judaism, both with deep roots in Spanish culture, which the Franco regime had actively sought to eradicate. In 1986, for example, Juan Carlos accepted the presidency of the commission organising the commemoration of the twelfth centenary of the construction of the Cordoba Mosque, one of Spain's most outstanding architectural jewels, and subsequently attended a seminar on Islamic architecture held at Granada. The king later presided the opening of Madrid's Islamic Cultural Centre, financed by the Saudis, which houses the largest mosque in Europe. Similarly, in the course of 1992 the royal family supported the 'Al Andalus' project, which celebrated eight hundred years of Arab presence in Spain.

The establishment of diplomatic relations with Israel in 1986 paved the way for a rapid improvement in Spain's relations with international Jewry. Juan Carlos played a leading role in this process, to the extent that in 1991 Nobel Prize winner Elie Wiesel claimed that the king had made up for the humiliation of the expulsion of the Jews in 1492. The following year Juan Carlos attended the opening of the Beth Yaacov synagogue in Madrid with Israeli president Herzog, at which he donned the *yarmulka* and was blessed by the rabbi in *ladino*, the ancient Sephardic language. As in the case of the Al Andalus events, the royal family was closely involved with 'Sefarad '92', which sought to heighten Spaniards' awareness of their Jewish heritage. For the first time ever, during his visit to Istanbul in 1993 Juan Carlos met representatives of the local Sephardic community and the following year Queen Sofía was awarded the Wiesenthal prize for her commitment to racial and religious tolerance.[48]

Like other European monarchs, the king and queen have dedicated much of their time to cultural and scientific activities. Juan Carlos's role as honorary patron of the eight Royal Academies, officially stipulated in the constitution, serves the purpose of demonstrating the support of the crown and therefore the state for the highest level of cultural and scientific achievement. The king and queen are also associated with less formal manifestations of Spanish cultural life, such as the annual open-air Madrid book fair and the Cervantes prize, the country's most prestigious literary award. Similarly, in the 1980s the monarch began to host a special reception for leading members of the academic, artistic and cultural community, which generally took the form of a garden party in the Royal Palace.[49]

The Spanish case is somewhat different to that of other European countries in that there is a clear political motivation behind this commitment to the world of culture. Juan Carlos has always partly attributed his grandfather's downfall in 1931 to the hostility of the Spanish intelligentsia, which turned against him during the Primo de Rivera dictatorship, and has worked hard to compensate for Alfonso XIII's lack of interest in intellectual or artistic pursuits. Indeed the king has gone out of his way to pay tribute to leading liberal intellectuals such as José Ortega y Gasset and Gregorio Marañón, who turned away from the monarchy in the late 1920s and placed their considerable prestige at the disposal of the Republican cause. In this, as in so many other spheres, Juan Carlos betrays an almost obsessive awareness of his family's recent past. This is one Bourbon of whom it will never be said that he had learnt nothing and forgotten nothing.

10 Looking to the Future

Juan Carlos's popularity since 1975 has sometimes been attributed to his ability to match the size and style of the monarchy to Spain's needs and possibilities. In this, the king has enjoyed the considerable advantage of being able to start afresh, but this also meant there were very few reliable precedents for him to follow.

Long before his proclamation Juan Carlos had decided he would have a small, functional household, free from the constraints of traditional court life. The decision to remain at La Zarzuela rather than move to the Royal Palace in central Madrid proved crucial in this respect, for it allowed him to maintain a distinction between his private and public persona. Additionally, it enabled his three children to grow up in an atmosphere more akin to that of a large country house rather than that of a palace. Unlike the Duke of Edinburgh, Juan Carlos has never had to worry about his tea arriving cold on account of the vast distance between the kitchens and his private apartments.[1]

According to the constitution, 'the king receives an overall amount from the state budget for the upkeep of his family and household and distributes it unrestrictedly' (article 65.1). In 1995 the Cortes allocated the sum of 956 million pesetas, approximately equal to the annual cost of the royal yacht *Britannia* alone.[2] This sum is intended to cover all household expenditure, including employees' salaries and meals (some two hundred a day), receptions, and the internal maintenance of the La Zarzuela complex. Strictly speaking there is no civil list in Spain, and in practice Juan Carlos allocates funds to his wife and three children as the need arises. Neither the king's parents nor his sisters have ever received salaries from the state, as they were not expected to perform public duties. The king's sisters, Pilar and Margarita, who settled in Spain in the 1970s, have led extremely private lives, generally staying away from La Zarzuela other than on family occasions. Indeed Spaniards are probably more accustomed to seeing Juan Carlos in the company of his brother-in-law Constantine and his family than in that of his own sisters. The queen's younger sister, Irene, has resided at La Zarzuela since her mother's death in 1981.

The Spanish Bourbons are often described as the least wealthy of Europe's royal families. Alfonso XIII is thought to have accumulated a small fortune during his reign, but his hurried departure in 1931 and a decade in exile deprived Don Juan of a substantial inheritance. Additionally, unlike the royal families of Britain and even some of the so-called 'bicycle monarchies', Juan Carlos and his family have never been exempt from any form of taxation, including income tax. Nevertheless the actual extent of their wealth is a closely guarded secret. On his death in 1993 Don Juan left his son and two daughters twenty million pesetas and a flat in Estoril, which Juan Carlos and Pilar subsequently ceded to their sister Margarita.[3]

On the whole the Spanish royal family has enjoyed a comfortable though not luxurious existence. Both La Zarzuela and Marivent in Majorca are owned by the state, and the skiing chalet they use in Baqueira belongs to the resort's developers. In 1988 there was talk of them spending part of their summer at Comillas on the Cantabrian coast, but these plans were dropped due to the cost of restoring the only suitable building available. The only outward symbol of luxury generally associated with the king is the royal yacht *Fortuna*, a present from the then Crown Prince Fahd, which is owned by the state. Given its frequent mechanical failures, Juan Carlos thought of replacing it with a newer model (which would have cost some one thousand million pesetas in 1989), but decided to modernise the *Fortuna* instead. A great lover of fast cars and motorcycles, the king takes great pride in showing visitors his collection, which consists largely of models given to him by friends and foreign statesmen.

While British governments have often been accused of being unduly lenient with the royal family when it comes to financial matters, in Spain the opposite has sometimes been the case. In the mid-1980s, for example, the king's flight consisted of two DC-8s, which had seen over twenty years' service and had left Juan Carlos and Sofía stranded on several visits abroad. In response to growing concern over their safety, in 1988 these aircraft were finally replaced with two ten-year old Boeing 707s.

Given that Spain is one of the great tourist destinations of the world, it would be incongrous for Juan Carlos to go on holiday abroad. Other than the occasional week's skiing at Aspen, Courchevel or Gstaad, the royal family has invariably spent its winter holidays in Spain. As to the summer, the king's presence in Majorca since 1971 is said to have attracted wealthy Spanish holidaymakers to the island.

Much of the king's success over the years has been attributed to his ability to surround himself with competent, loyal advisers. Between 1977 and 1990 the royal household was superbly run by Mondéjar and Fernández Campo, with the latter gradually playing the dominant role. In Spain the post of head of the royal household is of ministerial rank, and enjoys a far higher profile than its equivalent in other European monarchies. In early 1990 Mondéjar – whom Juan Carlos once described as a surrogate father – finally retired, and was replaced as head of the household by Fernández Campo. In turn the latter's post as secretary-general went to the former ambassador in London, Puig de la Bellacasa. As we saw above, Puig had already been attached to La Zarzuela in the early 1970s, but was removed shortly after the king's investiture by Armada, who thought him excessively liberal. Given the king's insistence that he return to his side after so many years, it is surprising that Puig was once again forced to leave abruptly in early 1991 after less than a year in the job. On this occasion he appears to have fallen out with Fernández Campo, who knew him to be his natural successor. Additionally Puig is thought to have attempted to impose a degree of discipline on the king's private life which Juan Carlos found intolerable.

Ironically, shortly thereafter Juan Carlos also dispensed with Fernández Campo, though not before making him Count of Latores and a grandee of Spain. This decision was officially justified on the grounds that he would soon be seventy-five and had long wanted to retire. Unofficially it was known that Fernández Campo had disapproved of the king's decision to grant an exclusive televised interview to the British journalist Selina Scott and opposed the publication of a so-called authorised biography by his friend the novelist, actor and aristocrat Vilallonga, who had acted as the *Junta Democrática*'s representative in Paris in the mid-1970s.[4]

Be this as it may, Juan Carlos was finally free to appoint an entirely new team to run his household, something he had been looking forward to for some time. In January 1993 the career diplomats Fernando Almansa and Rafael Spottorno became the new head and secretary-general of the *Casa Real* respectively, and proceeded to appoint a new team of assistants.[5] What is most significant about these changes is that, for the first time ever, La Zarzuela was exclusively in the hands of civilians. Additionally, and also for the first time, the king no longer found himself under the tutelage of older men.

It could of course be argued that this tutelage had served the king extremely well in the past. Though less so than before, Juan Carlos continued to practice dangerous sports, drive fast cars, and fly his own aeroplanes and helicopters. Indeed over the years he proved to be somewhat accident-prone. In mid-1981 he walked through a glass door as he was leaving the swimming pool at La Zarzuela, breaking an arm. Two years later he splintered his pelvis in a skiing accident, which required a second operation in 1985. In December 1990 his Porche 959 – a present from a group of wealthy friends – skidded off the road as he was driving to Baqueira.[6] A year later the king badly injured a knee in another skiing incident, forcing him to use crutches until well into the spring of 1992, possibly his busiest year ever. Finally, in December 1994, he hurt his right hand while skiing, which forced him to wear a cast during his eldest daughter's wedding three months later.

The staff at La Zarzuela sometimes regretted the casual, spontaneous approach cultivated by Juan Carlos, which was exceptional even by the standards of the Scandinavian royal families. In the late 1970s, for example, the king would sometimes turn up at La Moncloa on his motorbike to see Suárez unannounced. Similarly, the story has often been told of the occasion when he stopped to assist a motorist who had run out of petrol, and of the shock he gave him when he removed his helmet. Security considerations have gradually restricted his freedom of movement, but the king still frequents the restaurants of Madrid's old quarter – in particular his favourite, 'Casa Lucio' – and can still be seen dining *al fresco* in the streets of Palma in the summer. Indeed not many reigning monarchs have been photographed being thrown into a swimming pool fully clothed after winning a yacht race, as Juan Carlos was in the summer of 1993.

The king's apparently cavalier attitude towards security matters reflects more than a personal whim. As prince he soon became aware of the irritation Franco's elaborate security arrangements caused ordinary citizens trying to go about their business, and swore not to follow his example. Unlike Franco, who had a rigid 'court' of his own, the king has never sought to distance himself artificially from his fellow citizens and is widely perceived as being far more accessible than most reigning monarchs.[7] Spanish society is in some ways remarkably egalitarian and meritocratic, and Juan Carlos has wisely refrained from frequenting the country's aristocracy. Indeed some Spanish grandees have been heard to complain that, given the attention they get from La Zarzuela, they might as well be living under a republic.

Juan Carlos has very rarely given the impression of allowing his private life to interfere with his public duties, however. As we saw above, the Gulf crisis of 1990 provoked the first such incident. In mid-June 1992 the alarm bells were again set ringing, this time by González's admission that his new foreign minister could not take up office until Juan Carlos returned from abroad to preside the swearing-in ceremony. The royal household had not informed the media of the king's departure but it was not long before journalists traced him to Switzerland, where he spent over a week. The purpose of this visit, which triggered speculation as to the king's health, his love life and even his financial affairs, was never fully clarified. Given the size of his work load during 1992, however, in all likelihood Juan Carlos merely needed a rest.[8]

Although the king has been attributed several stable extra-marital relationships over the years, this has not undermined his popularity or credibility. This is no doubt partly because until recently the Spanish press were very reluctant to discuss the royal family's private life. This may in turn have reflected their awareness of the importance of the king's political

210 Juan Carlos of Spain

role, particularly in the wake of the 1981 coup, and their reluctance to undermine his authority. Ironically the increased coverage registered in recent years could be read as evidence of the monarchy's consolidation, as Spaniards begin to take their royal family for granted.

In connection with the above, it has become somewhat of a cliché to claim that the king's reputation as a womaniser – justified or otherwise – has probably contributed to his popularity more than it has detracted from it. This view is not uncommon amongst middle-aged men, but does not appear to be shared by women and younger people generally. Indeed studies conducted in 1993–4 revealed that Juan Carlos's standing was highest amongst middle-aged married women, who were also shown to be the least likely to condone infidelity.[9]

The king's private life suddenly became a political issue in the summer of 1992, when a succession of French and Italian magazines and newspapers published stories of his alleged long-term relationship with a resident of Majorca, Marta Gayá, which were reproduced in the Spanish press. Remarkably this prompted an intervention by González, who claimed there was a sinister campaign afoot, masterminded from abroad, aimed at counteracting the prestige acquired by Juan Carlos and Spain as a whole thanks to the Olympic Games and Seville's Expo '92. The head of the royal household, Fernández Campo, subsequently attributed the campaign to the monarchy's enemies within Spain. On a less dramatic note, a prominent left-wing politician, Pablo Castellano, came to the king's defence by announcing that 'the only night of his life which matters to me is that of 23 February 1981!'[10]

Inevitably these reports fuelled fresh speculation concerning the king's relations with queen Sofía. It has long been known that their marriage has experienced difficulties, but the queen has never allowed them to stand in the way of her public duties, which she performs with a mixture of Germanic efficiency and Mediterranean charm. The king himself has described her as 'a very great professional', attributing this to the fact that 'she has royalty in her blood'. As they have grown older, they appear to have become increasingly incompatible in their personal tastes and hobbies. Juan Carlos is known for his passion for technological gadgetry, and spends much of his free time keeping abreast of the latest audio and video equipment. Sofía, on the other hand, feels most at home in concert halls and art museums, and hosts an on-going private seminar on issues of special interest to her, mostly of a philosophical nature. The queen – who is something of a vegetarian and dislikes bullfighting – has often remarked that she would have liked to work as a paediatrician. The fact that the royal couple have very different tastes and temperaments may not have contributed to their personal happiness, but it has facilitated a division of labour that has undoubtedly enhanced the monarchy's popularity and prestige.[11]

Extra-marital relationships are not the only aspect of the king's private life to have come under growing scrutiny. In recent years Juan Carlos has been criticised for associating too closely with members of the international jet set, notably during his sojourns in Majorca. The concern underlying these criticisms was that these allegedly undesirable elements cultivated him in the hope of extracting favours that he was too generous to refuse. Indeed in late 1993 the former head of his household, Fernández Campo, claimed that the only threat to the crown was 'that parallel court which irresponsibly tells the monarch what he wants to hear ... a court of "buddies" who advise him out of self-interest, with no regard for the country's concerns'. Juan Carlos himself has admitted that it is both difficult and dangerous for a king to have friends, and that 'it isn't always easy to tell the difference between a friend and a courtier'. Although he has never been publicly associated with corrupt practices, the fact that foreign investors attempted to bribe him in the 1960s is indicative of the type of pressures he has been subjected to over the years.[12]

In recent years, safe in the knowledge of his own popularity, Juan Carlos's overriding goal has been the consolidation of the monarchy as an institution. This largely explains his efforts to bring Spaniards closer to the Bourbon dynasty and its recent history, something the Franco regime had actively prevented.

It was not until early 1981 that Juan Carlos was finally able to arrange the return of King Alfonso XIII's remains to Spain, something he had begun to discuss with his father as early as 1975. Given the political turmoil that marked the early years of the transition, it was agreed that the remains of the king who had been forced into exile in 1931 were best left in the Roman church where they were buried until the monarchy was fully recognised by the major parties of the left. Even then, the decision to land Alfonso XIII's coffin at Cartagena, the port from which he had sailed into exile, was seen by some as a misguided attempt to vindicate his reign and turn back the clock.[13]

Juan Carlos continued the sorry task of reuniting the Spanish royal family beyond the grave in 1985, when Queen Victoria Eugenia's remains, buried at Lausanne, were transported to the royal pantheon at El Escorial, where they will eventually join those of her husband. In October 1992 the same was done with the remains of the king's younger brother, Alfonso, who had been buried at Estoril in 1956.

The death of the king's seventy-nine-year-old father, Don Juan, in April

1993, in some ways marked a turning point in the consolidation of the monarchy in Spain. The Count of Barcelona had been hospitalised the previous September and his long struggle against cancer raised widespread sympathy. Following his death a week's official mourning was decreed by the government, and tens of thousands of people queued outside the Royal Palace to pay their last respects. This public display of sorrow was remarkable given both Franco's efforts to prevent Spaniards from becoming familiar with Don Juan and the discretion with which the latter had conducted himself since returning to Spain permanently in 1977. Although the Navy made him an honorary admiral, Don Juan was never provided an official role under his son's parliamentary monarchy.[14]

The wave of sympathy aroused by Don Juan's death reflected both widespread admiration for his life-long defence of the institution he embodied and popular affection for Juan Carlos and Sofía, who were photographed shedding tears of grief for the first time. By granting his father a state funeral and deciding to have him buried in the royal pantheon at El Escorial even though he had never reigned, the king succeeded in highlighting the dynastic and institutional dimension of these events. It was thus that Don Juan was able to make a significant posthumous contribution to the consolidation of the monarchy in Spain.

The popularity of the monarchy and the royal family were further enhanced by the *infanta* Elena's wedding to Jaime de Marichalar in March 1995, the first event of its nature held in Spain since 1906. In spite of Charles III's pragmatic sanction of 1776 excluding royals who married commoners from the line of succession, the king's household hastened to clarify that his eldest daughter would retain her rights in keeping with the 1978 constitution, a decision which only a handful of diehard monarchists appeared to resent. The decision to hold the wedding in Seville rather than Madrid, and the relatively informal, festive atmosphere which prevailed provided fresh evidence of Juan Carlos' and Sofía's sureness of touch in these matters.

The consolidation of the monarchy will increasingly rest not only on perceptions of the institution's role in the past, but also on its ability to prove useful in the future. In recent years the king's overriding concern has thus been to prepare his heir for the task that lies ahead. The Prince of Asturias's education has been a curious synthesis of the type of training imposed on Juan Carlos by Franco and the ideas Don Juan would have wished to implement had he been free to do so. Felipe initially attended a small, private though relatively inexpensive school in Madrid, where he mingled freely with children of different social backgrounds. In 1984 he spent the final year of his secondary education at a boarding school in

Canada, where he learnt to fend for himself and considerably improved his English. He then spent a year at each of the three military academies, as his father had done before him, passing out in 1988. This had the unexpected advantage of exposing Juan Carlos to a new generation of officers, who had grown up entirely under a democratic system of government. Felipe subsequently enrolled at Madrid's Autónoma University to study law and economics, and in 1993 he became the first Spanish crown prince ever to have obtained a degree. The prince later spent 1993–95 studying international relations at Washington's Georgetown University.[15]

In recent years Juan Carlos has increasingly delegated his official duties on his son. Felipe first represented his father abroad in 1983, at the age of fifteen, at the commemoration of the 450th anniversary of the foundation of the city of Cartagena de Indias in Colombia. Since then he has become increasingly active both abroad and at home, particularly in military-related activities such as the *pascua militar* celebrations. The publicity surrounding his relationship with Isabel Sartorius during the period 1989–93, which led some to fear that Spain had contracted the British media disease, at least had the advantage of providing him with a foretaste of the difficulties he will face as king.

Although Felipe has always been very close to his mother, his admiration and affection for his father are legendary. (As a child, for example, the prince began to wear his watch on his right wrist, like Juan Carlos, a habit he retains to this day.) A firm believer in the advantages of teaching by example, the king forced his son to stay awake at his side during the long night of 23 February 1981, when Felipe was only twelve. Whenever he fell asleep, Juan Carlos would wake him up and say: 'watch: this is what you have to do when you are king'. As he recently told a British journalist, 'the most important thing is that he should learn from me. I had nobody; I had to learn everything myself'.[16]

The king of Spain's current prestige and reputation largely reflect popular recognition of his decisive role during Spain's transition to democracy and beyond.[17] Ironically, Juan Carlos has long feared that the exceptional role he was called upon to play in recent Spanish history may stand in the way of the consolidation of the monarchy as an institution. Although he is naturally flattered when Spaniards, notably former republicans, describe themselves as *Juancarlistas*, he would much rather hear praise for the institution itself rather than the individual who currently personifies it.[18] In the king's own words: 'a monarchy does not root itself in the heart of a nation just like that. It takes time. And time passes so quickly. My own task is to see that Spaniards renew their links with the monarchical tradition. That is not easy after forty years during which the monarchy was so often denigrated. Three or four generations of Spaniards have heard more bad than good said of us. I have to show the people of Spain that the monarchy can be useful to their country. . . . God willing, I shall continue to work for the Spanish people to accept that the man they call Juan Carlos embodies an institution that counts. At present I am doing my best to see that my son, the prince of Asturias, follows the advice General Franco gave me: "Highness, let the Spanish people get to know you". And I hope Don Felipe will be loved by the Spanish people as it appears that I am. That is all I ask'.[19]

Public opinion research would suggest that the king has little to fear. A consistently high proportion of Spaniards value the monarchy for its contribution to 'order and stability', and a steadily increasing percentage see it as an institution firmly rooted in Spanish history and tradition. Furthermore, in the early 1990s three quarters of those polled still regarded the king's arbitrating and moderating functions as an essential element of Spanish democracy. Most importantly of all perhaps, many respondents believe that Juan Carlos has shown that the monarchy is capable of adapting to the changing needs of Spanish society. Although the king will not be able to transfer his hard-won charismatic legitimacy to his son, the latter is fast becoming a popular, respected figure in his own right. It will be up to the future Felipe VI to prove that the monarchy can continue to be of service to Spain in the twenty-first century.[20]

Notes and References

1 Years of Exile and Uncertainty

1. It is said to have been José María Oriol who decided that he be called Juan Carlos once he arrived in Spain, so as to differentiate him from his own father and ingratiate him with the Carlists (see note 6) Pérez Mateos, *Juan Carlos. La infancia desconocida de un Rey*, p. 35. His father, however, has attributed the decision to Franco himself. Sainz Rodríguez, *Un reinado en la sombra*, p. 276.
2. Some of the king's supporters would later claim that the absence of a suitable heir undermined his ability to defend the monarchy and stand up to his opponents in 1931. If this was the case, it remains unclear why Alfonso XIII did not attempt to make Don Juan his heir in the late 1920s.
3. Don Alfonso divorced his first wife in 1937, and later married another Cuban, whom he also divorced. He died without issue in 1938 in Miami, Florida, as a result of the injuries incurred in an automobile accident. In 1934 Alfonso XIII's fourth son, Don Gonzalo, died in Austria in similar circumstances.
4. In 1935 Don Jaime married the Italian aristocrat Emmanuela Dampierre, with whom he had two sons: Alfonso, born in 1936, and Gonzalo, born in 1941.
5. Borbón, *Mi vida marinera*, p. 11.
6. Carlism, which first emerged in the 1820s as the extreme clerical party, took its name from Don Carlos, brother of King Ferdinand VII, who in 1833 refused to recognise his niece Isabel II as queen. In claiming the right to succeed his brother, Don Carlos denied the validity of Charles III's pragmatic sanction (1776), and appealed instead to the Salic Law introduced into Spain by Philip V (1713). In the nineteenth century the Carlist programme was an amalgam of absolutism and the rural localism enshrined in the *fueros* (laws) of Navarre, inland Catalonia and the Basque provinces. The political climate of the Second Republic fostered the reunification of the movement into a single Traditionalist Communion (1932), under the octogenarian Don Alfonso Carlos.
7. Vegas Latapié, *Memorias políticas*, pp. 155–6, 237–9, 242–8.
8. Sainz Rodríguez, *Un reinado*, p. 347. This volume contains most of Franco's correspondence with Don Juan between 1936 and 1974.
9. In April 1937 Franco forcibly merged the Falange and the Traditionalist Communion (Carlists) into a single political organisation, Falange Española Tradicionalista y de las Juntas de Ofensiva Nacional Sindicialistas (FET y de las JONS). As his regime shed its more totalitarian trappings, this amalgam gradually came to be known as the *Movimiento Nacional* (National Movement).
10. Sainz Rodríguez, *Un reinado*, p. 48.
11. Instead of adhering to the strict law of succession and recognising Alfonso XIII as his heir, in 1936 the Carlist pretender Don Alfonso Carlos named

215

as regent and, implicitly, heir, his nephew Francisco Javier Borbón-Parma (henceforth, Don Javier).

12. Spain has never had a King Juan, but four Juans have ruled in the land, two each in the kingdoms of Castile and Aragon. The most famous were Juan II of Aragon, father of King Ferdinand, and King Juan II of Castile, father of Queen Isabella.

13. Sainz Rodríguez, *Un reinado*, pp. 349–51.

14. Sainz Rodríguez, *Un reinado*, pp. 351–3.

15. Sainz Rodríguez, *Un reinado*, pp. 354–8.

16. Sainz Rodríguez, *Un reinado*, pp. 358–9, 258.

17. Sainz Rodríguez, *Un reinado*, pp. 359–64.

18. Sainz Rodríguez, *Un reinado*, pp. 34–7.

19. López Rodó, *La larga marcha hacia la Monarquía*, p. 55.

20. According to Article 6, 'at any time the head of state may propose to the Cortes the person he considers should succeed him, either as king or as regent . . .' In order to be eligible, 'it shall be necessary to be a Spanish male, to have reached the age of thirty, to profess the Catholic religion, to have the qualities needed to undertake such a high mission and to swear allegiance to the Fundamental Laws and to the Principles of the National Movement'.

21. Anson, *Don Juan*, pp. 260–3.

22. Vilallonga, *The king*, p. 34; Noel, *Spain's English Queen*, p. 267; Pérez Mateos, *Juan Carlos*, pp. 92–3.

23. Pérez Mateos, *Juan Carlos*, pp. 84, 172; López Rodó, *Memorias*, I, p. 195; Vilallonga, *The king*, pp. 54–5.

24. Pérez Mateos, *Juan Carlos*, p. 134.

25. Vilallonga, *The king*, p. 35.

26. For the preparation of the meeting, see Pérez Mateos, *El Rey que vino del exilio*, pp. 21–30.

27. Gil Robles, *La Monarquía por la que yo luché*, pp. 265–73; Sainz Rodríguez, *Un reinado*, pp. 220–22; Créach, *Le Coeur et l'épeé*, pp. 234–5.

28. Sainz Rodríguez, *Un reinado*, p. 368; Pérez Mateos, *Juan Carlos*, pp. 195–9.

29. Vilallonga, *The king*, pp. 20–6, 30; Gil Robles, *La monarquía*, p. 284.

30. Pérez Mateos, *El Rey*, pp. 30–58.

31. Juan Carlos appears to have been very taken by the Spanish Foreign Legion as a child. When Vegas went to visit him in 1951, the prince asked him to sing famous legionnaires' songs.

32. Pérez Mateos, *El Rey*, pp. 93–5; Vilallonga, *The king*, pp. 30–1.

33. Gil Robles, *La Monarquía*, p. 287.

34. Gil Robles, *La Monarquía*, pp. 294, 301–5, 308–10; Sainz Rodríguez, *Un reinado*, p. 369.

35. For Juan Carlos's life at Miramar, see Pérez Mateos, *El Rey*, p. 133 ff.

36. Sainz Rodríguez, *Un reinado*, pp. 370–8.

37. Vilallonga, *The king*, p. 86.

38. Sainz Rodríguez, *Un reinado*, pp. 378–82; Anson, *Don Juan*, pp. 297–8.

39. Sainz Rodríguez, *Un reinado*, pp. 383–4; Franco Salgado-Araujo, *Mis conversaciones privadas con Franco*, p. 53.

40. Sainz Rodríguez, *Un reinado*, pp. 222–36; Franco Salgado-Araujo, *Mis conversaciones*, pp. 59–66.

41. On Martínez Campos and the Montellano period, see Armada, *Al servicio de la Corona*, p. 79 ff.

42. Juan Carlos has admitted that 'ever since I was a small child I'd heard our economic problems discussed at home. Money was a constant worry to us'. Vilallonga, *The king*, p. 62.

43. *ABC*, 15 April 1955; Franco Salgado-Araujo, *Mis conversaciones*, pp. 72–4, 83–4, 102, 110, 115.

44. Franco Salgado-Araujo, *Mis conversaciones*, pp. 92–4.

45. Much to the irritation of the Duke of La Torre, who was obsessed with protocol, most of his cadet friends called him Juan, or Carlos, or simply *Sar*, after the acronym for *Su Alteza Real* (His Royal Highness). Vilallonga, *The king*, pp. 33, 104.

46. *Daily Telegraph*, 11 April 1956. Amazingly, the Ministry of Education subsequently authorised a secondary school textbook entitled *Catholic Morality* which made use of this tragic accident to explore the limits of personal responsibility. Toquero, *Franco y Don Juan*, p. 384.

47. Anson, *Don Juan*, pp. 313–14.

48. Areilza, *Memorias exteriores, 1947–1964*, pp. 120–2.

49. Tusell, *Carrero Blanco*, pp. 252–3.

50. Franco Salgado-Araujo, *Mis conversaciones*, pp. 264–5; Toquero, *Franco y Don Juan*, p. 279.

51. On the Salamanca espisode, see Armada, *Al servicio*, pp. 95–101; Anson, *Don Juan*, pp. 324–5; Sainz Rodríguez, *Un reinado*, p. 393 ff.

52. Sainz Rodríguez, *Un reinado*, pp. 236–9; Franco Salgado-Araujo, *Mis conversaciones*, pp. 280–2.

53. The palace derives its name from the bramble bush (*zarza*). In the seventeenth century it was often the venue for popular light operas, hence the musical genre *zarzuela*. Badly damaged during the civil war, some of its outer walls still bear bullet holes.

54. During these years Fernández-Miranda was director general of secondary education (1955–56), of university education (1956–62), and of social promotion (1962–66). He was also the author of *El hombre y la sociedad* (Madrid, 1960), widely used by the regime as a politics textbook. Mondéjar's version is in Fernández-Miranda Lozana, 'La Reforma Política', unpublished PhD thesis, Complutense University, Madrid 1994, p. 82.

55. Armada, *Al servicio*, p. 138. Juan Carlos readily admits that Fernández-Miranda 'contributed a great deal to my training to be king ... he taught me patience and serenity, and above all he taught me to see things as they are, without illusions and without trusting appearances too much'; Vilallonga, *The king*, pp. 67–8.

56. López Rodó, *La larga marcha*, pp. 178–9.

57. Toquero, *Franco y Don Juan*, pp. 284–6; Anson, *Don Juan*, pp. 330–1; author's interview with Otero Novas.

58. Vilar, *Historia del antifranquismo 1939–1975*, pp. 298–9.

59. Some of his love letters, many of them written in French, were published in *Interviú*, 27 January 1988.

60. Frederica, *A Measure of Understanding*, p. 230.

61. Suárez Fernández, *Francisco Franco y su tiempo*, VI, p. 306 ff; Sainz Rodríguez, *Un reinado*, p. 405 ff; Pemán, *Mis encuentros con Franco*, p. 218.

62. The British ambassador to Spain informed London that 'I had imagined, as you will appreciate, that the engagement of Don Juan Carlos to Princess Sofía might result in the Royal Question being brought out into the open. In fact, up to the present, nothing of the sort has occurred'. G. Labouchere to E.E. Tomkins, 28 November 1961, FO 371/160786. López Rodó, *La larga marcha*, p. 193.

63. Frederica, *A measure*, p. 231; Sainz Rodríguez, *Un reinado*, p. 407 ff.

64. López Rodó, *La larga marcha*, p. 202; Franco Salgado-Araujo, *Mis conversaciones*, pp. 333–4.

65. Labouchere to Tomkins, 28 November 1961, FO 371/160786.

66. On taking up office as minister of information in July 1962, Manuel Fraga discovered a 'Green Book' containing instructions for the censors dealing with these events. Fraga Iribarne, *Memoria breve de una vida pública*, p. 37.

67. Labouchere to Tomkins, 18 May 1962, FO 371/163829.

68. Franco Salgado-Araujo, *Mis conversaciones*, p. 345.

69. Shortly after returning to Athens Sofía had her appendix removed. The British ambassador reported that 'I understand that she was at the time pregnant and the operation caused a good deal of anxiety for this reason, but there has been no official confirmation of her pregnancy'. Murray to Tomkins, 22 November 1962, FO 371/163829.

70. In his letter to Franco of 8 February 1963, Don Juan emphasised the perils of living in Madrid. In his reply of 18 February, Franco observed that Juan Carlos's visits to Estoril could prove far more harmful than residing in the Spanish capital. Sainz Rodríguez, *Un reinado*, pp. 409–11; Salgado-Araujo, *Mis conversaciones*, pp. 369, 374. Aurelio Vals to the Foreign Minister, 22 February 1963, MAE 7193/50.

71. *Daily Sketch*, 3 April 1963; *San Francisco Chronicle*, 11 April 1963.

72. Labouchere to the Earl of Home, 23 April 1963, FO 371/169512.

2 After Franco, Who?

1. Fraga, *Memoria breve*, p. 42.

2. Franco Salgado-Araujo, *Mis conversaciones*, pp. 374–5, 377; Vilallonga, *The king*, pp. 37, 150–1.

3. A baffled British ambassador duly reported that 'such is the curious set up in this to me still incomprehensible country that Franco and Doña Carmen were present with Don Juan at the small ceremony which I gather from one who was present was characterised by the greatest affability and cordiality on both sides'. Labouchere to D.S.L. Hodson, 31 December 1964, FO 371/174937.

4. On the eve of the military parade, an anonymous caller threatened to kill López Rodó if Juan Carlos was present at Franco's side. López Rodó, *La larga marcha*, p. 221; Salgado-Araujo, *Mis conversaciones*, pp. 421, 426–7.

5. In April 1964 Carlos Hugo married Princess Irene of the Netherlands, who took up her husband's cause with great zest. Franco Salgado-Araujo, *Mis conversaciones*, pp. 382–3.

6. Vilallonga, *The king*, pp. 59, 57.

7. Vilallonga, *The king*, p. 57.

8. *Keyhan International*, 9 February 1966. Ministerio de Asuntos Exteriores, Leg. R. 8309, Exped. 8.

9. Vilallonga, *The king*, pp. 57–8, 108–9.
10. Armada, *Al servicio*, p. 120; Vilallonga, *The king*, p. 107.
11. Fraga, *Memoria breve*, pp. 150–1.
12. López Rodó, *Memorias*, II, pp. 24–5; *Le Figaro*, 10 March 1966; Franco Salgado-Araujo, *Mis conversaciones*, p. 466; Armada, *Al servicio*, p. 111; Anson, *Don Juan*, pp. 350–2.
13. Anson, *Don Juan*, pp. 353–8.
14. López Rodó, *Memorias*, II, p. 29.
15. López Rodó, *Memorias*, II, pp. 40–1; Suárez, *Franco*, VII, pp. 328–9; Armada, *Al servicio*, pp. 110–13.
16. López Rodó, *La larga marcha*, pp. 248–9.
17. López Rodó, *La larga marcha*, p. 247. When asked by a French journalist which member of the royal family had the best claim to the throne, Alfonso replied that 'only the Spanish people will be able to decide that in the future'. *Le Figaro*, 27 December 1966. Much to Juan Carlos's irritation, in January 1967 his father hastened to congratulate Franco on the referendum results.
18. Suárez, *Franco*, VII, pp. 374, 395; Franco Salgado-Araujo, *Mis conversaciones*, pp. 488, 500, 505, 506.
19. López Rodó, *La larga marcha*, pp. 257–61.
20. Spain's first Bourbon monarch, Felipe V, was confirmed on the throne after defeating the Habsburg pretender, Charles VI, in the War of Spanish Succession; Alfonso XII was put on the throne in 1875 after a *pronunciamiento* by General Martínez Campos. López Rodó, *La larga marcha*, p. 268.
21. Suárez, *Franco*, VII, p. 412.
22. López Rodó, *Memorias*, II, p. 345. As one observer noted, the Greek case showed that 'an amiable young man, however ancient his lineage, and however loyal to him traditionalists among the officer corps may be, would lack the authority to control the country without the support of the Army – or to control the Army itself should it decide to seize power'. 'The affairs of Spain', *The Times*, 18 July 1969.
23. López Rodó, *La larga marcha*, p. 267. Ferdinand VII, who reigned in the early nineteenth century, had been one of Spain's most controversial monarchs. The general no doubt preferred the name Felipe because the Habsburg Philip II was his favourite Spanish king.
24. López Rodó, *La larga marcha*, p. 270; Peñafiel, *¡Dios salve a la Reina!*, p. 106. Don Juan saw the highly respected Army officer Manuel Díez Alegría, who agreed to stage a military coup in his favour if Franco were to die without having appointed a successor. Author's interview with García Trevijano.
25. 17 January 1968, *The Manila Chronicle*. López Rodó, *La larga marcha*, pp. 274–5.
26. Armada, *Al servicio*, pp. 120, 173; López Rodó, *Memorias*, II, p. 314.
27. Mérida, *Un rey sin corte*, pp. 212–13; *The New York Times*, 10 July 1968; López Rodó, *Memorias*, II, pp. 313–14; Sainz Rodríguez, *Un reinado*, pp. 264, 312–13, 342–4. Juan Carlos's reply, written in December 1968, has never been published. Armada, *Al servicio*, p. 124.
28. Tusell, *Carrero Blanco*, pp. 333–5.
29. The formal excuse for the expulsion was that it was illegal for a foreigner such as Carlos Hugo, a French national, to become involved in Spanish

politics. Carlos Hugo's supporters were jokingly referred to as 'hugonotes' (Huguenots).

30. *Point de Vue*, 22 November 1968; Armada, *Al servicio*, pp. 124–6; López Rodó, *La larga marcha*, pp. 279–81, 291–4; Fraga, *Memoria breve*, p. 235; author's interview with Elorriaga.
31. López Rodó, *La larga marcha*, pp. 294–9.
32. Franco Salgado-Araujo, *Mis conversaciones*, p. 537. According to López Rodó, Franco told Juan Carlos: 'Be perfectly calm, Highness. Don't let yourself be influenced by anything else. Everthing is prepared'. The prince is said to have responded 'Don't worry, General. I have already learned a great deal from your *galleguismo* [slyness],' and after both laughed, Franco added 'Your Highness does it very well'. López Rodó, *La larga marcha*, pp. 301–2; Armada, *Al Servicio*, pp. 124–6.
33. López Rodó, *La larga marcha*, p. 303.
34. López Rodó, *Memorias*, II, p. 415.
35. Sainz Rodríguez, *Un reinado*, p. 314; Anson, *Don Juan*, p. 18.
36. López Rodó, *La larga marcha*, pp. 316–25; Vilallonga, *The king*, p. 54.
37. According to López Rodó, Juan Carlos told his father: 'If you forbid me to accept, I'll pack my bags, take Sofi and the children, and leave. I have not intrigued in order to have the choice fall on me. I agree that it would be better if you became king, but if the decision has been made, what can we do?' López Rodó, *La larga marcha*, pp. 331–2, 359; Anson, *Don Juan*, p. 24. Vilallonga's version – which contains numerous factual errors – reflects the king's determination to prove that he was unaware of Franco's true intentions, when there is ample evidence to the contrary.
38. Díaz Herrera and Durán, *Los secretos del poder*, pp. 65–6.
39. López Rodó, *La larga marcha*, pp. 330–2, 335–6.
40. Vilallonga, *The king*, pp. 55–6.
41. López Rodó, *Memorias*, II, pp. 454–7, 367. Juan Carlos's letter, dated 15 July, begins 'I have just returned from El Pardo, where I had been called by the Generalissimo, and since we cannot speak on the telephone, I hasten to write these lines so that Nicolás, who is about to catch the *Lusitania*, can take them to you'. As we have seen, however, the prince's meeting with Franco had taken place three days earlier. Areilza, *Crónica de Libertad*, pp. 89–91; Anson, *Don Juan*, pp. 16, 33–4, 41, 61–2.
42. Some of Juan Carlos's supporters hastened to justify this choice of title on the grounds that it had once been favoured by the Habsburg monarch Philip II. López Rodó, *La larga marcha*, pp. 339–41, 346. As an adolescent, Juan Carlos had used a passport that bore the title of Prince of Gerona, one of the titles traditionally used by the heir to the crown. Osorio, *Escrito desde la derecha*, p. 42.
43. Dem, *Las memorias de Alfonso de Borbón*, pp. 92–3.
44. López Rodó, *La larga marcha*, pp. 349–53, 367; López Rodó, *Memorias*, II, p. 470; Areilza, *Crónica*, pp. 92–96; Anson, *Don Juan*, pp. 43–7.
45. Fernández-Miranda, *La Reforma*, pp. 84–9.
46. Author's interview with Ollero.
47. López Rodó, *La larga marcha*, pp. 356, 367; Girón de Velasco, *Si la memoria no me falla*, p. 208.
48. López Rodó, *La larga marcha*, pp. 362–6; Silva Muñoz, *Memorias políticas*, pp. 237–8.

49. *ABC*, 23 July 1969.
50. Salmador, *Las dos Españas y el Rey*, p. 236.
51. López Rodó, *Memorias*, II, pp. 469–70.
52. Sainz Rodríguez, *Un reinado*, pp. 313–15; Anson, *Don Juan*, p. 64.
53. López Rodó, *La larga marcha*, pp. 379–80; *ABC*, 20 December 1983.
54. 'The affairs of Spain', *The Times*, 18 July 1969.

3 Prince of Spain

1. Richard Eder, 'Juan Carlos promises a democratic regime', *The New York Times*, 4 February 1970.
2. *The Times*, 22 January 1970.
3. Vilallonga, *The king*, p. 108.
4. *El Socialista*, 30 July 1969; *Mundo Obrero*, 2 August 1969.
5. *The New York Times*, 4 February 1970; Vilallonga, *The king*, p. 109.
6. Silva Muñoz, *Memorias*, p. 279.
7. López Rodó, *La larga marcha*, pp. 401–2; López Rodó, *Memorias*, III, p. 25; Areilza, *Crónica*, pp. 97, 164–5.
8. López Rodó, *Memorias*, III, pp. 26, 47, 193.
9. Ziegler, *From shore to shore*, p. 226.
10. *The New York Times*, 4 February 1970.
11. Shortly before the prince's audience with the shah in 1969, the Iranian minister of court observed that the Spanish ambassador was 'sticking to him like glue'. Sofía discreetly informed the minister that her husband would rather be received on his own, in view of which he 'arranged for the limpet-like ambassador to be detached'. This episode illustrates Juan Carlos's determination to fend for himself. Alam, *The Shah and I*, p. 96.
12. On the French and German visits, see Armada, *Al servicio*, pp. 177–81. RTVE, *La transición española*, episode 3.
13. Juan Carlos enlisted Mountbatten's support in convincing Don Juan of the need to renounce his rights to the throne in his favour. In December 1969 Mountbatten informed Juan Carlos of a recent conversation with Don Juan, whom he had urged to 'execute a legal Instrument of Abdication to be issued by you on the evening before you become king so that the world can see you are the legal king in your own right and not the puppet of a dictator'. Ziegler, *Mountbatten*, p. 678.
14. On returning from Finland, which had a Socialist government, princess Sofía remarked on how ironical it was that the Danish royal family refused to have anything to do with them on the grounds that Spain was a dictatorship, but were happy to visit the Soviet Union. López Rodó, *Memorias*, IV, p. 130.
15. Walters, *Silent missions*, p. 552. 'During dinner I was able to talk to the President a bit about both Tino [Constantine] and Juanito to try and put over their respective points of view about Greece and Spain, and how I felt the US could help them. The President appeared to be so interested that he called over his Secretary of State to join the conversation and we had a three-cornered conversation lasting about twenty minutes'. Ziegler, *From shore to shore*, p. 204.
16. Vilallonga, *The king*, pp. 14–15. Armero owned a major news agency, Europa Press.

17. Armada, *Al servicio*, pp. 174–5; *The New York Times*, 25 January, 1 February 1971; *Chicago Tribune*, 27 January 1971; *Time*, 8 February 1971. One US journalist glibly observed that 'when he [Juan Carlos] takes over, the reign in Spain will plainly be humane'. *Newsweek*, 8 February 1971.

18. The *Chicago Tribune*, 27 January 1971; Bardavío, *Los silencios*, pp. 53–5.

19. Walters, *Silent Missions*, pp. 555–6.

20. Despite an official State Department denial, on 28 July 1971 *The Washington Post* claimed the Nixon administration was waging a low-intensity campaign to convince Franco to stand down in the prince's favour before his physical decline produced a crisis. Payne, *The Franco Regime*, p. 574.

21. López Rodó, *Memorias*, III, pp. 49, 75, 94, 13.

22. López Rodó, *Memorias*, III, p. 179.

23. Mountbatten later wrote to congratulate them for 'the tremendous way you have increased your popularity with the people – that is a great personal triumph for both of you'. Ziegler, *From shore to shore*, p. 226; Ziegler, *Mountbatten*, p. 678.

24. Opinion Poll number 1046, Cuestiones de Actualidad política II, July 1971, carried out by the Instituto de Opinión Pública (IOP). According to one observer, Juan Carlos 'has begun to project a more positive image both at home and abroad', and was proving to be 'more intelligent than was assumed, without being brilliant, which would have been a distinct disadvantage'. *The Times*, 11 October 1971.

25. Opinion Poll number 1050, Cuestiones de Actualidad política, I, November 1971, IOP. It should be noted that 50 per cent of those polled failed to pick out any of the names from the list offered to them, which excluded leaders of the illegal anti-Francoist opposition parties.

26. López Rodó, *La larga marcha*, pp. 417–18.

27. Opinion Poll number 1054, December 1971, IOP.

28. The poll did not please Carrero, and although the minister of information retained his portfolio, the director of the Institute of Public Opinion was summarily dismissed. Fraga, *Memoria breve*, p. 282; Vilallonga, *The king*, p. 70; Payne, *The Franco Regime*, p. 582.

29. López Rodó, *Memorias*, III, pp. 320, 333. For further evidence of the prince's obsession with his cousin Alfonso in late 1972, see De la Cierva, *Retratos que entran en la Historia*, pp. 288–90.

30. López Rodó, *Memorias*, III, pp. 334–5.

31. López Rodó, *Memorias*, III, pp. 349–50.

32. Fernández-Miranda, *La Reforma*, pp. 139–41, 90; López Rodó, *Memorias*, III, pp. 365–6.

33. Fraga would later remark that 'everyone is of the opinion that the prince's influence has played a decisive role in the crisis, within what was possible'. Fraga, *Memoria breve*, p. 296.

34. Carrero Blanco's first choice as minister of information was Suárez, an appointment Juan Carlos would have endorsed, even though he thought him excessively keen to become minister. When Franco imposed Arias Navarro as minister of the interior, Liñán was moved to the Ministry of Information, thereby depriving Suárez of a job. Forced to choose between Suárez and Liñán, Juan Carlos favoured the latter. López Rodó, *Memorias*, III, pp. 334, 344, 379, 385, 387.

35. Vilallonga, *The king*, pp. 158–60. The tunnel was built not far from the US Embassy in Madrid, at a time when the latter was preparing a visit by Kissinger. The ETA terrorists involved were apparently trained in South Yemen and Cuba by East German agents, and purchased the explosives from IRA members they had met in Algeria, at a camp run by the KGB.
36. When the admiral's sons subsequently thanked him for presiding the funeral, Juan Carlos replied: 'how could I have stayed away?' In February 1974 the prince gave Carrero Blanco's widow the pen with which he had signed the document by which he became Franco's successor in July 1969.
37. Fernández-Miranda, *La Reforma*, p. 321; Vilallonga, *The king*, p. 161.

4 The Succession Crisis

1. Gil, *Cuarenta años junto a Franco*, p. 140; Fernández-Miranda, *La Reforma*, pp. 143–9.
2. Silva Muñoz, *Memorias*, p. 299.
3. *ABC*, 5 January 1974. Fernández-Miranda, *La Reforma*, pp. 178–88. Fernández-Miranda retreated to the safety of a state-owned bank, though he remained active in the National Council and the Cortes and continued to be a regular visitor to La Zarzuela.
4. López Rodó, *Memorias*, IV, p. 24.
5. López Rodó, *Memorias*, IV, pp. 27–8; 42–3.
6. Author's interview with Puig de la Bellacasa; López Rodó, *Memorias*, IV, p. 42.
7. Bayod, *Franco visto por sus ministros*, p. 350.
8. *ABC*, 13 February 1974.
9. Bayod, *Franco visto por sus ministros*, pp. 311–12. Author's interview with Cisneros.
10. Morán, *Miseria y grandeza del Partido Comunista de España*, p. 94; Carrillo, *Memoria*, p. 592.
11. Author's interviews with Calvo Serer and García Trevijano; López Rodó, *Memorias*, IV, pp. 50–1; Anson, *Don Juan*, pp. 388–94; Morán, *Miseria*, p. 494.
12. Author's interview with Puig de la Bellacasa.
13. López Rodó, *Memorias*, IV, p. 57.
14. *ABC*, 10 August 1971.
15. Author's interviews with Osorio and Ortega y Díaz Ambrona. The article in question was 'La interinidad', *Ya*, 26 July 1976.
16. Utrera Molina, *Sin cambiar de bandera*, p. 163.
17. Vilallonga, *The king*, pp. 164–6.
18. López Rodó, *Memorias*, IV, pp. 73–4.
19. Inspired by events in Portugal, the Communist leader Carrillo had urged his friend Ceaucescu to invite Díez Alegría to Bucharest to explore the possibility of an Army-led coup against Franco. See Díez Alegría, *Primicias de una confesión*, p. 159 ff.
20. Bayod, *Franco visto*, p. 356. Amongst those who resigned were a number of future ministers under the monarchy, such as Marcelino Oreja, undersecretary

at the Information Ministry; Francisco Fernández Ordóñez, president of the Instituto Nacional de Industria (INI); and Miguel Boyer, head of the INI's research department.

21. Osorio, *Trayectoria política de un ministro de la Corona*, p. 33; López Rodó, *Memorias*, IV, p. 89; López Rodó, *La larga marcha*, p. 473.
22. Fraga, *Memoria breve*, p. 341.
23. Osorio, *Trayectoria política*, p. 34; Silva Muñoz, *Memorias*, pp. 302–7.
24. Fraga, *Memoria breve*, pp. 347, 349.
25. Vilallonga, *The king*, pp. 96–6. The dictator's nephew told López Rodó that he had seen the Communist Ramón Tamames, and the Socialist leaders Tierno Galván and González. López Rodó, *Memorias*, IV, p. 167. These meetings were detected by Utrera, and they no doubt fuelled his suspicions concerning Juan Carlos's intentions. Utrera, *Sin cambiar*, pp. 166, 183; Carrillo, *Mañana España*, p. 206.
26. Carrillo, *El año de la peluca*, pp. 37–8. The Communist leader claims to have received Juan Carlos's message somewhat later, in early 1976. Vilallonga, *The king*, pp. 73–6; *L'Europeo*, 10 October 1975.
27. 'Ante la monarquía de la guerra civil', *El Socialista*, September 1974. Summary of the report to the Executive Committee on the Spanish situation and the party's policy, XIII Congress, *El Socialista*, December 1974. See also the interview with Alfonso Guerra in *El Socialista*, February 1975.
28. González/Toledo. González did not meet Don Juan in person until October 1977. Anson, *Don Juan*, p. 415.
29. Papell, *Conversaciones con Luis Yáñez*, p. 85; Vilallonga, *The king*, p. 73; González/Toledo; Guerra, *Las Filípicas*, pp. 46–7.
30. Papell, *Conversaciones*, pp. 103–4; Brandt, *My life in politics*, p. 315.
31. Baeza and Morán, 'Testimonio Socialista', *ABC*, 18 April 1993.
32. Alvarez de Miranda, *Del 'contubernio' al consenso*, p. 81.
33. Utrera Molina, *Sin cambiar*, p. 156.
34. Pozuelo Escudero, *Los Ultimos 476 días de Franco*, p. 122.
35. Armada, *Al Servicio*, p. 187; Suárez/Toledo. Suárez denies having prepared a report for Juan Carlos on the attitude of the armed forces, as some authors have claimed.
36. Armada, *Al servicio*, p. 188. On 25 June, Juan Carlos expressed deep regret at Herrero Tejedor's death in the presence of López Rodó. López Rodó, *La larga marcha*, p. 480; Suárez/Toledo; Anson, *Don Juan*, p. 403; RTVE, *La transición española*, episode 6.
37. López Rodó, *Memorias*, IV, p. 120; Fraga, *Memoria breve*, p. 361.
38. Vilallonga, *The king*, pp. 5–6; Fraga, *Memoria breve*, p. 378.
39. Ziegler, *From Shore to shore*, p. 315.
40. Vilallonga, *The king*, pp. 167–68; Armada, *Al servicio*, p. 188.
41. Sales, *Don Juan de Borbón*, p. 181.
42. According to Enrique Múgica, a prominent member of the PSOE who watched the scene on television, it was only then that he began to suspect that under Juan Carlos the introduction of the monarchy would be accompanied by the restoration of democracy. Múgica, *Itinerario hacia la libertad*, p. 139.
43. Arnaud de Borchgrave, 'As Juan Carlos sees it', *Newsweek*, 3 November 1975. Author's interview with Borchgrave.

44. The prince had mentioned the possibility of appointing Fernández-Miranda president of the Cortes as early as May 1974. When he repeated the suggestion in June 1975, Franco had merely observed: 'He is not popular'. López Rodó, *Memorias*, IV, pp. 50, 131.
45. Fernández-Miranda, *La Reforma*, pp. 159–63; Vilallonga, *The king*, pp. 68–9.
46. Fernández-Miranda, *La Reforma*, p. 170.
47. López Rodó, *La larga marcha*, pp. 489–90.
48. Fernández-Miranda, *La Reforma*, pp. 168–75.
49. Spaniards' peculiar brand of black humour was very much in evidence during Franco's prolonged agony. That same evening, a French journalist overheard someone describing a meeting between Franco and Juan Carlos at which the former agreed to hand over power. 'But will it be for good this time?', the prince asked. 'What do you mean, for good?', came the reply. 'You will hand it back to me when you die!' Edouard Bailby, *España hacia la democracia?*, pp. 170, 172.
50. Armada, *Al servicio*, p. 190; Vilallonga, *The king*, pp. 171–2.
51. Armada, *Al servicio*, p. 192. See *The New York Times*, 3 November 1975. Author's interview with Carro. On 6 November the 'Green March' was allowed to enter the Spanish Sahara unhindered. Three days later King Hassan II ordered his followers to withdraw and talks were resumed. On 14 November Spain effectively agreed to cede the territory to Morocco and Mauritania, and to withdraw from the Sahara by 28 February 1976.
52. *Newsweek*, 3 November 1975.
53. López Rodó, *Memorias*, IV, p. 107; UMD document in Fortes and Otero, *Proceso a nueve militares demócratas*, p. 258.
54. Opinion Poll number E. 1085, November 1975, IOP. Pollsters were surprised to find that fewer than 5 per cent of those questioned refused to answer or expressed no opinion.
55. Vilallonga, *The king*, p. 210.
56. *Newsweek*, 3 November 1975.
57. According to Don Juan, 'they wanted me to know that the armed forces were on the side of the new king and would not pay me any attention'. Sainz Rodríguez, *Un reinado*, pp. 280, 319–20.
58. Juan Carlos's version is in Oneto, *Anatomía de un cambio de régimen*, pp. 190–1. Fernández-Miranda, *La Reforma*, pp. 180–1.
59. Fernández-Miranda, *La Reforma*, p. 183. On 18 November, however, Juan Carlos told López Rodó he would make Fernández-Miranda prime minister. López Rodó, *Memorias*, IV, p. 166.
60. Vilallonga, *The king*, pp. 58–9.
61. Vilallonga, *The king*, p. 59.
62. Vilallonga, *The king*, pp. 60, 175.
63. Vilallonga, *The king*, pp. 60–1. 'I did not approve of all the things Franco did', Juan Carlos told a British writer in 1989, 'but if anyone speaks ill of him in my presence I shut them up immediately'. Maclean, *Crowned Heads*, p. 67.
64. Vilallonga, *The king*, pp. 29–30. In his last conversation with Arias, which versed on Spain's political future, Franco never mentioned the *Movimiento* or the fundamental principles, and his twin obsessions had been the consolidation

of the monarchy and the preservation of Spanish national unity. Martín Villa, *Al servicio del Estado*, p. 25.

65. Vilallonga, *The king*, p. 69.
66. *ABC*, 23 November 1975.
67. *ABC*, 26 November 1975.
68. López Rodó, *La larga marcha*, p. 495.
69. Areilza, *Diario de un ministro de la Monarquía*, p. 20.
70. In February 1975 Juan Carlos had told Giscard that he could telephone him whenever he wished, an invitation the president appears to have taken quite literally. López Rodó, *Memorias*, IV, p. 107.
71. Ziegler, *Wilson*, p. 464.
72. During his visit, Giscard d'Estaing, who was sometimes referred to as Giscard d'Espagne by the French satirical press on account of his obsessive concern for Spanish affairs, advised Armada to 'proceed with care. Introduce changes slowly, *doucement*'. Armada, *Al servicio*, p. 197.
73. *ABC*, 28 November 1975; Martín Patino/Toledo.
74. *Mundo Obrero*, 27 December 1975; *El Socialista*, 22 November 1975; Claudín, *Santiago Carrillo*, p. 225; Areilza, *Crónica*, p. 168.

5   After Franco, What?

1.   *Newsweek*, 3 November 1975.
2.   *Newsweek*, 3 November 1975.
3.   Fernández-Miranda, *La Reforma*, pp. 193–6; author's interviews with Primo de Rivera and De la Mata.
4.   López Rodó, *La larga marcha*, pp. 476, 493; Tamayo, *Lo que yo he conocido. Recuerdos de un viejo catedrático que fue ministro*, p. 428 ff.
5.   Fernández-Miranda, *La Reforma*, pp. 186–92; Figuero and Herrero, *La muerte*, pp. 164–9. The king told Borchgrave that he was planning to appoint 'a fifty-year old centrist who calls himself an apolitical technocrat'. *Newsweek*, 8 December 1975. Author's interview with Oreja.
6.   Fernández-Miranda, *La Reforma*, pp. 211–13.
7.   Fernández-Miranda, *La Reforma*, pp. 213–16; Bayod, *Franco visto*, pp. 407–8, 417. In an interview with Silva on 3 December the king assured him that Arias would be replaced. Silva, *Memorias*, p. 324.
8.   Suárez/Toledo; Areilza, *Diario*, p. 13; Oneto, *Anatomía*, p. 141.
9.   Juan Carlos had no doubt read Fraga's article 'La Monarquía de España', *ABC*, 14 November 1975, in which he further elaborated his programme. Fraga, *En busca del tiempo servido*, p. 15.
10. Author's interview with Fraga. Fraga, *En busca*, pp. 20–1.
11. Author's interview with Ollero; Areilza, *Crónica* p. 168; Areilza, *Diario*, p. 16.
12. Areilza, *Diario*, p. 15; *ABC*, 7 November 1975. Silva Muñoz, *Memorias*, pp. 324–6; Garrigues y Díaz Cañabate, *Diálogos conmigo mismo*, p. 163.
13. Vilallonga, *The king*, p. 98.
14. Author's interview with Osorio; Osorio, *Trayectoria*, p. 124.
15. Author's interview with Suárez; Fernández-Miranda, *La Reforma*, pp. 217–20, 416.

16. Author's interview with Suárez.
17. Author's interview with Martín Villa.
18. San Martín, *Servicio especial*, pp. 116, 245.
19. Areilza, *Diario*, pp. 76–7; Gutiérrez Mellado, *Un soldado de España*, p. 40.
20. López Rodó, *Memorias*, IV, pp. 217, 226.
21. Areilza, *Diario*, pp. 20, 77; *Mundo Obrero*, 7 January 1976.
22. *Newsweek*, 5 January 1976.
23. Fernández-Miranda, *La Reforma*, pp. 233–4, 368–9.
24. Fernández-Miranda, *La Reforma*, pp. 314–16.
25. Areilza, *Diario*, p. 84; Fernández-Miranda, *La Reforma*, pp. 329–30.
26. Fernández-Miranda, *La Reforma*, p. 361.
27. Fernández-Miranda, *La Reforma*, pp. 331–2; Areilza, *Diario*, pp. 164, 168.
28. Sánchez-Terán, *De Franco a la Generalitat*, pp. 47–56.
29. Sánchez-Terán, *De Franco*, p. 51.
30. *Mundo Obrero*, 25 February 1976; López Rodó, *Memorias*, IV, pp. 225–6.
31. Opinion Poll number 1099, April 1976, IOP; *Newsweek*, 19 April 1976.
32. Areilza, *Diario*, p. 124. The visit to Andalusia was severely criticised by Carlos Alba in *Mundo Obrero*, 7 April 1976. Bau Carpi, *Crónica de veinte años*, pp. 286–7; 'Pancartas para el Rey', *El País*, 21 May 1976; Baón, *Fraga, genio y figura*, p. 79.
33. Fontán, *Don Juan entra en la Historia*, pp. 25–6; Areilza, *Diario*, pp. 21, 41, 44; López Rodó, *Memorias*, IV, pp. 241–2, 238–9; *El País*, 5 November 1994.
34. *Newsweek*, 4 November 1975; author's interview with Borchgrave.
35. Papell, *Conversaciones*, p. 86; 'Una prueba para el rey', *El Socialista*, December 1975 and 'Críticas a la Monarquía', January 1976; *Newsweek*, 8 December 1975.
36. *Discusión y convivencia*, December 1975.
37. Areilza, *Diario*, p. 97.
38. Author's interview with Puig de la Bellacasa; *Discusión y convivencia*, December 1975.
39. *Mundo Obrero*, 28 March 1976.
40. Author's interviews with Múgica and García Trevijano.
41. The telegram read as follows: 'I would ask you to convey to your government my extreme dismay, and that of the European Parliament, at a time when it was looking forward to a liberalisation of the political situation in Spain in the longer-term hope of a rapprochement between your country and the European Community. We should welcome with great relief any satisfactory assurances on your part'. When Juan Carlos was told that García Trevijano was amongst those arrested, his first reaction was to observe: 'this character ought to have his tax returns inspected'. Baón, *Fraga*, p. 54.
42. Alvarez de Miranda, *Del 'contubernio' al consenso*, pp. 104–6.
43. Gil Robles, *Un final de jornada*, pp. 163–72.
44. See his 'Esquema de un camino hacia la democracia', dated 26 May 1976, in Gil Robles, *Un final de jornada*, pp. 163–72; Areilza, *Diario*, pp. 148, 157.
45. Areilza, *Diario*, pp. 149–50, 174–5. González always suspected that Areilza's proposal had been made without the king's explicit consent. *Guadiana*, 18–24 May 1976.

228   *Notes and References*

46. Suárez/Toledo; González/Toledo; Osorio, *Trayectoria*, p. 143.
47. Fraga/Toledo; González/Toledo.
48. Author's interview with Fraga; Otero Novas, *Nuestra democracia puede morir*, p. 58.
49. *El País*, 22 May 1976; Otero Novas, *Nuestra democracia*, p. 62; Areilza, *Diario*, p. 179.
50. Morán, *Miseria y grandeza*, p. 515; 'La responsabilidad de Juan Carlos', *Mundo Obrero*, 5 May 1976.
51. *Mundo Obrero*, 26 May 1976.
52. *Newsweek*, 26 April 1976.
53. *The New York Times*, 19 June 1976; Fraga, *En busca*, pp. 49–52; Osorio, *Trayectoria*, p. 124; Otero Novas, *Nuestra democracia*, p. 58.
54. Suárez/Toledo; López Rodó, *Memorias*, IV, p. 255; Armada, *Al servicio*, p. 141; Osorio, *Trayectoria*, p. 167.
55. López Rodó, *Memorias*, IV, p. 254.
56. The king set aside the speech initially prepared for him by Areilza, which enumerated the Arias government's reform proposals in great detail, and only used the historical references it contained. López Rodó, *Memorias*, IV, p. 254.
57. Areilza, *Diario*, p. 189. One of the Spanish journalists present at the press conference observed that Areilza seemed to 'dominate the situation, to the point of behaving rudely towards his head of state, interrupting and qualifying the king's replies'. Ysart, *Quién hizo el cambio*, p. 57. The PCE was highly critical of the king's visit, and remained sceptical as to his intentions. *Mundo Obrero*, 9 and 16 June 1976.
58. López Rodó, *Memorias*, IV, p. 254.
59. Eaton, *The forces of freedom in Spain, 1974–79*, p. 37; *Newsweek*, 19 April 1976. According to Juan Carlos, Arias 'didn't have the necessary vision to face up to the radical changes the Spaniards were demanding'. Vilallonga, *The king*, p. 163; Fernández-Miranda, *La Reforma*, pp. 372–3; Areilza, *Diario*, pp. 106–7, 118, 133, 152. Under Suárez a new internal telephone system was installed, enabling the king to talk to ministers and senior military men without fear of being spied on.
60. Fernández-Miranda, *La Reforma*, pp. 373–81.
61. Fernández-Miranda, *La Reforma*, pp. 381–3.
62. Areilza, *Diario*, pp. 14–15, 35, 66, 196; Eaton, *The forces of freedom*, p. 40; *The Washington Post*, 8 and 19 June 1976.
63. López Rodó, *Memorias*, IV, p. 254; Areilza, *Diario*, p. 161; author's interview with Puig de la Bellacasa. The latter was briefly replaced by another career diplomat, Santiago Martínez Caro.
64. Fernández-Miranda, *La Reforma*, pp. 397–400.
65. Fernández-Miranda, *La Reforma*, p. 441.
66. Fernández-Miranda, *La Reforma*, p. 465; Areilza, *Diario*, pp. 146–8, 168.
67. Areilza, *Diario*, pp. 107, 134.
68. Areilza, *Diario*, pp. 78, 134, 204, 213.
69. Author's interviews with Otero Novas and Fraga.
70. Fernández-Miranda, *La Reforma*, pp. 417–18; Suárez/Toledo.
71. Osorio, *Trayectoria*, pp. 86–90.
72. Author's interview with Martín Villa.

73. Vilallonga, *The king*, p. 70; Suárez/Toledo; Salmador, *Las dos Españas*, p. 161. Fernández-Miranda later told a former minister he had selected Suárez because 'he will do as I tell him'. Fernández de la Mora, *Los errores del cambio*, p. 29.
74. Suárez/Toledo; Osorio, *Trayectoria*, p. 129; Areilza, *Diario*, pp. 197–9; 'Arias contra *Cambio 16*', *Diario 16*, *Historia de la transición*, pp. 283–4.
75. Suárez/Toledo.
76. Vilallonga, *The king*, p. 69.
77. Areilza, *Diario*, p. 214.
78. Bayod, *Franco visto*, pp. 312–13.
79. Fernández-Miranda, *La Reforma*, p. 423 ff. The Council of the Realm's secretary, De la Mata, told Silva Muñoz that Suárez would be appointed prime minister on 1 July. Silva Muñoz, *Memorias*, pp. 332–4.
80. Morán, Adolfo Suárez. *Historia de un ambición*, pp. 56–60; Enrique de la Mata, 'Aquella reunión del Consejo del Reino', *Diario 16*, *Historia*, pp. 291–3; *ABC*, 7 July 1976; Suárez/Toledo.
81. Silva Muñoz, *Memorias*, pp. 334–5.
82. Suárez/Toledo.

6 In the Driving Seat at Last

1. Suárez/Toledo.
2. Suárez/Toledo.
3. Fraga, *En busca*, p. 53; author's interview with Martín Villa.
4. Suárez/Toledo. Areilza had already allocated the presidency and foreign affairs portfolios to Oreja and Garrigues respectively. Author's interview with Oreja.
5. Osorio, *Trayectoria*, pp. 129–36. Author's interview with Oreja.
6. *El País*, 7 July 1976.
7. *El País*, 4 July 1976; *Mundo Obrero*, 7 July 1976; PSOE Executive Committee communiqué, 9 July 1976; *El Socialista*, 10 July 1976.
8. Osorio, *Trayectoria*, p. 146.
9. *El País*, 10 July 1976.
10. Suárez/Toledo.
11. *El País*, 16 July 1976.
12. *El País*, 22 July 1976.
13. *El País*, 16 July 1976.
14. Author's interview with Oreja.
15. Author's interview with Suárez.
16. Author's interview with Suárez.
17. Otero Novas, *Nuestra democracia*, p. 34; Felipe González, 'Línea política del PSOE', in *Socialismo es Libertad*; Escuela de verano del PSOE 1976, pp. 49–58; De la Cierva, *Retratos*, p. 302.
18. Interview with Suárez in *Paris Match*, 3 August 1976.
19. Author's interview with Armero.
20. Suárez/Toledo; Fernández-Miranda, *La Reforma*, pp. 507–13, 710 ff; Martín Villa, *Al servicio*, p. 52.

21. *El País*, 12 September 1976.
22. *Mundo Obrero*, 15 September 1976; *El Socialista*, 20 September 1976.
23. Author's interview with Múgica.
24. Suárez/Toledo; Gutiérrez Mellado/Toledo; author's interview with Vega Rodríguez; Vilallonga, *The king*, pp. 91–2.
25. Gutiérrez Mellado/Toledo; Suárez/Toledo.
26. Osorio, *Trayectoria*, pp. 188–9.
27. *El Pais*, 16 July 1976.
28. Fernández de la Mora, *Los errores*, p. 162.
29. *El País*, 17 November 1976.
30. De la Cierva, *Retratos*, p. 299; López Rodó, *Memorias*, IV, p. 276; Fernández de la Mora, *Río arriba*, pp. 272–3.
31. Areilza, *Cuadernos de la transición*, pp. 71–5.
32. The German politician would later write: 'I have met the King from time to time, and on a particularly critical occasion he telephoned me. King Juan Carlos has turned out to be a piece of great good fortune for Spanish democracy'. Brandt, *My life in politics*, p. 315.
33. *Mundo Obrero*, 16 December 1976.
34. *El País*, 30 October 1976.
35. Carrillo, *El año*, pp. 64, 66.
36. Areilza, *Diario*, p. 99; letter to Juan Carlos, dated 22 November 1976, quoted in Ziegler, *Mountbatten*, p. 678. Juan Carlos and Sofía had not been invited to the King of Sweden's wedding in June 1976 due to the opposition of the Swedish government.
37. *El País*, 15 December 1976.
38. *ABC*, 26 December 1976.
39. See *IV Informe FOESSA*, vol. 1, pp. 121–48.
40. Suárez/Toledo; author's interview with Otero Novas.
41. Vilallonga, *The king*, p. 91; Osorio, *Trayectoria*, p. 282.
42. Carrillo/Toledo; Carrillo, *El año*, pp. 146–7.
43. Osorio, *Trayectoria*, pp. 285–7.
44. Suárez/Toledo.
45. Suárez/Toledo.
46. Author's interview with Alvarez Arenas; Osorio, *Trayectoria*, p. 289.
47. Osorio, *Trayectoria*, p. 290; Vilallonga, *The king*, p. 127.
48. Armada, *Al servicio*, pp. 145, 151; Calvo Sotelo, *Memoria viva de la transición*, p. 21; author's interview with Osorio; Oneto, *Anatomía*, pp. 193–4. According to Armada, following this incident with Suárez the latter admitted having bugged his telephone, in view of which the king gave him a direct line to La Zarzuela. Vilallonga, *The king*, p. 152.
49. *Mundo Obrero*, 20 April 1977.
50. Author's interview with Oreja.
51. With reference to the Spanish transition, the former German chancellor has written that 'prime minister Adolfo Suárez, the opposition leader (later prime minister) Felipe González, and especially King Juan Carlos played their parts to perfection'. Schmidt, *Men and Powers*, p. 168.
52. Tierno Galván, *Cabos sueltos*, p. 640.
53. González/Toledo; Márquez Reviriego, *Felipe González, un estilo ético*, pp. 97–8; Vilallonga, *The king*, pp. 3–5, 71–2.

54. De la Cierva, *Retratos*, p. 301; Fraga, *En busca*, p. 74; Sainz Rodríguez, *Un reinado*, p. 318.
55. Suárez/Toledo.
56. Sainz Rodríguez, *Un reinado*, p. 266 ff. Don Juan and Fernández-Miranda did not meet in person until May 1977, and would only see each other again once, in 1980, shortly before the latter's death.
57. See the editorial in *El Pais*, 'No hay "hombres del Rey",' 31 May 1977.
58. *El País*, 1 June 1977.
59. Suárez/Toledo.
60. Alcocer, *Fernández-Miranda, agonía de un Estado*, p. 107; Suárez/Toledo.
61. The coat of arms of the Duke of Fernández-Miranda bears the motto '*Semper et ubique fidelis*'.
62. Suárez/Toledo.
63. Fraga, *En busca*, pp. 60, 66–7; López Rodó, *Memorias*, IV. p. 416.
64. Author's interview with Osorio; Juan Van-Halen, *Objetivo: ganar el futuro. Conversaciones con Alfonso Osorio*, p. 167.
65. *El País*, 4 May 1977.
66. Armada, *Al servicio*, pp. 210–13.
67. Amongst the 557 deputies and senators were 77 former members of Franco's Cortes.
68. Vilallonga, *The king*, pp. 97–8; Carrillo, *Memorias*, pp. 723–4; Otero Novas, *Nuestra democracia*, p. 59; Juan Luis Cebrián, 'La izquierda en palacio', *El País*, 26 June 1977. The newspaper *El País* proposed that 24 June (the king's saint's day) be declared a national holiday in recognition of Juan Carlos's role in the democratising process, but the suggestion fell on deaf ears. Since 1985 Spain has celebrated its national holiday on 12 October, in commemoration of the discovery of America by Columbus.
69. Alam, *The Shah and I. The Confidential Diary of Iran's Royal Court, 1969–77*, pp. 552–4. According to the royal household, there is no trace of this letter in the archive at La Zarzuela.
70. It is a well-established fact that both the German SPD and the Venezuelan Acción Democrática provided the PSOE with substantial financial as well as political support during the transition. When Venezuelan president Carlos Andres Pérez visited Spain in December 1976, he jokingly told Juan Carlos, who greeted him at Madrid airport, that he had a stowaway on his plane. Pérez had picked up González in Geneva, and appears to have taken pleasure in embarrassing the Spanish authoritites, who were mortified to find the leader of an as yet illegal party arriving in this manner.
71. The closing paragraph reads thus: 'Should my request meet your approval, I take the liberty to recommend a visit to Tehran by my personal friend, Alexis Mardas, who can take receipt of your instructions'.
72. Earlier in the letter Juan Carlos thanked the shah 'for sending your nephew, Prince Shahram to see me, thus providing me with a speedy response to my appeal at a difficult moment for my country'. This would suggest the king had obtained financial assistance from him in the recent past.
73. In January 1980 the king would tell Ricardo de la Cierva, minister of culture under Suárez, that 'it was your grandfather who was right on 14 April 1931, and not mine'. He was referring to Juan de la Cierva y Peñafiel, a minister under Alfonso XIII, one of the few people who spoke out against his decision

to surrender power in the wake of the municipal elections. De la Cierva, *Retratos*, p. 304.

7 King of a Parliamentary Monarchy

1. Vilallonga, *The king*, p. 7. Some PSOE deputies would have preferred to show greater courtesy towards the monarchs, but were overruled by their leaders. Peces-Barba, *La elaboración de la Constitución de 1978*, p. 16; Carrillo, *Memorias*, p. 683.
2. Otero Novas, *Nuestra democracia*, pp. 32–4; Peces-Barba, *La elaboración*, pp. 16–17.
3. The committee consisted of Miguel Herrero de Miñón, Gabriel Cisneros, José Pedro Pérez Llorca (representing UCD); Gregorio Peces-Barba (PSOE); Jordi Solé Tura (PCE); Manuel Fraga (AP); and Miguel Roca (Catalan and Basque nationalists).
4. Osorio, *Trayectoria política*, pp. 231–2; Josep Tarradellas, *Ja sóc aquí*, pp. 89–90; Ortínez, *Una vida entre burgesos*, pp. 133–45.
5. Tarradellas, *Ja sóc aquí*, pp. 94–104.
6. López Rodó, *Memorias*, IV, pp. 327–9.
7. Tarradellas, *Ja sóc aquí*, p. 117.
8. Tarradellas, *Ja sóc aquí*, pp. 133–8, 158; López Rodó, *Memorias*, IV, pp. 327–8.
9. *ABC*, 19 October 1977.
10. Peces-Barba, *La elaboración*, pp. 27–8.
11. Attard, *La Constitución por dentro*, pp. 23, 31.
12. Peces-Barba, *La elaboración*, p. 38; Herrero y Rodríguez de Miñón, *Memorias de estío*, p. 234.
13. López Rodó, *Memoras*, IV, pp. 338–9.
14. Herrero, *Memorias*, pp. 127–30, 133–5; López Rodó, *Memorias*, IV, p. 368.
15. *El País*, 2 November 1977.
16. See for example Julián Marías, 'El Rey', *El País*, 24 January 1978.
17. Herrero, *Memorias*, pp. 124, 135–7; Oneto, *Anatomía*, p. 178.
18. Peces Barba, *La elaboración*, pp. 38–9.
19. Silva Muñoz, *Memorias*, p. 375; Anson, *Don Juan*, p. 415; Oneto, *Anatomía*, pp. 194–5.
20. Carrillo, *Memoria*, p. 725.
21. Oneto, *Anatomía*, pp. 188–9, 194–5.
22. The *pascua militar* was originally instituted as a military celebration by King Carlos III to commemorate the recovery of Menorca from the British in 1782. Since 1975, Juan Carlos has marked this occasion with an official reception at the Royal Palace attended by senior officers from the three services.
23. At the time the Cortes was beginning to debate the new military ordinances. Gutiérrez Mellado, *Un soldado de España*, pp. 143–4.
24. López Rodó, *Memorias*, IV, p. 366. Attard was prevented from visiting La Zarzuela more frequently by Suárez, who discouraged fellow UCD leaders from seeking direct access to the king.
25. López Rodó, *Memorias*, IV, p. 367; Attard, *La Constitución*, p. 111.

26. Fraga, *En busca*, pp. 112–13.
27. *El País*, 30 April 1978.
28. *El País*, 10 May 1978.
29. *El País*, 10 May 1978.
30. *El País*, 10 May 1978.
31. *El País*, 10 May 1978.
32. *El País*, 10 May 1978.
33. Fraga, *En busca*, p. 121; Silva Muñoz, *Memorias*, pp. 390–6.
34. According to López Rodó, in April 1978 Juan Carlos told him that both Fernández-Miranda and Hernández-Gil were also in favour of a Council of the Crown. López Rodó, *Memorias*, IV, p. 366.
35. *El País*, 19 July 1978.
36. De la Cuadra and Gallego-Díaz, *Del consenso*, p. 92; Tico Medina, 'La cara inédita del Rey', *Blanco y Negro*, 22 November 1978.
37. *El País*, 6 August 1978.
38. See Emilio Romero, 'Los viajes del Rey', and Ricardo de la Cierva, 'Seis razones para un viaje histórico', *El País*, 26 August 1978.
39. In September Juan Carlos told López Rodó that he had come to resent Areilza's phrase to the effect that he was 'the engine of change'. López Rodó, *Memorias*, IV, p. 434. See Enrique Sánchez, '¿Quien pretende servirse de la Corona?', *El País*, 16 September 1978, and the editorial 'Añoranza de una Monarquía franquista', *El País*, 20 September 1978. López Rodó, *Memorias*, IV, pp. 423–4, 433–4.
40. Martín Villa, *Al servicio*, pp. 148–50; Gutiérrez Mellado, *Un soldado*, pp. 114–15. In August 1978 the publication of an open letter to the king entitled 'No more blood, your Majesty' had already won Tejero a two-week arrest. After the Galaxia fiasco, he received a seven-month sentence.
41. Vilallonga, *The king*, pp. 183–4.
42. Author's interview with Oreja. In September 1993, at a reception held at the Ortega y Gasset Institute in Madrid, the author witnessed a moving encounter between the king and Mario Paoletti, an Argentinian writer released as a result of this visit.
43. Some members of the PSOE executive opposed the visit on the grounds that it entailed a definitive renunciation of the Republican ideal. Feo, *Aquellos años*, pp. 83–3.
44. The closest historical precedent for this decision was that of Alfonso XII, king of Spain from 1874, who sanctioned the constitution of 1876.
45. *El País*, 28 December 1978.

8 Consolidating – and Defending – Democracy

1. Gutiérrez Mellado, *Un soldado*, pp. 107–8.
2. *El País*, 11 May 1977.
3. In October 1977 Milans had been removed from the Brunete armoured division, which was fast becoming an 'ultra' stronghold, and appointed captain-general of the Third Military Region, based in Valencia.
4. *ABC*, 26 December 1979.
5. *ABC*, 21 February 1980. *Il Messagero*, 22 March 1980.

6. *El País*, 25 April 1980; Fraga, *En busca*, pp. 201–2.
7. Urbano, *Con la venia, yo indagué el 23F*, pp. 38–40.
8. *El País*, 7 May 1980; *ABC*, 15 June 1980.
9. Prieto and Barbería, *El enigma del 'Elefante'*, p. 85; Vilallonga, *The king*, p. 125. In November Juan Carlos received a report compiled by the secret service, CESID, which outlined the various initiatives currently under way, aimed at dislodging Suárez by both parliamentary and extra-parliamentary means. See 'Panorámica de las operaciones en marcha', reproduced in Prieto and Barbería, *El enigma*, pp. 280–93.
10. For Múgica's version, see *El País*, 13 March 1981; Armada, *Al servicio*, pp. 223–4; Prieto and Barbería, *El enigma*, pp. 92–6; Oneto, *La noche de Tejero*, p. 16; Antich, *El virrey*, pp. 83–5.
11. Fraga, *En busca*, pp. 223–4; Urbano, *Con la venia*, pp. 41–2; Carrillo, *Memorias*, p. 710; Semprún, *Federico Sánchez se despide de ustedes*, pp. 192–94.
12. Armada, who was at La Zarzuela on 18 December, claims to have been shown a draft of the Christmas speech by the king, but does not explain for what purpose. Armada, *Al servicio*, p. 225.
13. Suárez/Toledo.
14. Armada, *Al servicio*, p. 230; Merino and Segura, *Jaque al Rey*, p. 57–8. Armada had already discussed the king's views with Milans on 17 November.
15. *ABC*, 7 January 1981.
16. Suárez/Toledo; Urbano, *Con la venia*, pp. 52–4.
17. Meliá, *Así cayó Adolfo Suárez*, pp. 75–6; Calvo Sotelo, *Memoria viva*, pp. 23–32; De la Cierva, *Retratos*, pp. 305–7; Suárez/Toledo.
18. Suárez/Toledo. Unlike Arias, in the wake of his resignation the Duke of Suárez made full use of his title, to the extent of having his shirts embroidered with a ducal crown.
19. Author's interview with Suárez. Martín Villa, *Al servicio*, p. 116. Vilallonga, *The king*, p. 124.
20. *El País*, 6 February 1981.
21. The book in question was Cernuda, Oneto, Pi and Ramirez, *Todo un Rey*. Oneto, *Los últimos días de un presidente*, pp. 174–8.
22. Fraga, *En busca*, p. 298.
23. Suárez/Toledo; Armada, *Al servicio*, pp. 231–3.
24. After the coup Armada requested the king's permission to use the contents of their conversation of 13 February in his defence, but was turned down. Armada, *Al servicio*, pp. 154, 230, 234–5; Gutiérrez Mellado/Toledo.
25. Author's interviews with Alfaro Arregui and Robles Piquer; Vilallonga, *The king*, p. 133.
26. Author's interview with Fernández Campo. Vilallonga, *The king*, pp. 127–28.
27. Vilallonga, *The king*, p. 119.
28. Urbano, *Con la venia, yo indagué el 23F*, p. 251.
29. According to Juan Carlos, 'if I had wanted to carry out an operation "in the king's name" but without his consent, the first thing I'd have thought of doing would have been to isolate him from everyone'. Vilallonga, *The king*, p. 131. This, however, would have rendered Armada's plan inviable, since its success largely depended on the king's consent.
30. In the wake of the coup, a direct link was set up between La Zarzuela and TVE, enabling royal messages to be relayed directly.

31. *El País*, 24 February 1981.
32. Vilallonga, *The king*, pp. 134–5.
33. Carrillo, *Memoria*, pp. 716–17; author's interview with Suárez.
34. Carrillo, *Memoria*, p. 718; Vilallonga, *The king*, pp. 145–6; Fraga, *En busca*, p. 235.
35. Vilallonga, *The king*, p. 178.
36. Since 1984 the official Centro de Investigaciones Sociológicas has conducted an annual study on the level of support enjoyed by Spain's major political institutions. The proportion of those who agree with the statment that 'the king, by stopping the coup of 23 February 1981, won the respect of Spanish democrats' has never fallen below 80 per cent.
37. Vilallonga, *The king*, p. 112.
38. Author's interview with Calvo Sotelo. Nevertheless, on one occasion the latter is said to have reprimanded the king for leaving the country without informing him. Fuente, *El caballo cansado*, p. 240.
39. *ABC*, 6 March 1981.
40. Author's interview with Calvo Sotelo.
41. Author's interviews with Oreja and Calvo Sotelo. Nourry, *Un Rey*, p. 309. A facsimile of this letter is reproduced in Andrew and Gordievsky, *Instructions from the Centre*, pp. 147–51.
42. *ABC*, 7 January 1982.
43. According to Juan Carlos, Milans del Bosch 'was the victim of subtle poisoning of the mind more than anything else'. Vilallonga, *The king*, pp. 118, 123. When the general's father died in February 1983, the king, Don Juan, Mondéjar and Fernández Campo all sent him their condolences. Their telegrams are reproduced in Merino and Segura, *Jaque al Rey*, p. 217. Juan Carlos described Armada as a traitor in the original (French) text of his conversations with Vilallonga, a reference that was removed from the English and Spanish versions.
44. Vilallonga, *The king*, p. 3. *Il Messagero*, 22 March 1980.
45. *El País*, 28 October 1982.
46. *El País*, 26 November 1982.
47. Peces-Barba, *La elaboración*, p. 16.

9 Juan Carlos at Home and Abroad

1. Nevertheless it is believed that in June 1985 a small group of officers planned to blow up Juan Carlos and González as they watched a military parade in La Coruña. *El País*, 25 April 1991.
2. Peter Bruce, 'González plays the King card for all its worth', *Financial Times*, 20 September 1991.
3. *ABC*, 7 January 1983.
4. Morán, *España en su sitio*, pp. 186–7; Martínez, *En la sombra del Rey*, pp. 101–7.
5. *El País*, 18 January 1986.
6. *Expresso*, 11 April 1992.
7. 'El Rey toma partido', *Hechos*, 30 September 1991; *Expresso*, 11 April 1992; Fuente, *El caballo cansado*, pp. 14–17.
8. *Epoca*, 15 July 1991; *Tribuna*, 31 December–6 January 1991.

9.   '¿Qué hace el Rey?' *Tiempo*, 27 February 1995.
10. According to Tarradellas, 'it may be the profound melancholy he can't hide which makes the king's charm so engaging, so that even if you aren't the kind of royalist who supports the monarchy as an institution, you can't help being a royalist who supports this particular monarch'. Juan Carlos recalls that on several occasions Tarradellas told him: '"I am a staunch defender of your majesty's monarchy". I'd rather he had simply said "the monarchy", for there is quite a difference'. Vilallonga, *The king*, pp. 9, 101. In 1986 the king granted the Catalan politician the title of Marquis of Tarradellas.
11. Antich, *El virrey*, pp. 164–76. More recently, after a routine visit to La Zarzuela, journalists asked Pujol if Juan Carlos had raised the language issue, to which he replied: 'He used to ask me about it, but he doesn't any more, because he knows he has nothing to fear'. *El País*, 17 September 1993.
12. Antich, *El virrey*, pp. 176–7.
13. The British press inevitably compared the affection and pride prompted by Juan Carlos's spontaneous enthusiasm with the more distant respect accorded British royalty when they preside at sporting events. According to journalist Charles Bremner, one veteran Fleet Street Olympic hand who marvelled at the way the king had caught the mood and rallied his country was quick to observe that 'you couldn't imagine one of ours having this kind of effect'. *The Times*, 10 August 1992.
14. Feo, *Aquellos años*, pp. 287–8.
15. According to one poll, 56 per cent of Basques were in favour of the visit, 26 per cent were indifferent, and only 7 per cent opposed it. The same study revealed that approximately 10 per cent of the population still favoured outright independence. *Tribuna*, 5–11 August 1991.
16. According to a poll conducted in early 1994, the king was favourably regarded by 61 per cent of the Basque population, unfavourably by 12 per cent, and neither one nor the other by 22 per cent. *El País*, 6 February 1994.
17. *ABC*, 7 January 1994.
18. According to a November 1993 CIS poll (Percepción del escenario internacional), two out of every three Spaniards believed the crown's role abroad to be beneficial. *ABC*, 16 May 1994.
19. Author's interview with Oreja.
20. See for example, Reventós, *Misión en Paris*, pp. 23–4.
21. Howe, *Conflict of Loyalty*, p. 406.
22. *The Wall Street Journal*, 8 July 1985.
23. On this occasion the state banquet at the Royal Palace compared very badly with the return dinner laid on by the French at Aranjuez. Outraged, Carrillo complained to Mondéjar that 'offical dinners given by their majesties should be as good as the dinners given by our foreign guests, if not better! The prestige of our monarchy is at stake!' Vilallonga, *The king*, pp. 72–3.
24. Morán, *España*, p. 56.
25. Mitterrand, *L'Abeille et l'architecte*, p. 153. In June 1971 Mitterrand had asked Areilza whether Juan Carlos, whom he regarded as Franco's puppet, would resist the growing demand for democratic change, to which the Count of Motrico replied that he would lead the process himself. The future president of France, however, remained unconvinced. Areilza, *Crónica*, p. 108.

26. Morán, *España*, p. 50; Acuña, *Como los dientes de una sierra*, pp. 91–2, 110–14; Reventós, *Misión*, pp. 215–19.
27. Helmut Schmidt, 'Una suerte para España', *El País*, 27 February 1986.
28. In 1975 the Duke of Edinburgh had asked Juan Carlos: 'why the hell don't you get in touch with the people in Gibraltar and make some progress there in favour of an arrangement? We're fed up with the story anyhow and it is very expensive at that'. Areilza, *Diario*, p. 21.
29. *El País*, 21 May 1982.
30. Significantly, Alastair Burnett, the BBC commentator covering the event, wondered out loud whether the Gibraltar issue was not best left to the Spanish government. He thus failed to realise that, unlike the Queen, who speaks exclusively on behalf of her government, Juan Carlos is expected to express his own views, which in this case merely echoed those of a majority of his countrymen. The king reiterated Spain's claim when he addressed the United Nations General Assembly in September 1986, and again in October 1991.
31. The US press claimed the king 'did not hide his discomfort' over González's propensity to give in to public opinion over the bases issue. *The Washington Post*, 23 September 1987.
32. Vilallonga, *The king*, p. 183; Galvani, *El Rey y la Comunidad Iberoamericana*, p. 6.
33. Morán, *España*, pp. 187–9. For the Spanish ambassador's account, see Gómez Jordana, *Diplomacia cálida*, pp. 270–85.
34. CIS poll number 1357, May 1983.
35. Vilallonga, *The king*, p. 184.
36. In the king's view, Spaniards gave the peoples of America something far more important than their language, namely 'our blood', for 'unlike the Anglo-Saxons, the Spaniards mingled their blood with that of the inhabitants of all the Latin American countries'. Determined to avoid the empty rhetoric of the past, when he is in Latin America Juan Carlos refers to Spain as '*vuestra patria hermana*' (your sister country), and not as '*la Madre Patria*' (the mother country). Vilallonga, *The king*, pp. 182–4.
37. Vilallonga, *The king*, p. 183.
38. Hassan II, *La memoria de un Rey*, pp. 286–8.
39. Vilallonga, *The king*, p. 182.
40. Vilallonga, *The king*, pp. 179–82.
41. José Antonio Lisbona, 'Rey de Jerusalén', *El País*, 7 November 1993.
42. Vilallonga, *The king*, pp. 180–1.
43. Pedro J. Ramirez, 'Un verano en Mallorca', *El Mundo*, 9 September 1990; *Tribuna*, 17–23 September.
44. Vilallonga, *The king*, p. 150.
45. Vilallonga, *The king*, pp. 178–9.
46. See the interview with Father Bartolomé Vicens Fiol in *El País*, 24 October 1985.
47. Faced with a similar situation in April 1992, King Baudouin of Belgium opted for a temporary abdication, which could have proved highly damaging for the monarchy.
48. *Time*, 13 April 1992.
49. Partly at the queen's suggestion, Juan Carlos has conferred titles of nobility on a number of artists and musicians, notably Salvador Dalí, Andrés Segovia and Joaquín Rodrigo.

10   Looking to the Future

1. Vilallonga, *The king*, pp. 63–4.
2. In 1994, the budgets for continental Europe's major royal families (in millions of pesetas) were as follows: Norway, 1121; Sweden, 1225; Belgium, 980; Denmark, 798. (Note: £1 = approx. 200 pesetas).
3. Prince Felipe is said to have inherited some 400 million pesetas from Don Juan in deeds and shares, which had been left to him by Victoria Eugenia. *Tribuna*, 22 March 1993. After a long dispute with the Greek authorities, Queen Sofía has recently come into part of her inheritance, estimated at some 3500 million pesetas. *Tiempo*, 4 March 1991; *FIES*, Periódico de la Fundación Institucional Española, July–September 1994, p. 10.
4. The Scott documentary for ITV, a highly flattering account of the events of 1992 seen through royal eyes, was watched by five million viewers, or 38 per cent of the total audience, when finally shown in Spain.
5. Almansa's appointment was attributed to the influence of the banker Mario Conde, president of Banesto, who studied at Deusto University with him. In June 1993 the king presided over the ceremony at which Conde was awarded an honorary doctorate by Madrid's Complutense University. In January 1994, however, Conde was publicly disgraced when the Bank of Spain removed him from Banesto in order to avoid its collapse; a year later, he was imprisoned for several months.
6. The author happened to be with a senior royal household official when he was informed of the accident. His first question was not 'how is the king?', but 'who was he with?'.
7. Vilallonga, *The king*, pp. 185–8.
8. El Mundo, 2 August 1992. Remarkably, according to one poll, 60 per cent of those consulted did not see why the king should adapt his private life to the interests of the state. *Tiempo*, 6 July 1992.
9. Amando de Miguel, *La sociedad española, 1993–94*, pp. 764–9.
10. One Spanish newspaper even attributed this campaign to the Italian industrialist Agnelli, on the ground that most of the publications involved belonged to his Rizzoli group. See *Point de Vue*, 11 August 1992; El *Mundo*, 12, 20 August 1992; *Oggi*, 18 August 1992; *Cambio 16*, *Epoca*, 31 August 1992.
11. Vilallonga, *The king*, p. 148.
12. Among those mentioned in this connection are the Georgian aristocrat and businessman Zourab Tchokonia ('Prince' Tchokonia) and the Aga Khan. 'Los errores del Rey', *Tribuna*, 17–22 September 1990; *El País*, 5 October 1993; Vilallonga, *The king*, pp. 35–6; Maclean, *Crowned heads*, pp. 68–9.
13. Don Juan had requested Franco's permission to take his father's remains back to Spain as early as 1967, but failed to obtain a reply.
14. Ironically, it appears to have been Carrero Blanco who first suggested the possibility of making Don Juan an honorary admiral to his son in early 1970. The precedent cited for this by Carrero was Mountbatten. López Rodó, *Memorias*, III, p. 13.
15. According to a major poll conducted in late 1990, 74 per cent of those questioned believed Felipe was receiving an adequate education for a future king, while 5 per cent thought it inadequate and 21 per cent failed to express an opinion. See 'XII Años de Constitución y Democracia en España', *Revista Española de Investigaciones Sociológicas*, 56, October–November 1991.

16. Vilallonga, *The king*, p. 139. Television interview with Selina Scott, 1992.
17. According to CIS polls conducted during the period 1984–90, between 62 per cent and 71 per cent of respondents agreed with the statement 'without the presence of the king democracy would not have been viable in Spain'.
18. The CIS polls conducted over the period 1983–93 reveal that between 73 per cent and 81 per cent of respondents believed that 'the king has won the support and affection of Spaniards, including those who were not initially in favour of the monarchy'.
19. Interview with Juan Carlos, *El Figaro Magazine*, 16 October 1994; Vilallonga, *The king*, p. 179.
20. According to the CIS polls, 71–79 per cent of those polled appreciated the monarchy's contribution to 'order and stability'; on average, 70 per cent attributed its importance to history and tradition; and 77–79 per cent expressed faith in its adaptability. The crown prince's popularity has increased steadily in recent years as a result of his higher public profile. In late 1990, 79 per cent of those questioned had a good or excellent opinion of him, while 10 per cent were indifferent and only 3 per cent were critical.

Bibliography

PRIMARY SOURCES

Unpublished Sources

(i) Official archives
A. Ministerio de Asuntos Exteriores (Madrid)
   Archivo General: Serie de Archivo Renovado (MAE/R files)
B. Public Record Office (London)
   FO General Correspondence

(ii) Interviews
This book is partly based upon individual and collective interviews with many of the leading protagonists of Spain's recent political history. The collective interviews took place at the Symposium on Spain's Transition to Democracy organised by the author for the José Ortega y Gasset Foundation and held at San Juan de la Penitencia, Toledo, in May 1984. Amongst those interviewed at length were: Leopoldo Calvo Sotelo; Manuel Fraga Iribarne; Felipe González; Manuel Gutiérrez Mellado; José María Martín Patino; Adolfo Suárez; and Josep Tarradellas. In the notes, these interviews appear as Suárez/Toledo (for example). The individual interviews carried out by the author over the period 1983–1993 are referred to by the interviewee's name.

(iii) Opinion polls conducted by the Centro de Investigaciones Sociológicas (formerly Instituto de Opinión Pública).
Opinion Poll number 1046, Cuestiones de Actualidad Política VI, July 1971.
Opinion Poll number 1050, Cuestiones de Actualidad Política I, November 1971.
Opinion Poll number 1054, Boda del príncipe D. Alfonso de Borbón y María del Carmen Martínez-Bordiú, December 1971
Opinion Poll number 1085, Visita del Príncipe D. Juan Carlos al Sahara, November 1975.
Opinion Poll number 1099, Visita de los Reyes a Andalucía, April 1976.
Opinion Poll number 1357, Viaje de SSMM los Reyes al Uruguay, May 1983.
Opinion Poll number 1993, Percepción del escenario internacional, November 1993.

Published Sources

(i) Newspapers and periodicals

ABC	Le Monde
Cambio 16	Mundo Obrero
Epoca	El País
FIES. Periódico de la Fundación	Point de Vue
Institucional Española	Newsweek
Hola	The New York Times
Informaciones	El Socialista
Interviú	Tiempo

Time   Tribuna
The Times   Ya

(ii) Diaries, memoirs, letters, etc.
Alam, Asadollah (1991) *The Shah and I. The confidential Diary of Iran's Royal Court, 1969–1977* (London).
Alderete, Ramón (1974) *. . . y estos borbones nos quieren gobernar. Recuerdos de veinte años al servicio de SAR Don Jaime de Borbón* (Paris).
Alvarez de Miranda, Fernando (1985) *Del 'contubernio' al consenso* (Barcelona).
Anson, Luis María (1994) *Don Juan* (Barcelona).
Areilza, José María de (1977) *Diario de un ministro de la Monarquía* (Barcelona).
Areilza, José María de (1983) *Cuadernos de la transición* (Barcelona).
Areilza, José María de (1984) *Memorias exteriores* (Barcelona).
Areilza, José María de (1985) *Crónica de libertad* (Barcelona).
Armada, Alfonso (1983) *Al servicio de la Corona* (Barcelona).
Attard, Emilio (1983) *La Constitución por dentro* (Barcelona).
Bau Carpi, Fernando (1991) *Crónica de veinte años* (Tortosa).
Bayod, Angel (1981) *Franco visto por sus ministros* (Barcelona).
Borbón, Juan de (1978) *Mi vida marinera* (Madrid).
Borbón y Borbón, Juan Carlos (1974) *Palabras de Su Alteza Real el Príncipe de España Don Juan Carlos de Borbón y Borbón* (Madrid).
Brandt, Willy (1992) *My Life in Politics* (London).
Calvo Sotelo, Leopoldo (1990) *Memoria viva de la transición* (Barcelona).
Carrillo, Santiago (1975) *Mañana, España* (Paris).
Carrillo, Santiago (1983) *Memoria de la transición* (Barcelona).
Carrillo, Santiago (1987) *El año de la peluca* (Barcelona).
Carrillo, Santiago (1993) *Memorias* (Barcelona).
Cierva, Ricardo de la (1994) *Retratos que entran en la historia* (Barcelona).
Dem, Marc (1990) *Las Memorias de Alfonso de Borbón* (Barcelona).
Díez Alegría, Manuel (1984) *Primicias de una confesión* (Madrid).
Eaton, Samuel D. (1981) *The forces of freedom in Spain* (Stanford).
Feo, Julio (1993) *Aquellos años* (Barcelona).
Fernández de la Mora, Gonzalo (1986) *Los errores del cambio* (Barcelona).
Fernández de la Mora, Gonzalo (1995) *Rio arriba. Memorias* (Barcelona).
Fraga Iribarne, Manuel (1980) *Memoria breve de una vida pública* (Barcelona).
Fraga Iribarne, Manuel (1987) *En busca del tiempo servido* (Barcelona).
Franco Salgado-Araujo, Francisco (1976) *Mis conversaciones privadas con Franco* (Barcelona).
Frederica, Queen of the Helenes (1982) *A Measure of Understanding* (London).
Fuentes Gómez de Salazar, Eduardo (1994) *El pacto del capó* (Madrid).
Garrigues y Díaz Cañabate, Antonio (1978) *Diálogos conmigo mismo* (Barcelona).
Gil, Vicente (1981) *Cuarenta años junto a Franco* (Barcelona).
Gil Robles, José María (1976) *La Monarquía por la que yo luché: páginas de un diario, 1941–1954* (Madrid).
Gil Robles, José María (1977) *Un final de jornada* (Madrid).
Girón de Velasco, José Antonio (1994) *Si la memoria no me falla* (Barcelona).
Gómez Jordana, Rafael (1994) *Diplomacia cálida* (Madrid).
Gutiérrez Mellado, Manuel (1983) *Un soldado de España* (Barcelona).
Hassan II (1994) *La memoria de un Rey* (Barcelona).

Hernández Gil, Antonio (1982) *El cambio político español y la Constitución* (Barcelona).

Herrero y Rodriguez de Miñón, Miguel (1993) *Memorias de estío* (Madrid).

Howe, Geoffrey (1994) *Conflict of Loyalty* (London).

López Rodó, Laureano (1977) *La larga marcha hacia la Monarquía* (Barcelona).

López Rodó, Laureano (1990) *Memorias I* (Barcelona).

López Rodó, Laureano (1991) *Memorias II. Años decisivos* (Barcelona).

López Rodó, Laureano (1992) *Memorias III. El principio del fin* (Barcelona).

López Rodó, Laureano (1993) *Memorias IV. Claves de la transición* (Barcelona).

Lora Tamayo, Manuel (1985) *Lo que yo he conocido. Recuerdos de un viejo catedrático que fue ministro* (Barcelona).

Martín Villa, Rodolfo (1984) *Al servicio del Estado* (Barcelona).

Martínez Inglés, Amadeo (1994) *La transición vigilada* .(Madrid).

Meliá, Josep (1981) *Así cayó Adolfo Suárez* (Barcelona).

Merino, Julio and Santiago, Segura (1983) *Jaque al Rey* (Barcelona).

Merino, Julio and Santiago, Segura (1984) *Las vísperas del 23-F* (Barcelona).

Mitterrand, François (1979) *L'Abeille et l'architecte* (Paris).

Morán, Fernando (1990) *España en su sitio* (Barcelona).

Múgica, Enrique (1986) *Itinerario hacia la libertad* (Barcelona).

Ortínez, Manuel (1993) *Una vida entre burgesos. Memories* (Barcelona).

Osorio, Alfonso (1980) *Trayectoria política de un ministro de la Corona* (Barcelona).

Otero Novas, José Manuel (1987) *Nuestra democracia puede morir* (Barcelona).

Papell, Antonio (1993) *Conversaciones con Luis Yáñez* (Barcelona).

Peces-Barba, Gregorio (1988) *La elaboración de la Constitución de 1978* (Madrid).

Pemán, José María (1976) *Mis encuentros con Franco* (Barcelona).

Pozuelo Escudero, Vicente (1980) *Los últimos 476 días de Franco* (Barcelona).

Reventós, Joan (1993) *Misión en Paris. Memorias de un embajador* (Barcelona).

Sainz Rodríguez, Pedro (1981) *Un reinado en la sombra* (Barcelona).

Sánchez-Terán, Salvador (1988) *De Franco a la Generalitat* (Barcelona).

San Martín, José Ignacio (1983) *Servicio especial* (Barcelona).

Satrústegui, Joaquín (1990) 'La política de Don Juan III en el exilio', *ABC*, 23 December.

Schmidt, Helmut (1990) *Men and Powers. A political retrospective* (London).

Semprún, Jorge (1993) *Federico Sánchez se despide de ustedes* (Barcelona).

Silva Muñoz, Federico (1993) *Memorias políticas* (Barcelona).

Tarradellas, Josep (1990) *Ja Sóc Aquí* (Barcelona).

Tierno Galván, Enrique (1981) *Cabos sueltos* (Barcelona).

Utrera Molina, José (1989) *Sin cambiar de bandera* (Barcelona).

Van-Halen, Juan (1986) *Objetivo: ganar el futuro. Conversaciones con Alfonso Osorio* (Barcelona).

Vegas Latapié, Eugenio (1983) *Memorias políticas* (Barcelona).

Vilallonga, José Luis de (1994) *The King. A Life of King Juan Carlos of Spain* (London).

Walters, Vernon (1978) *Silent missions* (New York).

Ziegler, Philip (ed.) (1989) *From shore to shore. The final years. The Diaries of Earl Mountbatten of Burma, 1953–1979* (London).

SECONDARY SOURCES

Acuña, Ramón Luis (1986) *Como los dientes de una sierra* (Barcelona).

Alcocer, José Luis (1986) *Fernández-Miranda, agonía de un Estado* (Barcelona).

Andrew, Christopher, and Gordievsky, Oleg (1991) *Instructions from the Centre* (London).

Antich, José (1994) *El virrey* (Barcelona).

Apezarena, José and Carmen Castilla (1993) *Así es el Príncipe* (Madrid).

Bailby, Edouard (1977) *¿España hacia la democracia?* (Barcelona).

Baón, Rogelio (1985) *Fraga, genio y figura* (Madrid).

Bardavío, Joaquín (1974) *La crisis* (Madrid).

Bardavío, Joaquín (1979) *El dilema* (Madrid).

Bardavío, Joaquín (1979) *Los silencios del Rey* (Madrid).

Bardavío, Joaquín (1980) *Sábado Santo Rojo* (Madrid).

Bardavío, Joaquín (1989) *La ráma trágica de los Borbones* (Barcelona).

Carr, Raymond and Juan Pablo Fusi (1979) *Spain, dictatorship to democracy* (London).

Cernuda, Pilar, José Oneto, Ramón Pi, and Pedro J. Ramírez (1981) *Todo un Rey* (Madrid).

Cierva, Ricardo de la (1992) *Victoria Eugenia. El veneno en la sangre* (Barcelona).

Cierva, Ricardo de la (1992–3) *Franco y Don Juan, los reyes sin Corona* (Madrid).

Claudín, Fernando (1983) *Santiago Carrillo: crónica de un secretario general* (Barcelona).

Créach, Jean (1959) *Le couer et l'épeé* (Paris).

Cuadra, Bonifacio de la and Soledad Gallego-Díaz (1981) *Del consenso al desencanto* (Madrid).

Díaz Herrera, José and Durán, Isabel (1994) *Los secretos del poder* (Barcelona).

Fernández-Fontecha, Manuel and Alfredo Pérez de Armiñán (1987) *La Monarquía y la Constitución* (Madrid).

Fernández-Miranda Lozana, Pilar (1994) 'La Reforma Política', PhD thesis, Universidad Complutense (Madrid).

Figuero, Javier and Luis Herrero (1985) *La muerte de Franco jamás contada* (Barcelona).

Fontán, Antonio (1994) *Don Juan entra en la Historia* (Madrid).

Fortes, José and Luis Otero (1983) *Proceso a nueve militares demócratas: las Fuerzas Armadas y la UMD* (Barcelona).

Fuente, Ismael (1991) *El caballo cansado. El largo adiós de Felipe González* (Madrid).

Fuente, Ismael (1992) *Don Juan de Borbón* (Madrid).

Fusi, Juan (1987) *Franco* (London).

Galvani, Victoria (1987) *El Rey y la Comunidad Iberoamericana* (Madrid).

Gilmour, David (1985) *The transformation of Spain* (London).

González-Doria, Francisco (1962) *Juan Carlos y Sofía, boda real* (Madrid).

González-Doria, Fernando (1990) *Don Juan de Borbón* (Madrid).

Guerra, Antonio (1992) *Las Filípicas* (Barcelona).

Gunther, Richard, Giacomo Sani and Goldie Shabad (1986) *Spain after Franco* (London).

Lafuente Balle, José María (1987) *El Rey y las Fuerzas Armadas en la Constitución* (Madrid).

Laot, Françoise (1987) *Juan Carlos y Sofía* (Madrid).

Linz, Juan J. (1993) 'Innovative Leadership in the Transition to Democracy and a New Democracy: The Case of Spain', in Gabriel Sheffer (ed.), *Innovative Leaders in International Politics* (New York).

Linz, Juan et al. (1981) *IV Informe FOESSA. Vol. 1. Informe sociológico sobre el cambio político en España, 1975–81* (Madrid).

Lucas Verdú, Pablo (ed.) (1983) *La Corona y la Monarquía parlamentaria en la Constitución de 1978* (Madrid).

Maclean, Veronica (1993) *Crowned heads* (London).

Márquez Reviriego, Victor (1982) *Felipe González, un estilo ético* (Barcelona).

Martínez Durbán, Rafael (1990) *En la sombra del Rey* (Almeria).

Mérida, María (1994) *Un rey sin corte* (Barcelona).

Morán, Gregorio (1979) *Adolfo Suárez. Historia de una ambición* (Barcelona).

Morán, Gregorio (1986) *Miseria y grandeza del Partido Comunista de España* (Barcelona).

Noel, Gerard (1984) *Ena. Spain's English Queen* (London).

Nourry, Philippe (1986) *Juan Carlos, un Rey para los republicanos* (Barcelona).

Oneto, José (1975) *Cien días en la muerte de Francisco Franco* (Madrid).

Oneto, José (1981) *La noche de Tejero* (Barcelona).

Oneto José (1981) *Los últimos días de un presidente* (Barcelona).

Oneto, José (1985) *Anatomía de un cambio de régimen* (Barcelona).

Osorio, Alfonso (1985) *Escrito desde la derecha* (Barcelona).

Palacio Attard, Vicente (1989) *Juan Carlos I y el advenimiento de la democracia* (Madrid).

Payne, Stanley (1987) *The Franco Regime 1936–1975* (Madison).

Peñafiel, Jaime (1993) *¡Dios salve a la Reina!* (Madrid).

Pérez Mateos, Juan Antonio (1980) *Juan Carlos. La infancia desconocida de un Rey* (Barcelona).

Pérez Mateos, Juan Antonio (1981) *El Rey que vino del exilio* (Barcelona).

Powell, Charles T. (1989) 'Reform vs. "ruptura" in Spain's transition to democracy', DPhil thesis (Oxford).

Powell, Charles T. (1991) *El piloto del cambio* (Barcelona).

Preston, Paul (1986) *The triumph of democracy in Spain* (London).

Preston, Paul (1993) *Franco* (London).

Prieto, Joaquín and José Luis Barbería (1991) *El enigma del 'Elefante'* (Madrid).

Rayón, Fernando (1993) *Sofía de Grecia, La Reina* (Barcelona).

RTVE (1994) *La transición española* (Madrid).

Salmador, Victor (1981) *Las dos Españas y el Rey* (Madrid).

Seco Serrano, Carlos (1988) *Juan Carlos I* (Madrid).

Suárez Fernández, Luis (1984) *Francisco Franco y su tiempo*, 8 volumes (Madrid).

Toquero, José María (1989) *Franco y Don Juan. La oposición monárquica al franquismo* (Barcelona).

Toquero, José María (1992) *Don Juan de Borbón, el Rey padre* (Barcelona).

Tusell, Javier (1993) *Carrero Blanco* (Madrid).

Ubboldi, Raffaello (1985) *Juan Carlos* (Milan).

Urbano, Pilar (1982) *Con la venia, yo indagué el 23F* (Barcelona).

Vidal Sales, José Antonio (1993) *Don Juan de Borbón* (Madrid).

Vilar, Sergio (1982) *Historia del antifranquismo 1939–1975* (Barcelona).

Ysart, Federico (1984) *¿Quién hizo el cambio?* (Barcelona).

Ziegler, Philip (1985) *Mountbatten* (London).

Ziegler, Philip (1994) *Wilson. The authorized life* (London).

Index

Note: JC is used as an abbreviation for Juan Carlos.